DRUGS AND DOPING
IN SPORT
SOCIO-LEGAL PERSPECTIVES

Cavendish
Publishing
Limited

London • Sydney

DRUGS AND DOPING IN SPORT

SOCIO-LEGAL PERSPECTIVES

Edited by

John O'Leary, LLB, M Phil
Lecturer in Law
Anglia Polytechnic University

Cavendish
Publishing
Limited

London • Sydney

First published in Great Britain 2001 by Cavendish Publishing Limited,
The Glass House, Wharton Street, London WC1X 9PX, United Kingdom
Telephone: +44 (0)20 7278 8000   Facsimile: +44 (0)20 7278 8080
Email: info@cavendishpublishing.com
Website: www.cavendishpublishing.com

O'Leary, John
Drugs in sports
1 Doping in sports   2 Doping in sports – law and legislation
I Title
362.2'9'088796

ISBN 1 85941 662 4
Printed and bound in Great Britain

For Lesley, Niamh and Orfhlaith

CONTRIBUTORS

Paul M Anderson is Adjunct Assistant Professor of Law and Assistant Director of the National Sports Law Institute at Marquette University Law School. He is a Consultant to The Leib Group, LLC, advisors to the sports and entertainment industry, Mequon, Wisconsin, and contributing author of the company listed Front Office Publications, Mequon, Wisconsin. He is also Secretary of the State Bar of Wisconsin's Sports and Entertainment Law Section; Secretary of the Society for the Study of the Legal Aspects of Sport and Physical Education; and a Research Associate at the Sports Law Centre at Anglia Polytechnic University.

The Honourable Michael J Beloff QC is President of Trinity College, Oxford, a Master of the Bench of Gray's Inn, a Judge at the Court of Appeal in Jersey and Guernsey and a member of the Court of Arbitration for Sport. He served on panels at the Atlanta and Sydney Olympics and is a Steward of the Royal Automobile Club.

Simon Boyes is a member of the Sports Law Centre at Anglia Polytechnic University. He is currently working towards a PhD relating to the impact of globalisation upon the regulation of sport.

Andy Curtis is the European Blind 200 m and 400 m athletics champion, World Blind 400 m silver medallist and winner of 20 other international athletics medals. He is currently conducting PhD research into the 'Use of discretion in sports administration' at Hull University.

Ken Foster is Lecturer in Law at the University of Warwick. He has been teaching a course on sports law since 1987 and has written widely in this area. He is currently researching international aspects of sports law.

Andy Gray, Solicitor, is Head of Legal Affairs to the Amateur Swimming Federation of Great Britain, the national governing body for swimming. He is a professional member of the Sports Dispute Resolution Panel and Consultant Sports Adviser to Leftley Mallett Solicitors, King's Lynn. He also lectures in sport and media law on the Legal Practice Course at De Montfort University.

Edward Grayson is a Barrister of the Middle Temple and of the South Eastern Circuit, and Visiting Professor of Sport and the Law in the Law School, Anglia Polytechnic University. He is the Founding President of the British Association for Sport and the Law and is a Fellow of the Royal Society of Medicine.

Barrie Houlihan is Professor of Sport Policy at Loughborough University. His research interests include the domestic and international policy processes for sport. His most recent books include *Sport, Policy and Politics: A Comparative Analysis* (1997) and *Dying to Win: The Development of Anti-Doping Policy* (1999).

Gregory Ioannidis is Research Associate and part time Lecturer in the Law School, Anglia Polytechnic University. His PhD thesis is entitled 'Drug testing and legal regulation'. He is an Advocate of the Greek Bar, specialising in criminal law and sports law.

Jason Lowther is Lecturer in Law at the University of Wolverhampton. He was formerly a needle exchange worker and drug counsellor in Portsmouth. His research interests include drugs in sport issues and environmental law.

David McArdle is Research Fellow in Sports Law at De Montfort University and a Research Associate at the Sports Law Centre, Anglia Polytechnic University. He is author of *From Boot Money to* Bosman: *Football, Society and the Law* (2000, Cavendish Publishing) and has published widely on the application of employment law and European law within sports organisations and on the history and sociology of sport. David is co-editor of the journal, Entertainment Law.

John O'Leary is Lecturer in Law and member of the Sports Law Centre at Anglia Polytechnic University. He is a co-author of *Sports Law* (1998, Cavendish Publishing). He has written extensively on contractual and doping issues in sport and is currently researching into the Court of Arbitration for Sport on behalf of the European Commission.

JanWillem Soek is Senior Research Officer at the TMC Asser Instituut in The Hague, The Netherlands. He is co-editor of the International Sports Law Journal, *Basic Document of International Sports Organisations* (1998) and *Doping Rules of International Sports Organisations* (1999).

Michele Verroken is Director of Ethics and Anti-Doping at UK Sport. She was a member of the International Olympic Committee Sub-Commission on Harmonisation of Anti-Doping and is the author of several articles and chapters on the drugs and sport issue. Michele guided the Directorate to be the first to achieve ISO 9002 certification in 1987 for the management of drug testing in human sports and oversaw the UK Sport Nandrolone Review in 1999.

Emile N Vrijman is an attorney with Lamsma Veldstra & Lobé, Rotterdam, The Netherlands. Before starting his career as an attorney, he worked in the field of anti-doping for almost 10 years as the Director of NeCeDo, the national anti-doping organisation of The Netherlands. He has published extensively on anti-doping policies and legal issues concerning doping, and is the author of *Doping* (1997) in the *Sport en Recht* series.

Roger Welch is Senior Lecturer in Law at the University of Portsmouth. He is a co-author of *Sports Law* (1998, Cavendish Publishing) and has published extensively in the areas of employment law and industrial relations.

PREFACE

The aim of this book is to paint a picture of the ongoing socio-legal tensions in the system of doping control within sport. The law plays an increasingly important role in the regulation of sporting activity generally and doping is no exception. There is a growing awareness on the part of sportsmen and women, sports doctors, administrators and others of the influence of the law, and this awareness has impacted on all facets of doping control, from the construction of the rules of sports' governing bodies to the desire on the part of competitors to mount legal challenges.

The contributors to this book come from a variety of backgrounds and present, therefore, a variety of perspectives. They are administrators, lawyers, academics and participants and their contributions reflect their beliefs, concerns and anxieties. If this book had been written 15 years ago, before the Ben Johnson revelations, the issues raised may have been very different, as, at least in the eyes of the public, doping control was not perceived to be the problem it is today. The contemporary issues raised in this book reflect the determination of administrators to get the rules right and the problems they have yet to overcome. They reflect the importance of emerging bodies such as the Court of Arbitration for Sport (CAS) and the World Anti-Doping Agency (WADA). They examine the anxiety of competitors post-*Modahl* and they challenge the philosophy and efficacy of the current system of doping control. In a few years' time, it is likely that many of the issues raised in this book will have to have been been answered, and analysis will have moved on from CAS and WADA to an examination of, say, human rights, or even doping's equivalent of the *Bosman* case – a high profile example of the law's ability to rewrite the rules of sport. In one sense, therefore, this book provides a snapshot of the contemporary issues in doping at the turn of the 21st century.

When compiling this book, it was not my intention to provide the reader with a comprehensive description of the workings of doping control in sport – there are other texts that provide this function. Nor was it the contributors' brief that they should be controversial. However, many views expressed are undoubtedly controversial and I hope that the contributions both enlighten and challenge the reader's understanding of this dynamic and volatile area of socio-legal study.

John O'Leary
December 2000

ACKNOWLEDGMENTS

I would like to thank my colleagues for their perceptive and thoughtful contributions to this book. I would also like to thank Jonathan Fitchen for his assistance in revising and editing the text. I thank Anglia Polytechnic University for providing me with the facilities to undertake this task and colleagues in the Law School and Sports Law Centre for the contributions they have made to the discussions about the book. Last, but by no means least, I would like to thank my family for their love, encouragement and support.

John O'Leary

CONTENTS

TABLE OF CASES

TABLE OF UK LEGISLATION

TABLE OF INTERNATIONAL LEGISLATION

TABLE OF SPORTS RULES AND REGULATIONS

Table of Sports Rules and Regulations

TABLE OF ABBREVIATIONS

ACAS ....Advisory, Conciliation and Arbitration Service
ACMD ....Advisory Council on the Misuse of Drugs
ADSA ....Australian Sports Drug Agency
AFA ....Amateur Fencing Association
AIBA ....Association Internationale de Boxing Amateur
(International Amateur Boxing Association)
AS ....anabolic steroids
ASCA ....Anabolic Steroid Control Act 1990
ASFGB ....Amateur Swimming Association of Great Britain
ATP ....Association of Tennis Professionals

BAF ....British Athletic Federation
BOA ....British Olympic Association

CAS ....Court of Arbitration for Sport

DEA ....Drug Enforcement Agency (US)

EAT ....Employment Appeal Tribunal
EPO ....erythropoietin
EU ....European Union

FA ....Football Association
FFTri ....Fédération Française de Triathlon
(French Triathlon Federation)
FIBA ....Fédération Internationale de Basketball Amateur
(International Amateur Basketball Federation)
FIBT ....Fédération Internationale de Bobsleigh et du Tobogganing
(International Bobsleigh and Tobogganing Federation)
FIC ....Fédération Internationale de Canoe
(International Canoeing Federation)
FIE ....Fédération Internationale d'Escrimage
(International Fencing Federation)
FIFA ....Fédération Internationale de Football Association
FIG ....Fédération Internationale de Gymnastique
(International Gymnastic Federation)
FIH ....Fédération Internationale de Hockey
(International Hockey Federation)
FIL ....Fédération Internationale de Luge
(International Luge Federation)

FILA ....Fédération Internationale des Luttes Associées
(International Amateur Wrestling Federation)

FINA ....Fédération Internationale de Natation Amateur
(International Amateur Swimming Federation)

FIS ....Fédération Internationale du Ski
(International Skiing Federation)

FISA ....Fédération Internationale des Sociétés d'Aviron
(International Rowing Federation)

FITA ....Fédération Internationale de Tir à l'Arche
(International Archery Federation)

FIVB ....Fédération Internationale de Volleyball
(International Volleyball Federation)

GHB ....Gammahydroxybutyrate

GDR ....German Democratic Republic

HIV ....human immuno-deficiency virus

HGH ....human growth hormone

IAAF ....International Amateur Athletic Federation

IADA ....International Anti-Doping Agency

IBA ....International Baseball Association

IBF ....International Badminton Federation

IBU ....International Biathlon Union

ICCPR ....International Covenant on Civil and Political Rights

IF ....international federation (general)

IHF ....International Handball Federation

IIHF ....International Ice Hockey Federation

IJF ....International Judo Federation

IOC ....International Olympic Committee

IOC MC ....International Olympic Committee Medical Code

ISAF ....International Sailing Federation

ISF ....International Softball Federation

ISSF (UIT) ....International Sport Shooting Federation

ISU ....International Skating Union

ITF ....International Tennis Federation

ITTF ....International Table Tennis Federation

ITU ....International Triathlon Union

IWF ....International Weightlifting Federation

LSD . . . . .lysergic acid diethylamide

MCA . . . . .Medicines Control Agency
MDA . . . . .Misuse of Drugs Act 1971

NeCeDo . . . . .Netherlands Centre for Doping Affairs
NCAA . . . . .National Collegiate Athletic Association (US)
NCO . . . . .National Olympic Committee (general)

TCCB . . . . .Test and County Cricket Board

UCI . . . . .Union Cycliste Internationale
UIPM . . . . .Union Internationale de Pentathlon Moderne
(International Union for Modern Pentathlon)
UIT (ISSF) . . . . .Union Internationale de Tir
(International Sport Shooting Federation)

WADA . . . . .World Anti-Doping Agency
WCF . . . . .World Curling Federation
WTA . . . . .Women's Tennis Association
WTF . . . . .World Taekwondo Federation

CHAPTER 1

THE STATE OF PLAY

John O'Leary

The Sydney Olympics was heralded by many, including Juan Antonio Samaranch, President of the International Olympic Committee (IOC), as the best Games ever. From a British perspective, the Games were certainly successful in terms of medals won, but perhaps the plaudits were meant in a wider context: the Games appeared to run smoothly, sportsmen and women appeared complimentary – certainly nothing comparable to the transport and accommodation problems encountered in Atlanta – and relatively few competitors 'cheated'.[1]

Not all breaches of the rules of sport are considered to be cheating. Most breaches, such as the false start, the faulty baton change or the walker who 'runs', are dealt with instantaneously by officials. The penalty imposed for this type of breach may be the subject of a challenge by the competitor, but this is unusual. Almost invariably, there is no intention on the part of the competitor to break rules of this nature. However, the reason for their exclusion is axiomatic – they flout the principle of fair competition. These banned activities, identified by the rules of the relevant sports governing body, are reinforced by a general consensus that the behaviour is undesirable.

Conversely, some activities that may have the hallmark of cheating about them are deemed legitimate. Although one might argue, for example, that technological advantages such as high-tech bicycles, swimming and running suits and the sophisticated drinks of some marathon runners are cheating, in that they establish an advantage which may be considered unfair; they are not necessarily examples of cheating as prescribed by the governing bodies.

One area, however, where the outlawing of activities by the governing bodies of sport has become synonymous in the minds of the public with cheating is doping. Cheating is one of the fronts on which the crusade by the IOC against doping is fought. The unyielding position adopted by the IOC and governing bodies is based on the premise that doping is wrong, although the logic which underpins this rather simplistic statement of principle is, at least, a little shaky. In 1999, the IOC restated its stance in a press release:

---

1   Or, at least, were discovered to have cheated.

> The IOC wishes to reiterate its total commitment to the fight against doping, with the aim of protecting athletes' health and preserving fair play in sport. Any declarations which go against these principles are both wrong and misplaced.[2]

In order to achieve these lofty ideals, a complex structure of institutions and mechanisms has been developed. Initially, governing bodies of sport felt free to impose, through contract, any system of regulation they deemed fit. These anti-doping rules were often drafted without legal advice, containing unworkable provisions and inappropriate sanctions. The law has played an active role in refining them and the courts stand as final arbiter should those rules remain unlawful.

Today, the campaign against doping by the governing bodies is a systematic one. Rules cover testing both during competition and outside. Positive tests are tested again, in the presence of the competitor or representative. All national governing bodies provide a system of hearings and appeals. There are further appeals to the international governing body. If the case is proven against the competitor, there are penalties that can be imposed. These would normally allow some latitude for a first offence. The penalties and other regulations are contained in the rulebooks of governing bodies and are freely available.

Governing bodies and doping control agencies, the bodies charged with the task of actually administering the tests, have a difficult and unenviable task. Get the testing wrong and, increasingly, legal action will follow. An inevitable consequence of the increased rewards available[3] to sportsmen and women is that banned competitors are far more likely to seek to overturn bans and fines of national governing bodies in appellate tribunals and courts of law. Sandra Gasser, a Swiss athlete who tested positive and was banned for two years by the International Amateur Athletics Federation (IAAF), was estimated to have lost over US $250,000 in endorsements and appearance fees. The cost to the IAAF of defending the legal action was more than £100,000. The US courts initially awarded Butch Reynolds $27 million in damages and American shot putter Randy Barnes commenced an action for $55 million after suspension for a positive drugs test.[4] If the constitution or procedures of the national governing bodies are defective, then athletes are now in the financial position to commission highly paid lawyers to exploit those flaws.

The job of the sports administrator, therefore, is an exacting one. The brief must be to eliminate the possibility of legal challenge wherever possible. In

---

2   IOC press release, Lausanne, 8 July 1999.

3   'Olympic winners of 10 years ago went home with gold medals, today they take with them a portfolio of contracts worth six figure sums.' Cashmore, E, *Making Sense of Sport*, 1990, London: Routledge, p 122.

4   Gay, M, 'Doping control: the scope for a legal challenge', Seminar on Doping Control, 1994, Sports Council Doping Control Unit.

Chapter 2 of this volume, Andy Gray of the Amateur Swimming Association examines the responsibilities of governing bodies to produce fair and workable anti-doping regulations.

Although the governing body formulates its regulations, the task of administering the doping test system itself is, in most instances, franchised to another body detailed with the task of overseeing the testing of competitors. In Britain, this function is performed by the Ethics and Anti-Doping Unit of UK Sport. The unit carries an enormous burden of responsibility, testing in the region of 5,000 sportsmen and women a year, across a range of sports, applying various regulations that the governing bodies deem appropriate for their particular sport. The unit is recognised, primarily, for its policing function. The duties are broader than this in practice, however, for its responsibility for proving innocence is arguably as important as, if not more important than, catching the cheats. In Chapter 3, below, Michele Verroken, Director of Ethics and Anti-Doping at UK Sport, explains the competing rationales behind the work of the Unit.

In order that doping and other sport-related disputes, as they arise, can be contained within the sporting world, the Court of Arbitration for Sport (CAS) was conceived in 1981. The working group charged with its formulation was headed by Judge Keba Mbaye, a judge at the International Court of Justice, now President of the CAS. The court is based in Lausanne, but ad hoc committees were formed for the Atlanta and Sydney Olympic Games, the Commonwealth Games in Kuala Lumpur and the Nagano Winter Games. The idea of these ad hoc committees was to deal with any disputes arising from the various games within a 24 hour period. With the exception of the Fédération Internationale de Football Association (FIFA) and the IAAF, all major sports governing bodies now use the CAS as their forum of final arbitration.

The CAS consists of up to 150 arbitrators, who apply the various rules of the governing bodies. Matthieu Reeb, counsel to the CAS, acknowledges that 'the CAS has not finished growing'.[5] This is perhaps true both structurally and jurisprudentially. In Chapter 4 of this book, Michael Beloff QC, a CAS arbitrator, analyses the emergence, traceable through CAS judgments, of a body of sports jurisprudence, or *lex sportiva*.

In doping cases, the nature of the actions against athletes have a quasi-criminal character. The sportsman or woman stands accused of a drug 'offence', the action being prosecuted by the governing body. However, there are some marked differences in the standards and burdens applied. Take, for example, the recent case of Dougie Walker, one of a number of recent high profile nandrolone cases that have also involved famous international athletes such as Linford Christie, Dieter Baumann and Merlene Ottey. Walker escaped

---

5   Reeb, M (ed), *Digest of CAS Awards 1986–1998*, 1998, Berne: Staempfli Editions SA, p xxxi.

a ban from Athletics UK. David Moorcroft, Chief Executive, confirmed that Walker was cleared because he made no knowing attempt to enhance his performance. The concept of *mens rea*, or 'guilty mind', is well known to criminal lawyers. Although there is a considerable difference between doping proceedings and criminal trials, many lawyers have suggested that the strict liability provisions of many sports governing bodies are fundamentally unjust. Strict liability in doping regulations allows a governing body to ban an athlete without showing that the athlete intended to take the substance – a positive test is sufficient. The rules of the IAAF do allow, in exceptional cases, for the governing body to find the athlete 'not guilty' if there is sufficient evidence to warrant such a finding. However, without such evidence, it would usually be insufficient for the athlete to claim that he or she did not know how the substance got into their urine. Despite the obvious concerns over a rule of this nature, the English High Court in the case of *Gasser v Stinson*[6] did hold that a strict liability rule was lawful, bearing in mind that it may be the only way to police the doping problem effectively. It may, therefore, seem a little odd that Walker should be cleared, and understandable why the IAAF would be perplexed at the decision. The IAAF certainly thought so, and Walker was subsequently banned.

Even though Athletics UK cleared Linford Christie of a doping offence, the repercussions of the positive test continued to affect him. The IAAF, unhappy with Athletics UK's apparent reluctance to act on the positive test, instigated its own proceedings. Clearly, the relationship between the different levels of governing body is problematic. It is also hard on Christie, whose suspension by the IAAF meant that he was refused access to Australian State-owned athletics facilities that he wished to use to train his team of athletes. Australia has a policy of refusing facilities to athletes serving suspensions for doping related offences. The ban seems unreasonable on Christie in two ways. First, the suspension covers Christie's ability to compete – not to coach. Secondly, until the IAAF conducted its hearing, Christie could not have been 'guilty' of any offence. Unlike the law, where there is a presumption that one is not guilty until proven otherwise, it seems that sport applies the more questionable presumption of 'no smoke without fire'. In Chapter 5, below, JanWillem Soek considers the rights of sportsmen and women to fair hearings and the degree to which a competitor's doping hearing will be conducted in a way that is consistent with trials under national law.

In order for a governing body to regulate doping in sport, it is necessary that they be able to identify accurately which substances are not permitted. 'Banned lists' can be exhaustive, giving not only a list of substances outlawed, but also their metabolites (further substances present as a result of the body converting banned substances) and other related substances.

---

6   (1988) unreported, 15 June.

The list of banned substances has been the subject of considerable controversy. The reported decrease in positive tests in Sydney could be accounted for by a strategic move by some competitors away from detectable drugs to undetectable ones, such as human growth hormone. At the World Swimming Championships in Australia in January 1998, events were overshadowed by the alleged discovery of synthetic human growth hormone in the luggage of Chinese breaststroke swimmer Yuan Yuan. Yuan and her coach have received 15 year bans for trafficking in performance enhancing drugs. As well as being on the International Amateur Swimming Federation's (FINA's) list of banned substances, it is also an offence to import the substance into Australia. The national courts have the power to impose fines of up to £20,000 for this offence. Human growth hormone is favoured by drug taking athletes over anabolic steroids because it produces greater improvements in performance and is also difficult to detect. However, human growth hormone is significantly more expensive than other drugs on the banned lists of sports governing bodies. Steroids are becoming the poor man's alternative. If this theory is correct, expect to see a decrease in positive tests among First World countries but a maintained level of positive tests among poorer athletes from poorer nations. As Andrew Jennings predicted before the Atlanta Games:

> Two classes of dopers can be expected in Atlanta. Rich athletes can afford the drugs that don't show up in tests: human growth hormone, erythropoietin – which increases the number of red blood cells and so provides more oxygen in competition – and other hormonal drugs taken in dosages so low that they clear the body in hours. They'll stay ahead of the testers with new versions of steroids coming out of commercial and illicit labs. Poor athletes who rely on steroids that show up in tests and who don't come off them well before competition are the most likely to be caught.[7]

Equally, the list contains some substance that, at first sight, may seem incongruous – cannabis being a good example. Had not Ross Rebagliati been able to convince the ad hoc CAS that the detected presence of cannabis in his urine was as a result of passive smoking, he would have been stripped of his snowboarding gold medal for ingesting a substance that could not have enhanced his performance. In Chapter 6, below, Roger Welch considers the efficacy of banning 'recreational drugs' and, in particular, the impact of such positive tests on sports employees.

Although drug regulations are supposed to protect the rights of clean competitors, one might sympathise with them if the testing programme caused them some concern. The 'A' test of Diane Modahl showed significant levels of testosterone in her body. Testosterone makes an athlete stronger and more aggressive. However, it does little to aid endurance – one of the key characteristics of a successful middle distance runner. Modahl emphatically

---

7 Jennings, A, *The New Lords of the Rings*, 1996, London: Simon & Schuster.

denied taking any drug. In the time between her suspension and ultimate absolution, the case revealed a catalogue of medical, procedural and administrative problems that could well undermine a competitor's faith in the system. In Chapter 7 of this volume, David McArdle looks at the *Modahl* case and examines its legacy from the competitor's perspective.

The strict liability nature of the drugs regulations has caused problems for the nandrolone athletes, who have argued that there may be innocent reasons for their positive tests. However, there was a setback when a four month study led by Professor Vivian James of the University of London reported that there was no evidence to suggest that dietary substances can influence the production of nandrolone within the body. The report also rejected claims that nandrolone could be metabolised following the consumption of vegetables and meat. There are legitimate concerns over the number of positive tests for nandrolone in the last year. In 1998, there were four reported cases, and in 1999 the number rose to 17. David Moorcroft of Athletics UK advises athletes not to take supplements of any description. Athletics UK, like many other governing bodies, supports a system providing a helpline to competitors who are unsure as to which substances may or may not be taken. Anxiety amongst sportsmen and women persists, however. In Chapter 8 of this book, athlete Andy Curtis considers the anxieties of competitors and provides an athlete's perspective on ways of lessening the concerns of compliance with the anti-doping regulations.

In an effort to ward off criticisms of the existing system of regulation, the IOC announced at the end of 1999 the establishment of the World Anti-Doping Agency (WADA) to 'promote and co-ordinate the fight against doping in sport in all its forms at the international level'. The board is composed of between 10 and 35 members from, principally, the Olympic movement and public authorities. Those from the Olympic movement will represent the IOC, international sports federations and athletes. From public authorities there will be representatives from Member States of the European Union and the Supreme Council for Sport in Africa. The first Chairman of the Board has been confirmed as Dick Pound, Vice President of the IOC. As well as being seen as an independent body, WADA hopes to achieve a degree of uniformity in both the development of the rules and their implementation. These are, indeed, lofty ambitions. WADA has already been criticised for being identified too closely with the IOC and the IOC has done little to dispel this concern by the appointment of Dick Pound. In Chapter 9, below, Barrie Houlihan analyses the role of WADA and assesses its chances of success.

Harmonisation is the current buzzword of drug policy and an admirable ambition. It may, however, prove difficult to achieve. Governing bodies have been happy to go along with WADA thus far, but may prove more intransigent if changes in drug rules are imposed upon them. Equally, countries such as Germany have shown in the past that they will not allow their State laws to become subservient to sports regulations. With some countries apparently little concerned with doping in sport, and others, such as Greece and Belgium, creating specific criminal offences capable of being imposed on the competitors themselves, WADA has been ambitious in its objectives. In Chapter 10, below, Emile Vrijman evaluates the progress made towards a harmonised approach to doping control across a range of sports.

The aims of WADA and efforts to harmonise doping regulations can be viewed as part of a process of globalisation. The IOC leads the way, imposing its own cultural perspectives on the sporting world. The danger of such 'cultural imperialism', it is argued, is that it fails to allow for cultural, economic and political diversity. An example of this might be that doping control may concentrate on identifying those doping techniques which, because they are cheap, are those relied on by competitors from poorer socio-economic backgrounds – a sort of institutionalised racism. In Chapter 11 of this volume, Simon Boyes analyses the process of globalisation in sport and its relevance to doping regulations.

In the absence of a satisfactory system of self-regulation, the law is always available as the institution of ultimate recourse. The *Bosman* case[8] is the most obvious example of the law re-regulating an area of sporting activity where an inability, or unwillingness, to self-regulate led to a conflict with fundamental individual rights. However, to what degree does and should the law interfere with the right of the sporting world to conduct its own affairs? The law must tread carefully in considering the various interests or discourses at work within doping regulation if it is to intervene successfully. In Chapter 12, below, Ken Foster analyses the competing discourses and balances of power within doping regulation.

The implementation of the Human Rights Act 1988 in 2000 coincided with the introduction at Sydney of blood tests aimed at detecting erythropoietin (EPO) – one of the 'new' breed of performance enhancing drugs. There is an interesting juxtaposition between the two initiatives. The object of the Act is to reinforce individuals' human rights in accordance with the European Convention on Human Rights. Doping tests, particularly those requiring blood samples, raise human rights issues. The degree to which the Human Rights Act 1998 may provide a further example of re-regulation is questionable at the moment – it's a case of wait and see. Sport in the US has already undergone a similar legal examination, and there is considerable case law interpreting the Fourth Amendment to the US Constitution in the context of testing in amateur sport. In Chapter 13 of this book, Paul Anderson considers how the US courts have dealt with testing and the constitutional rights of sportsmen and women.

---

8   Case C-41 5/93 *ASBL Union Royale Belge des Sociétés de Football Association and Others v Jean Marc Bosman* [1996] 1 CMLR 645.

The ultimate sanction of any modern society towards conduct it deems unacceptable is to criminalise it. The process of criminalisation of doping would wrest jurisdiction entirely from the control of governing bodies and would represent the most overt intervention that could be made by the law. Most countries have made some attempt to criminalise the supply of certain performance enhancing drugs. Britain does so under Pt 1 of Sched 4 to the Misuse of Drugs Act 1971. The dangers of criminalising the use of drugs generally, such as forcing the problem 'underground', is well documented. There is little in the way of evidence, however, as to how criminalisation of steroids under the Misuse of Drugs Act has impacted on sport. The issue was particularly pertinent in the light of an increase in calls in Australia for more extensive criminal sanctions prior to the Sydney Games. In Chapter 14, Jason Lowther examines the impact on sport on the criminalisation of doping.

It is difficult to imagine legislatures criminalising doping in order to protect the tarnished image of sport. However, if the logic was to protect the health of competitors – a logic that would have a resonance in society generally – then governmental action is not beyond the realms of possibility. A reason given by the IOC for doping regulation – which governing bodies often promulgate – is that drugs damage your health. On this point, there can be little disagreement. It would seem logical that, to most observers, the potential side effects of these drugs outweigh the advantages of taking them. However, at the highest level, the competitive instincts of many participants may blind them to the dangers.[9]

The issue is more than one of simple paternalism, however. The competitor who wishes to compete without recourse to doping faces the problem that, without drugs, he may stand little chance of success. To this competitor, the decision to use doping is a desire not to gain an advantage, but merely to re-establish the status quo whereby his superior natural abilities may prevail. This competitor is being coerced into doping by other competitors. It is argued, therefore, that the doping regulations are not only waging war against those who seek to cheat, but also aim to protect those 'innocent' competitors who feel that they have no choice.

Health is not the only reason put forward by governing bodies for the anti-doping regulation, however. Other reasons include the unfair advantage argument. However, in Chapter 15, below, Edward Grayson and Gregory Ioannidis argue the importance of emphasising health issues as the main focus of anti-doping policy.

Doping in sport is a complex issue, partly because many of the themes are unrelated. They concern the governance of sport; the jurisdiction of the courts and the interaction between the law and the governing bodies; politics, both at

---

9   Goldman, R and Klatz, R, *Death in the Locker Room 2*, 1992, Chicago: Elite Sports Medicine, p 23.

a national level and within sport; as well as medicine, philosophy and sociology. Consequently, there may be no simple means of establishing a consensus of how doping regulation can be improved. In Chapter 16, I conclude that the present system can never be philosophically acceptable and the law can never provide a satisfactory remedy. The most satisfactory way of dealing with doping in sport is to allow competitors the freedom to use doping techniques.

In the 12 years since the Seoul Olympics and the Ben Johnson disqualification, doping in sport has been recognised as one of the major issues in sport. Despite those 12 years of soul searching and introspection, the revamping of the rules of governing bodies, initiatives aimed at harmonisation and political and sociological examination, we are no nearer to resolving the outstanding issues and, perhaps more importantly, restoring confidence in the 'purity' of sporting standards and excellence. If the subsequent chapters do not provide the reader with all the answers to the problems of doping in sport, they will present contemporary and challenging perspectives, provoke debate, and enhance our understanding of this fascinating area of socio-legal study.

DOPING CONTROL: THE NATIONAL GOVERNING BODY PERSPECTIVE

Andy Gray

BACKGROUND

Doping control raises many emotive issues, upon which there will inevitably be diverse views. What must surely be common ground is that any set of doping control rules has to be built on sound foundations. In particular, the rules need to recognise the principles of natural justice (of which more later) and, in addition, the procedures must be such as to produce fair and consistent outcomes.

This need to ensure 'consistency' warrants further consideration. British Swimming,[1] in common with many other governing bodies, has recently been involved in a substantial review of its doping control procedures, following on from a wide ranging consultation exercise.

As a consequence of this review, a revised set of doping control rules and protocols were put in place which sought to achieve the following:

- speedy and efficient resolution of cases in the interest of all parties;
- doping control rules drafted in a comprehensible fashion and widely disseminated to the athletes and coaches, with a possibility for feedback and ongoing dialogue, recognising that the rules, by their nature, must continue to evolve;
- transparency in procedures and full communication of outcomes at all stages;
- the creation of an independent review board with responsibility for considering 'quality control' issues such as compliance with chain of custody procedures. This review board, to be empowered to determine whether, on the facts and in the circumstances of a particular case, there is evidence of the commission of a doping offence;
- the establishment of an independent judiciary under the chairmanship of an independent qualified lawyer. 'Judges' are no longer to be drawn from representatives of the governing body executive, but from an independent judiciary comprising both qualified lawyers and key volunteers in the sport with the requisite skills and experience.

---

1   British Swimming is the trading name of the Amateur Swimming Federation of Great Britain Ltd, the national governing body with responsibility for doping control.

I will deal further with these various topics below.

Sport has learnt, through experiences in the civil courts in many jurisdictions, of the need to ensure that sanctions are 'proportionate'.[2] There is, therefore, a compelling and overwhelming need to differentiate between sanctions that are to be imposed upon offenders using drugs for performance enhancing effect (cheating), as distinct from the detection in a person's body fluids of other drugs which do not have the same effect. That is not to say that sport should turn a blind eye to the use of such substances, but it is merely to recognise that a key element in an effective doping control programme in sport is to concentrate on those substances with an established performance enhancing effect.

All relevant factors should be put before a tribunal to enable the appropriate sanction to be imposed.

The sport of swimming has had its problems. There was the very well publicised incident involving the Chinese national swimming team upon its arrival in Australia for the World Championships in January 1998. It was as if a flask of growth hormone had been issued as part of the necessary survival kit for the Championships. The nature of the problems highlighted was such as to create a widespread backlash amongst the world's media. Sports administrators have to recognise that the media is, on this occasion, actually reflecting the views of the general public and not seeking to create, for its own purposes, a particular public reaction. In Australia, the host of the World Championships, the response of the swimming press was characteristically robust. It was not long before 'alternative' world record lists were being produced, from which were omitted the record times of alleged drug cheats.

Governing body doping control procedures considered

Under typical doping control procedures, a sport's world governing body (or international federation (IF)) will reserve to itself jurisdiction to regulate doping control at international level, and will impose an obligation upon constituent national federations to undertake doping control in domestic events. There is a need for domestic governing bodies to dovetail their rules/procedures clearly with those of the world governing body to ensure the minimum of confusion as to issues such as jurisdiction.

A domestic governing body, like an IF, must clearly elucidate the basis of its doping control programme, and communicate this to participants. It is submitted that this is a key element in assisting the enforceability of any sanctions which may be imposed for contravention of the doping control

---

2   See, eg, *Edwards v BAF and IAAF* [1997] Eu LR 721.

rules. For instance, the Doping Control Rules and Protocols[3] of the Amateur Swimming Federation of Great Britain (ASFGB), the national governing body for elite swimming, state that:

> The purpose of the doping control programme of ASFGB, of which these Rules and Protocols form part, is to protect the health and rights of individuals through education and controlled doping tests. ASFGB considers doping to be contrary to the ethics of sport and in furtherance of the objectives of the Fédération Internationale de Natation Amateur (FINA), the world governing body for the sport of swimming, one of the objectives of ASFGB is to provide drug free sport.[4]

A comprehensive doping control programme must comprise not only appropriate sanctions for offenders, but must be underpinned with an education programme designed to promote healthy, fair and ethical competition.

Clear communication of the nature and extent of the doping control rules is important for two reasons: first, to emphasise that the rules do not exist in a vacuum, but have a legitimacy founded upon health and education as well as fair competition principles; and, secondly, to assist in ensuring that participating athletes are within the jurisdiction of the governing body for the purpose of regulation and sanction. As is well established, the relationship between a governing body and its membership is dependent upon principles of private law[5] and, in particular, the existence of a legally binding contract to give the governing body the requisite controls:

> To be eligible to participate or assist a participant in any event or activity promoted or authorised by ASFGB or any of its constituent associations (or any body directly or indirectly affiliated to those associations or to which ASFGB or any of its constituent associations is directly or indirectly affiliated) wherever held, a person shall agree to be bound by and comply with these Rules and the Protocols set out in Appendix A and further agrees to subject himself to unannounced testing by ASFGB, FINA and other member federations of FINA when under their jurisdiction.[6]

The above provision makes it clear that the very eligibility to participate of an athlete is dependent upon 'acceptance' of the jurisdiction of the governing body with regard to doping control. Particular care must be taken with those sports in which there is a prominent (even predominant) number of participants who are 'minors' in legal terms. There may be good arguments based upon the enforceability of such contracts with minors under established contract law principles (for example, contracts made for the benefit of a

---

3   ASFGB, Doping Control Rules and Protocols, October 1999.

4   *Ibid*, r 1.2.

5   *R v Football Association ex p Football League Ltd* [1993] 2 All ER 833.

6   *Ibid*, ASFGB, r 1.4.

minor). However, to avoid potential legal problems, best practice would suggest that an appropriate form of acknowledgment be taken from the parents of, or person(s) with parental responsibility for, the minor.

The doping control rules must clearly set out the actions which are prohibited, and again, it is recommended that the document should as far as possible be expressed in plain English, with suitable explanatory notes to accompany any unavoidable use of technical language. IFs/governing bodies will invariably follow the International Olympic Committee's (IOC's) list of prohibited classes of substances and prohibited methods, which list is then made the subject of particular sports specific modification. Again, the list is updated on an annual basis (typically, January in each year), consequent upon which the IF will typically modify its own list with an obligation for this new list to be adopted by the national governing body. Not only must the doping control rules contain the appropriate flexibility to allow for an updating of the lists on a periodic basis, but there must also be a practical mechanism for dissemination of information to athletes.

Again, matters must always be viewed from an education/health perspective and, for that reason, it is recommended that use be made of multiple channels of communication to involve direct contact with athletes/parents, coaches (both individual and through appropriate coaching organisations) and team managers and other support staff. With many governing bodies having established internet websites, this provides an important means of rapid dissemination of changes to rules/procedures, although this can by no means be considered to be an answer in itself.

Strict liability

It is the fundamental cornerstone of the doping control rules of the overwhelming majority of sports that doping is strictly forbidden – so called 'absolute', or strict, liability. Under such rules, the finding of a prohibited substance in a person's body fluids constitutes a doping offence.[7] Circumstances under which the substance came to be ingested are of no relevance to a finding of guilt, although such evidence may (subject to the rules) be introduced by way of mitigation against sanction. Such provisions are considered by many to be unconscionable. The counter-argument is that, in the absence of strict liability offences, the ability of sports administrators to combat the scourge of doping in sport would be severely restricted, perhaps to the point of rendering such efforts futile. It is submitted that, were a governing body obliged to establish not only that a prohibited substance had been found to be present within a participant's body tissue or fluids but that, in addition, that person had intended to consume the substance for the purpose of securing a competitive advantage, the difficulties of establishing the requisite

---

7   See, eg, *op cit*, ASFGB, fn 3, r 3.1.1.

'intent' would have a significant detrimental effect on the efficacy of doping control programmes. For this reason, the governing body's doping control rules may place the onus upon the participant to accept personal responsibility for substances found within their bodies. For instance:

> Many of the substances in the list set out in Appendix B below may appear either alone or as part of a mixture within medications which may be available with or without a doctor's prescription. Each person is responsible for any substances detected in samples given by him and must ensure that prohibited substances do not enter or come to be present in his body tissue or fluids and that prohibited techniques are not used. Each person (or where applicable that person's parent or other person with parental responsibility) is responsible for notifying their personal doctor(s), coach(es) and other relevant parties of the provisions of the Rules and Protocols.[8]

It is, however, submitted that the mere statement of this strict liability principle within a set of rules, without more, would be woefully insufficient and that the most important ramifications of this principle need to be clearly and consistently conveyed to athletes, their parents and coaches in the manner described above. Furthermore, the commission of a doping offence must not depend upon the success or otherwise of an attempt at doping and this point should be made clear:

> The success or failure of the use of a prohibited substance or prohibited technique is not material to the commission of a doping offence. It is sufficient that the prohibited substance or prohibited technique was used or attempted for the commission of a doping offence.[9]

It may be considered, viewed from the perspective of the individual athlete accused of a doping offence, that such provisions are unduly onerous. Reference is often made to the fact that the consequences of finding of guilt of a doping offence are akin to the finding of guilt in a criminal case and, accordingly, evidence of intent, or at the very least recklessness, should be a prerequisite. However, the concept of strict liability is not unknown in the criminal arena: one need only consider drink driving laws, which similarly provide for strict liability.

Furthermore, a governing body must carefully balance the rights of an individual athlete accused of doping with those of fellow competitors endeavouring to compete on a level playing field. In the absence of effective measures, confidence of the athlete body and the public in the effectiveness of doping control is eroded. One has only to recall the Tour de France cycling event in 1998, with what was reported to be an endemic culture of the use of

---

8   *Op cit*, ASFGB, fn 3, r 2.8.
9   *Op cit*, ASFGB, fn 3, r 3.3.

prohibited substances amongst some participating teams. This led to calls, from some quarters, for the removal of the prohibition on the use of certain substances in the interest of restoring competitive balance: this rather perverse call for 'equalising down' to the lowest common denominator of participation has thankfully not gained much support, either amongst politicians or the sporting public. Further, with the creation of the World Anti-Doping Agency, it is believed that there remains the political will to work towards the restoration of ethical competition and the maintenance of effective anti-doping programmes.

Nature of the offences

As mentioned above, the key offence under the doping control rules may relate to the 'use' of prohibited substances or methods. Care must be taken in the drafting of such provisions to ensure that liability is not dependent upon consumption of a particular substance in its final form, but that they regulate the consumption of substances which have the effect of 'metabolising' within a person's body into a banned substance. Thus, an athlete is guilty of an offence 'if a prohibited substance is found to be present within a person's body tissue or fluids'.[10]

The rules of many federations go further than simply restricting the use of or taking advantage of prohibited substances/techniques; they legislate for those individuals involved in the supply chain of prohibited substances. It is not uncommon for specific doping offences to be committed by any person who 'assists, induces, encourages or causes'[11] a participant to use a prohibited substance, and also for trafficking in or supplying such substances.[12] Again, it has to be recognised that there may be limitations upon the effective measures that can be taken by a domestic governing body where it seeks to regulate the behaviour of individuals/organisations outside the sport. Whilst a period of suspension may prevent an individual/organisation from becoming involved/continuing to be involved within a sport, and whilst this, of itself, may have a beneficial effect, in the absence of any contractual relationship (the privity of contract conundrum), sanctions may prove to be of little effect. Indeed, the doping control rules of some governing bodies go still further. Article 111 of the International Paralympic Medical and Anti Doping Code states that:

> Use of, counselling of the use of, permitting the use of or condoning the use of any substance or method included in the definition of doping ... is prohibited.[13]

---

10 *Op cit*, ASFGB, fn 3, r 3.1.1.

11 *Op cit*, ASFGB, fn 3, r 3.1.5.

12 *Op cit*, ASFGB, fn 3, r 3.1.7.

13 Available at www.paralympic.org.

Readers will immediately recognise the potentially far reaching ramifications of a specific offence committed by a person 'condoning' the use of prohibited substances, and there is, of course, the issue of effective enforceability mentioned above. For this reason, moves on a political level to extend the scope of the criminal law to dealings involving prohibited substances are to be welcomed.

Presumptions

Another common feature of doping rules is the inclusion of a provision to the effect that the IOC accredited laboratory is presumed to have undertaken the testing with appropriate care and in accordance with established procedures:

> A doping test shall consist of sample collection, the separation of the sample into two parts ('A' and 'B' samples) and analysis. Samples will be analysed at an IOC accredited laboratory. Analysis of all samples undertaken by an IOC accredited laboratory shall be presumed to have been conducted in accordance with the highest scientific standards. Further, such IOC accredited laboratories will be presumed to have conducted custody procedures which comply with acceptable and prevailing standards of care. Such presumptions may be rebutted by evidence to the contrary but there shall be no burden upon any IOC accredited laboratory to establish its procedures.[14]

Accordingly, the governing body is not faced, as a preliminary matter, with establishing the credibility of the test result, though evidence may be adduced to the contrary by the athlete.

Out-of-competition testing

It has been well recognised within sport that a comprehensive doping programme is dependent not only upon effective in-competition testing at events, but also an out-of-competition testing programme. For instance, the pharmacological qualities of many banned substances are such that the presence of a substance in a person's body fluids or tissues may be identified for a very short period after consumption. This is the so called 'wash through' effect. It follows from this that only the most ill-prepared or naïve of athletes (or perhaps those with the most skilled pharmacologists and most advanced masking agents) would take the risk of using prohibited substances/prohibited methods immediately before or during events. Use of anabolic agents, with their powerful body building effects, may thus be

---

14   *Op cit*, ASFGB, fn 3, r 5.2.

confined to the out-of-competition pre-season period. With this in mind, the governing bodies in the UK, particularly encouraged by the UK Sports Council (now called UK Sport) and its anti-doping secretariat, are becoming further engaged in out-of-competition testing. The importance of such testing was starkly illustrated in the case involving the Irish swimmer Michelle Smith. Smith was found guilty by the world governing body of swimming (FINA) of tampering with a sample provided as part of a routine out-of-competition test, for which the athlete was made the subject of a four year ban, the maximum allowed for a first offence under the FINA doping rules.[15]

Out-of-competition testing, of itself, raises a number of questions relating to individual civil liberties, which are discussed further below in consideration of the potential impact of the Human Rights Act 1998. Notwithstanding the potential implication of the Act, it is most important that doping control rules contain the necessary 'licences' to allow for effective out-of-competition testing. The starting point for this must be provisions which oblige an athlete to keep the governing body informed of his or her whereabouts:

> As part of its general unannounced out-of-competition testing programme, ASFGB may from time to time maintain a register of elite athletes. Anyone appearing on such register will be notified. Upon receiving notification a person must –
>
> • keep the ASFGB informed of the addresses or location and contact telephone numbers where he may be contacted to undergo a doping test at any time; and
>
> • should at all times carry with him a valid and conclusive form of identification.[16]

However, for the avoidance of doubt, individuals who do not appear on the register may also be the subject of unannounced out-of-competition testing:

> A person on the register who fails to notify ASFGB of a change of address or location where he may be contacted for a doping test at any time within 48 hours of such a change may be deemed to have committed a doping offence.[17]

> If ASFGB attempts to conduct unannounced out-of-competition testing on a person on the register of elite athletes but is twice unable to locate that person at the address(es) or location(s) provided to ASFGB for such purposes, then ASFGB shall send written notice regarding the situation to such person and request more detailed information as to his schedule. If the person cannot be located thereafter for a doping test at any time during a period of up to 12

---

15 FINA Doping Control Rules, June 1999, r DC 9.2.
16 *Op cit*, ASFGB, fn 3, r 4.6.
17 *Op cit*, ASFGB, fn 3, r 4.7.

(twelve) months from the first date that the person was unable to be located he may be considered to have refused and/or failed to submit to a doping test.[18]

The last of the above provisions represents a deterrent designed to 'encourage' due compliance with the reporting obligations. Again, the rules allowing for out-of-competition testing must be underpinned by fair and transparent procedures, in order that the athlete may be fully aware of what to expect:

Persons may be required to undergo unannounced out-of-competition doping tests. Unannounced out-of-competition testing may be conducted with respect to any prohibited substance or prohibited method. Every effort will be made to collect the sample speedily and efficiently with the minimum of interruption to the training, social or work arrangements of the person tested.

The UK Sports Council may conduct unannounced out-of-competition doping tests on request from ASFGB.

The FINA may also undertake unannounced doping tests.

ASFGB shall maintain a list of ASFGB registered athletes in the current FINA world ranking lists.

The Medical Officer shall send to the FINA information about world-ranked ASFGB registered athletes currently taking Salbutamol, Terbutaline, Salmeterol or Corticosteroids by inhalation.

When a person has been selected for an unannounced doping test, the ISO/Independent Testing Agent (IT) may arrive without an appointment at the person's training camp, accommodation or any other place where the person is likely to be found.

Upon introducing himself to the person the ISO/IT shall show his identification card with photograph and an authorisation letter.

The ISO must prior to commencing the sample collection procedure satisfy himself as to the identity of the person who will be the subject of a doping test.

The ISO/IT must give the person reasonable time to complete any activity in which he is engaged but testing should commence as soon as possible. The person must stay in view of the ISO/IT at all times until the sample collection, division and sealing is concluded.

The ISO/IT shall make every effort to collect the sample as discreetly as possible, with maximum privacy and with a minimum of interruption to the person's training plans or to his social or work arrangements.

If the person refuses to provide a sample the ISO/IT shall record the fact on the Sample Collection Form (Urine), sign his name on the Sample Collection Form (Urine) and ask the person to sign the Sample Collection Form (Urine). If the person refuses to sign it, the ISO shall record the fact on the Sample Collection Form (Urine).[19]

---

18   *Op cit*, ASFGB, fn 3, r 4.8.
19   *Op cit*, ASFGB, fn 3, protocols 9.1–9.11.

The collection procedure as far as reasonably practicable shall comply with those procedures set out in ASFGB Doping Control Protocols 4–6.[20]

'Restricted' substances

Whilst the overwhelming majority of substances contained within the IOC list are considered to be absolutely prohibited, there remain categories of substances which are permitted, typically subject to the following qualifications:

(a) genuine clinical need based upon medical prescription; and

(b) regulation as to the means of ingestion (for example, whether administered orally or by absorption, etc).

Included within this category of substances are prescription medicines for conditions such as asthma, many of the medications for which fall within the categories of Beta 2 agonists, stimulants or corticosteroids under the IOC list. Whilst such substances may enhance the performance of an athlete not suffering from an asthma condition, their permitted use by sufferers is justified on the basis of enabling fair competition by reducing the adverse physical effects of a medical condition.

Rules may contain a further residual authority on a designated individual, typically, the federation medical adviser, to grant individual exemptions permitting the use of substances otherwise prohibited by the relevant governing body rules. Governing bodies must take care in this regard to ensure effective dovetailing with the relevant regulations administered by their world governing body. Again, both governing bodies and participants must be scrupulous in attention to detail with regard to arrangements for the use of restricted substances. In so far as permitted use is dependent upon proven clinical need, it is submitted that such need must be continually the subject of review:

> A person may request the medical officer of ASFGB ('ASFGB Medical Officer') to grant him an exemption allowing him to take a prohibited substance. An application for an exemption must contain a valid certificate from a qualified medical practitioner setting out the reasons why the administration of a prohibited substance is necessary. Such an exemption will only be granted where the ASFGB Medical Officer is satisfied that the exemption is medically justified and will not create a competitive advantage for such person. An exemption may be granted subject to such conditions as the ASFGB Medical Officer deems appropriate to ensure that no competitive advantage may be gained. The decision of the ASFGB Medical Officer in relation to the granting

---

20 *Op cit*, ASFGB, fn 3, protocol 9.12.

or withholding of any exemption, and as to any conditions imposed, shall be final.[21]

Provisional suspensions

Under established doping control protocols, the participant will be asked to provide a urine sample, which will be divided into two, each portion to be preserved within sealed containers bearing the same unique identifying number and designation respectively as 'A' and 'B' samples. The 'A' sample is, as a matter of course, made the subject of testing at, typically, an IOC accredited laboratory and the 'B' sample is stored pending the outcome of the 'A' sample test. If the 'A' sample test proves negative, then no further action is taken and the athlete is advised accordingly. If the 'A' sample test proves positive of any prohibited substance, the governing body will need to consider the imposition of a provisional or temporary suspension.

This, again, is perhaps one of the most contentious issues in the area of doping control: why should an athlete, who has not yet been afforded the opportunity of a hearing, be made the subject of a suspension which may have the effect of rendering the person ineligible to compete in a major championships, with a potentially disastrous effect upon a medal winning opportunity as well as dire financial consequences? But then, let us consider the position of other competitors in the same event where there are limited opportunities for team selection for the relevant championship. What of the position of an individual who will be denied the opportunity to attend, and possibly obtain a medal, by virtue of the fact that another athlete who has failed a doping test is allowed to compete?

It may be that, subsequently, a doping offence is found to have been committed and a period of suspension imposed upon the offender, which may include the retroactive cancellation of performances in that championship. This may well benefit other participants in the championship, but what of the unlucky athlete who is denied the opportunity even to attend?

A real dilemma for a sporting governing body!

There appear to be two means of dealing with this situation: some governing bodies opt for a compulsory suspension upon an adverse 'A' sample test, whereas other governing bodies prefer to retain an element of discretion:

ASFGB shall be entitled to impose a provisional suspension from any event or activity promoted or authorised by ASFGB or any of its constituent

---

21 *Op cit*, ASFGB, fn 3, r 4.10.

associations (or any body directly or indirectly affiliated to those associations or to which ASFGB or any of its constituent associations is directly or indirectly affiliated) wherever held in the following circumstances:

- at any time after receipt of notification that the 'A' sample analysis or 'B' sample analysis of a doping test carried out on behalf of or arranged by ASFGB under these Rules indicates the presence of a prohibited substance or use of a prohibited technique; or

- where ASFGB shall have received notification that FINA has determined that a provisional suspension should be imposed on a person under the jurisdiction of ASFGB in accordance with any provision of the FINA Doping Control Rules.[22]

One advantage of the compulsory suspension approach is that it ensures absolute consistency (which may, of course, be equal unfairness) to the entire body of athletes. This may be contrasted with the discretionary approach, where decisions of governing bodies may be viewed cynically as being dependent to no small extent upon the identity of the alleged offender. However, the major disadvantage of the compulsory approach is that it affords the governing body no opportunity to satisfy itself as to the 'safety' of the 'A' test result. I am sure that it is no surprise to readers to learn that the overwhelming majority of 'A' test results (meaning well in excess of 99.9%) are subsequently confirmed by the 'B' test analysis. All things being equal, there is no reason why such results would not be exactly the same. However, there does remain that small proportion of cases where proper procedures have not been followed or there is otherwise some doubt as to the integrity of the results obtained. For this reason, many governing bodies have now introduced within their rules a review stage, where the 'A' sample test results may be made the subject of legal/medical/pharmacological deliberations. Such provision may be drawn as follows:

If the analysis of a person's 'A' sample indicates the presence of a prohibited substance or use of a prohibited technique then subject to Rule 3.2 the following procedure will apply:

ASFGB will appoint a Review Panel which shall consist of up to three independent people who shall undertake a preliminary review of such facts and circumstances relating to the 'A' sample test as they consider necessary to determine whether they believe a doping offence may have been committed. The Review Panel will not be notified of the identity of the person tested.

If the Review Panel does not unanimously decide that there is sufficient scientific or factual basis to proceed further it shall notify ASFGB. ASFGB shall notify the person tested in writing and no further action will be taken.

If the Review Panel unanimously decide that there is sufficient scientific or factual basis to proceed further with the case it shall notify ASFGB. ASFGB

---

22 *Op cit*, ASFGB, fn 3, r 6.

shall notify the person tested of his 'A' sample test result and may ask that person for an explanation of the finding. ASFGB shall offer the person tested the opportunity for the 'B' sample to be analysed at the IOC accredited laboratory where the 'A' sample analysis was carried out. ASFGB shall inform the person tested.[23]

If circumstances allow, it would clearly be of significant comfort to a governing body executive considering the imposition of a temporary suspension to subject the 'A' test result to further scrutiny, concentrating on issues such as the so called 'chain of custody' of the athlete's sample, from the moment that the test was completed, through transportation, to the conclusion of the laboratory analysis.

Judicial procedures

It is well established that governing body disciplinary procedures are subject to the rules of natural justice. What is less clear is whether governing bodies will be 'public authorities'[24] for the purposes of the Human Rights Act 1998 or whether the provisions of the Act will otherwise affect governing body actions (the so called horizontal effect of the Act).[25] See below, pp 27–28, for further consideration of these issues. What is clear is that, whilst the attitude of the English courts to sporting governing bodies has been largely supportive, and applications for judicial review for governing body decisions in a sporting context have been singularly unsuccessful,[26] the courts will intervene where a governing body fails to follow its own rules appropriately (see *Jones v Welsh Rugby Union* (1998) *The Times*, 6 January (CA)), particularly where its disciplinary hearings fail to follow the principles of natural justice, of which the following are key elements:

- the opportunity of an individual to be 'heard' and to present witness evidence in their defence;
- the opportunity to test by cross-examination the witness evidence put forward against them;
- to be subject to a fair process and to be judged by person(s) untainted by bias.

A familiar format for the judicial procedures might be as follows:

In any case where:
- a person who is the subject of a doping test admits that he has committed a doping offence or accepts the results of the 'A' sample analysis; or

---

23 *Op cit*, ASFGB, fn 3, r 7.

24 Human Rights Act 1998, s 6.

25 See the statement of the Lord Chancellor, *Hansard* col 783, 24 November 1997.

26 *R v Disciplinary Committee of the Jockey Club ex p Aga Khan* [1993] 1 WLR 909.

- a person fails, within the time period specified in Rule 7.2.4, to confirm in writing that he wants the 'B' sample analysed and is therefore deemed to accept the results of the 'A' sample analysis; or

- the result of a person's 'B' sample analysis indicates the presence of a prohibited substance or use of a prohibited method; or

- ASFGB otherwise believes any doping offence under these Rules may have been committed; or

- ASFGB is notified of the results of a doping test carried out by a sporting body other than FINA (or its member federations) in accordance with Rule 12.2 below and where such doping test was carried out on a person participating in any event or activity promoted or authorised by ASFGB or any of its constituent associations (or any body directly or indirectly affiliated to those constituent associations),

ASFGB shall appoint a Judicial Tribunal that shall ordinarily comprise three individuals under the chairmanship of a legally qualified person who may be a practising solicitor or barrister.

The chairman of the Judicial Tribunal or his designee shall arrange the time and place of the hearing which shall take place as soon as reasonably practicable. He shall inform the parties (who shall be ASFGB and the person or persons whom ASFGB believe may have committed a doping offence) directly giving them at least 21 days' notice of the date, time and place of the hearing and the names of the Tribunal members. The parties shall have seven days from receipt of this notification in which to lodge with the chairman or his designee any objection to any Tribunal member(s) stating the grounds for the objection. The chairman shall consider any objections made and if he deems it appropriate select a new Tribunal member or members. The parties shall be notified of the name(s) of the new member(s). The decision of the chairman in respect of an objection shall be final. The parties will be required to confirm in writing whether they, with or without their representative(s), will attend the hearing.

The non-attendance of a party or his representative(s) will not prevent the Judicial Tribunal from dealing with the matter in his absence although the Tribunal members may take into account the written representations of either party in arriving at any decision.

The procedure prior to and at a hearing shall be at the discretion of the chairman. The Tribunal will not be bound by judicial rules governing procedure or the admissibility of evidence. Each party will be given a reasonable opportunity to give and call evidence, address the Tribunal and present his case. At the hearing each party or his representative(s) shall have the right to state his case, to call witnesses, to give evidence personally, to cross-examine witnesses called by the other party and, finally, to summarise his or that party's case. The Chairman may require the parties to submit to the Tribunal and the other party in advance of the hearing an outline of the party's case, copies of any written evidence upon which the party seeks to rely and the identity of any persons the party proposes to call as witnesses.

> In proceedings before the Judicial Tribunal involving doping offences ASFGB shall have the burden of proving on the balance of probabilities that a doping offence has been committed.
>
> After the hearing the chairman of the Judicial Tribunal may inform the parties orally of the decision of the Judicial Tribunal. The decision of the Judicial Tribunal shall be binding immediately upon notification to the parties. Within 14 days of the conclusion of the hearing the decision, together with the reasons for it shall be sent in writing to the parties giving them details of their entitlement to appeal to the Chairman of the Appeals Tribunal. If the Judicial Tribunal does not hold that a doping offence has been committed subject to any appeal to the Appeals Tribunal any provisional suspension that may have been imposed shall be withdrawn immediately and no further action will be taken.
>
> The Judicial Tribunal shall be entitled to impose penalties in accordance with s 10 of these Rules and to make any such cost orders in relation to Judicial Tribunal proceedings as it deems fit. The decision of the Judicial Tribunal shall be published.[27]

A safeguard included for the benefit of the individual athlete is the requirement for an independent, legally qualified chairman, as distinct from an individual within the executive of the sporting governing body. Under the above rules, the burden of proof corresponds with the civil standard of the 'balance of probabilities', as opposed to the criminal standard – 'beyond reasonable doubt'. Whilst there has been much professional and academic debate concerning the appropriate standard in such cases, it is submitted that there is very little practical difference in the application of the two tests in a doping scenario. By analogy with other cases decided in the disciplinary field, it is to be seen that the civil standard itself is a moving target, the quality of evidence needed to establish a guilty finding being correspondingly higher the greater the adverse consequences of a finding of guilt upon the accused: see *R v Hampshire CC ex p Ellerton* [1985] 1 WLR 749.

Sanctions

Typically, governing body rules will draw distinctions between the various classes of substances contained within the IOC/IF list. Further, as a rule of thumb, those substances which are considered to have the greatest performance enhancing effect/most damaging effect upon an athlete's health will be subject to the most stringent sanctions. The most severe sanctions are reserved for the use of anabolic steroids and prohibited techniques such as blood doping and the use of EPO. In the sport of swimming, a first offence for anabolic steroids would render the individual subject to a minimum period of suspension of four years, together with the retroactive cancellation of results

---

27   *Op cit*, ASFGB, fn 3, r 8.

for the six month period prior to the offence.[28] By contrast, the world governing body for international athletics (IAAF) in 1997 reduced the comparable period of suspension to that of two years for a first offence. At the World Doping Conference hosted by the IOC in Lausanne in February 1999, a minimum period of suspension (subject to exceptional circumstances) of two years was endorsed. The concern of many governing bodies, particularly those of the major professional sports such as football, tennis and cycling, is over the potential enormous adverse financial consequences of a successful (or even unsuccessful) challenge to their procedures.

Certainly, the attitude of the courts in some jurisdictions has been to place restrictions upon the ability of governing bodies to impose long term periods of suspension; for instance, the decision of the German Federal Courts in the case brought by Katrin Krabbe against the IAAF. It is perhaps not surprising given the decisions in some jurisdictions that many governing bodies are troubled by the prospects of legal challenge to their decisions. However, this is perhaps to be contrasted with the attitude demonstrated by the English courts in recent years. In the case of *Edwards v BAF and IAAF* [1997] Eu LR 721 (Ch D), Lightman J stated:

> Community Law is applicable to sport only in so far as it constitutes an economic activity and does not apply to matters, rules or events which are of sporting interest only ...

> The imposition of penalties for cheating is essential if cheats are to be kept out of sport and the rules against cheating are to be effective.

This, it is submitted, is a very welcome acknowledgment by the judiciary of the fundamental importance of ensuring that sporting governing bodies, when acting in relation to matters of sporting interest (for example, in setting the regulatory framework of sport rules), should not readily be made the subject of legal challenge. Perhaps this decision recognises the nature of sporting governing bodies as essentially accountable 'political' organisations operating within a defined area of particular sports. The sanctions imposed by IFs are commonly made the subject of consideration at annual or quadrennial congresses, where individual participating federations have the opportunity to lobby and consider in the interests of the sport what are the appropriate sanctions for offenders. Whilst it would be disingenuous to suggest that this is an ideal democratic process, there is clearly a degree of accountability of national governing bodies to reflect in the international forum the wishes of the participants within the sport as to the appropriate sanctions. Furthermore, it is perhaps not surprising that, where soundings are taken from participating athletes at an elite level, the overwhelming majority favour the imposition of

---

28 *Op cit*, ASFGB, fn 3, r 10.1.

the most stringent sanctions possible to eradicate doping cheats. See below for comments on the athlete's perspective.

It is not only the English courts that have reflected both the public's and athletes' mood on these issues. In the case of Ben Johnson before the Canadian courts, Caswell J commented as follows:

> It is necessary to protect Mr Johnson for the sake of his own health from the effects of consistently using prohibited substances. It is necessary to protect the right of the athlete, including Mr Johnson, to fair competition, to know that the race only involves his own skill, his own strength, his own spirit and not his own pharmacologist.[29]

Position of the athletes: the swimming perspective

At the World Short Course Swimming Championships held in Hong Kong in 1999, the overwhelming number of participating nations voluntarily submitted to blood testing of athletes in competition. This issue has been a regular topic of discussion within the sport, through the forum of the Swimming Athletes' Council. The overwhelming view of the athletes, whilst noting the ethical issues arising, is that blood tests were to be supported as a further measure necessary to combat the scourge of doping. The view of the athletes is plain and simple: governing bodies should take whatever steps are necessary to identify and dispose of the cheats.

It has, however, to be recognised that a wider ethical debate must be undertaken, both within the sport of swimming and in sport generally, with regard to the use of blood testing.

There are moves within the athlete body within the sport of swimming for the publication of all doping tests (positive and negative) as a matter of course. There is even the suggestion that the test results should be published on the internet. Whatever the practicalities, the message from the athletes is loud and clear: 'We are clean; we want the opportunity to demonstrate that we are clean and we want others to be the subject of the same rigours.'

The Human Rights Act 1998: new challenges

A detailed consideration of the implications to sporting governing bodies of the Human Rights Act 1998 is outside the scope of this chapter. For detailed consideration of this subject in a very practical manner, readers are referred to Keir Starmer's publication, *European Human Rights Law*.[30]

---

29 *Benjamin Johnson v Athletics Canada and IAAF* (1997) unreported, 25 July, Ontario Court (General Division).

30 Starmer, K, *European Human Rights Law*, 1999, London: Legal Action Group.

Professional and academic opinion is divided as to whether national governing bodies will be subject to the provisions of the Act, which, with effect from 2 October 2000, brings into direct effect under English law the provisions of the 1950 European Convention on Human Rights and Fundamental Freedoms. The Act relates primarily to the activities of 'public authorities', which includes 'courts and tribunals' and other persons 'certain of whose functions are functions of a public nature'.[31] Acts of a private nature of private bodies are, on the face of it, outside the ambit of the Act.

Some commentators see this as precluding the application of the Act to sporting governing bodies who have been consistently regarded by the courts as private bodies, certainly in so far as applications for judicial review have been concerned.[32] However, the contrary argument is that previous determinations of the English courts with regard to the nature and status of any organisation will not be determinative upon a court considering any matter under the Human Rights Act, which itself, under established principles of Strasbourg jurisprudence, must adopt an autonomous interpretation of any expression in the Act (in this case, 'public authority') in the light of Convention jurisprudence. Furthermore, certain speeches of the promoters of the Human Rights Bill reported in *Hansard* seem to be supportive of a wide scope of interpretation for application of the Act.[33] An additional line of argument suggests that as courts and tribunals are themselves clearly public authorities for the purposes of the Act, then, in exercising their duty under the Act to act in a manner compatible with Convention rights, this will necessarily mean that the Act will have a 'horizontal' effect, as, inevitably, courts and tribunals will feel obliged to impose Convention rights considerations on private litigants.

Whatever the respective merits of the arguments in this area, what is clear at this stage, pending any judicial determination, is that sporting governing bodies must be aware of the potential implications of the Act to their procedures. In particular, two Convention rights may have particular effect on doping control procedures: Art 6 (the right to a fair trial) and Art 8 (the right to privacy). It is submitted that Art 6, as interpreted by the European Court of Human Rights,[34] develops and extends principles of natural justice recognised under English law as affecting disciplinary procedures.

Governing bodies will, however, need to consider particular elements of Art 6, including the requirements of an 'independent and impartial tribunal' and the requirement that 'judgment shall be pronounced publicly'. With regard to the constitution of the tribunal, it is suggested that both actual

---

31 Human Rights Act 1998, s 6(3).

32 *R v Disciplinary Committee of the Jockey Club ex p Aga Khan* [1993] 1 WLR 909.

33 See statements of the Lord Chancellor in connection with the Human Rights Bill, *Hansard* cols 783, 811, 24 November 1997.

34 See, eg, *Konig v Germany* (1978) 2 EHHR 170.

impartiality and the appearance of impartiality are required, and this will be an important consideration for any regulatory body. In addition, the tribunal must be 'established by law'. The basis of jurisdiction of the tribunal is a major practical consideration and governing bodies must ensure that their disciplinary functions are discharged by properly constituted tribunals acting in accordance with all relevant rules/procedures. Whilst Art 6 rights may be waived by contract, it is suggested that a sporting governing body may have difficulty in establishing a genuine and voluntary agreement to waive individual human rights if this consists of no more than a 'deeming provision' where, by virtue of membership of an affiliated club, a participant is deemed to accept the jurisdiction for doping control purposes of a national governing body. It is felt to be unlikely that a court will accept a voluntary waiver in the absence of full equality of bargaining power.

Article 8 has potentially wide reaching ramifications for doping control procedures. Under Art 8, 'everyone has the right to respect for his private and family life, his home and his correspondence'. Furthermore, there is to be no interference by a public authority with such rights 'except such as is in accordance with the law and is necessary' for one of a number of legitimate aims, one of which is the 'protection of the rights and freedom of others'.

Clearly, doping control procedures involving testing for human body fluids are, by their nature, invasive, but this of itself will not necessarily render such procedures unlawful under the Act, even if it applies. Indeed, the Act recognises the legitimate interests of other persons, and this chapter has already identified one of the key features of an effective doping control programme as the preservation of a level playing field for the benefit of all competitors. Governing bodies will, however, need to review their procedures to determine the 'proportionality' of the measures taken. Under this principle, a particular measure will only be legally permissible if it is proportionate, that is, a necessary measure for the pursuit of some legitimate purpose, provided, further, that the governing body can establish that the legitimate purpose may not be achieved by some other means which is less intrusive with the Convention right.[35]

Conclusion

There is far more to doping in sport than mere acknowledgment of the relevant legal rules. As stated at the outset, no set of rules can or should exist in a vacuum. If a person is guilty of committing a doping offence, then the sanctions should reflect 'the crime'. And what is the crime? The crime is in undermining the very essence of sport. At the 1999 IOC World Conference on

---

35   For consideration of this principle see *Barthold v Germany* (1985) 7 EHRR 383.

Doping in Lausanne, one of the speakers, the former athlete Sebastian Coe, spoke very eloquently regarding the very privileged place that sport occupies in the affections of the general public. If those participating in sport are, or are perceived to be, cheating, then the spectacle of sport is tarnished.

CHAPTER 3

A TIME FOR RE-EVALUATION: THE CHALLENGE TO AN ATHLETE'S REPUTATION

Michele Verroken

TESTING TIMES

Testing is only one way to tackle the issue of drugs and sport; sadly, it is the highest profile response to the problem of drug misuse in sport and is a very necessary part of the programme to protect athletes and their reputations. The very fact that more money is spent on testing than on information or education in virtually every country in the world demonstrates how important testing is considered within sport. Testing is a recent phenomenon; it was first introduced in the 1960s and has been improved and refined to reflect doping practices, although problems remain.

It is important to emphasise that identifying those competitors who break the rules of sport is only one application of doping regulations. Indeed, testing performs three interlinking functions:

(a) it is relied upon by athletes to protect them from other athletes who break the rules;

(b) it can be the means by which an athlete's reputation as a drug free athlete is confirmed;

(c) sadly, it may also be the way in which an athlete is found to have broken the rules.

An example of drug testing as a 'defender of reputations' occurred in a High Court case where Linford Christie relied upon his history of negative drug tests as part of his evidence in a libel case. His legal representatives argued that suggestions that he has abused drugs were untrue and relied upon his test history to show how regularly he had been tested. The counter-argument used by his opponent, John McVicar, was that the gaps between tests could have provided sufficient opportunity for drug misuse. Athletes need supporting evidence; how many times do we hear suggestions of drug-induced performance when an athlete breaks a record, or when a competitor plays out of his or her socks? Part of the function of testing is to reduce the doubt about sports performance.

On a broader level, the public rely on testing to ensure that the sport they see is fair, and the sponsors want to see a return on their investment – so there is more to the issue than a purely moral responsibility to get it right.

Surveys of athletes have demonstrated that there is a heavy reliance upon the testing programme as the means to protect athletes from others who might try to break the rules. Many athletes want to see more testing; the calls for blood testing as a means of addressing the previously undetectable substances are evidence of the need to remove any remaining doubt about 'indetectable' substances. Insufficient testing and inadequate coverage across sports was also identified by athletes as a reason why testing may not produce its intended deterrent effect.

Sadly, testing has to be regarded as *the health and safety* programme for sport, and relied upon as *the* way to rid sport of the scourge of drugs. If the system of drug testing is to work effectively, it is essential that it is comprehensive and watertight. This is because the challenge made by an athlete who does test positive will seek to exploit any loophole or weakness that can be identified. Often, the athlete's representatives will attack the findings on a number of fronts, such as the following:

- the testing procedures were wrong;
- the analysis is inaccurate;
- there has been a breach of security or integrity of the sample transport;
- the organisation had no authority to test;
- the rules do not cover a specific metabolite of a banned substance;
- there is no reason why the athlete would have used a doping substance at this stage in his or her career;
- the substance is naturally produced, or grew in the sample/body;
- the substance came from an unidentified source and was taken inadvertently;
- the athlete strongly supports drug free sport and would never have done such a thing.

As Angela Issajenko said in her evidence to the Dubin Inquiry in Canada, 'deny, deny, deny'. It goes without saying that an athlete is innocent until proven guilty, but perhaps the bounds of credibility are stretched when the challenge being made includes all of the lines of attack listed above.

TESTING SYSTEMS

Testing systems have grown up around the issues and demands for testing. The UK has a world leading reputation in the area of anti-doping programmes. Previously, testing programmes were organised and controlled by the sports bodies themselves: some achieved their purpose, but suspicion surrounded the inescapable conflict of interest that such bodies experienced in delivering a watertight testing programme. This suspicion led to a closer involvement of governments in testing systems. UK Sport represents the British Government policy interest in this area. As with most national anti-doping organisations, there is a twofold purpose: on a practical level, the delivery of an independent high quality testing service to sport bodies; and, on a policy level, a responsibility to identify best practice and to ensure that sport operates by the highest ethical standards; if you like, a publicly accountable watchdog on the drugs and sport issue.

Despite media reports to the contrary, the UK's interest is to ensure fairness, and it is balancing the need for fairness with the focus upon an athlete's reputation that causes tension in the programme. Of course, if you are taking a leading position, you are in a position to be attacked. By delivering high quality testing programmes, inevitably these programmes identify issues that may have their own controversies – for example, nandrolone.

Some critics claim that we disadvantage our athletes. Typical comments include 'no wonder we win so few medals, if we don't allow them to compete on the same platform as others'; 'is there anything we can give to our cricket/football/rugby teams who are doing so badly'; and 'never mind, nice guys finish last!'.

In the UK, not only has the focus been on the standards of testing, protecting the quality of the testing process to achieve a reliable result by achieving ISO 9002 certification and encouraging other countries to do the same, but the context within which the testing process is delivered is also set out in clearly stated standards. The policies and regulations that set out the procedures following a finding or report of a possible doping offence should adhere to high standards, too. Unfortunately for most governing bodies, the early regulations prohibiting doping were drafted by the medical officer, without the benefit of legal advice. Consequently, the regulations of a sport were often inconsistent, inadequate and lacking the proper authority to follow a fair and due process.

In the past, the regulations have included no clear definition of doping, or have not explained what the rules actually ban. Where there was an inconsistency among the rules of the home countries, that is, England, Wales, Scotland and Northern Ireland, the unfairness was obvious. Now, most governing bodies will not refer to following the rules of the sports councils who drafted the guidance document for them. There should be a connection between national and international bodies, as well as the UK organisation and its constituent bodies. Once the policies and regulations have been completed, the next step is the application of these regulations. At an international event in the UK, it is easy to assume that the British body's regulations would be adequate, but do they actually cover the international competitors? The standard that UK Sport looks for is adequate jurisdiction to undertake testing, then ability to progress to a finding. It is so easy to get caught up in the debate about the correctness of including certain substances under the rules, without addressing the adequacy of the rules to actually carry out testing.

If the quality of the regulations or the quality of the programme of testing is poor, it is difficult to achieve quality throughout. Once a finding has been reported, it must be properly and independently investigated. The standards that UK Sport has proposed to governing bodies in the national anti-doping policy to achieve consistency with the human rights legislation is that there should be three stages, namely, an independent review, disciplinary hearing and appeal, under the management of a legally qualified individual who is experienced in anti-doping matters. If an independent review determines that there is a case to answer, then the disciplinary process must be properly managed to achieve integrity of the whole process; all decisions must be communicated to the parties; and, if there is an objection to the disciplinary process or decision, this may form the grounds for appeal by either party.

It is no longer appropriate to expect governing bodies to have the internal resources to protect athletes and to discipline them when the rules are broken. This is a clear conflict of roles, so bringing into the equation independent, legally qualified chairs of the panels introduces an element to the process that might reduce the pressures of an aggressive defence lawyer on a governing body panel.

The disciplinary process being aimed for will require a co-operative relationship between governing bodies and athletes to get to the truth and to allow for a return of the athlete to the sport. The ultimate objective must be an independent disciplinary system for sport.

TESTING PROGRAMME STANDARDS

There are many aspects of the overall testing process that need to be considered. The framework of testing is complicated by the number of organisations that could be involved in delivering testing programmes. This can complicate any monitoring of test results to ensure that results have actually been reported in time for an athlete to be declared eligible for an event.

Originally, testing was based solely on competitions. This left athletes free to misuse drugs with impunity during training and to clear the drugs from their system before a competition. Testing out-of-competition was introduced; however, presently, it lacks the necessary co-ordination among the various testing organisations to avoid duplication and overlap and achieve maximum effectiveness.

The next area of debate is whether the selection processes are fairly applied and give adequate coverage. Are the right athletes being selected, if the selection policy is random? Is it wrong to target individual competitors, on the grounds of suspicion? Certainly, the Human Rights Act 1998 will be relevant here. There are some targeting policies that have a greater acceptability, such as confirming a record performance. What about the adequate management of reports of an athlete not being available; how do we strike the balance between rights to privacy and the responsibility that comes with receiving public funding and protecting the reputation of the athlete?

Presently, the testing programmes are based upon the collection of a urine sample. There is progress towards the analysis of blood for certain types of substance, but it is not clear whether this body fluid will provide the answer for all of the prohibited substances. Blood testing is perceived to be more sophisticated than urine, yet, to date, urine has been more than adequate in identifying substances. In the future, it is possible that DNA testing will assist us in providing a comprehensive testing programme that has its own unique identification system built in. This could aid the sample identification process and perhaps even reduce the need for supervised collection. Questions of sample manipulation could be dealt with more easily.

The present procedures require the urine sample to be divided into an 'A' and a 'B' sample; this provides a reserve sample in case the 'A' sample analysis produces a finding. The samples are sealed in the presence of the athlete, and the unique numbering is fully documented and confirmed by the athlete's signature. The athlete keeps a copy of this document. The samples are then transferred by a secure chain of custody to the International Olympic Committee (IOC) accredited laboratory. In the UK, the standard set is by signature-required courier. The sampling officer makes a report of the collection procedure followed and submits this contemporaneous report with copies of the sample collection form and chain of custody form to UK Sport.

The next stage is the laboratory analysis. For these quality standards, the process is in the hands of scientists and the IOC. The counter-arguments that have been advanced are that the scientists have not adequately proved their methods, that the quality of the analysis is in some way lacking in an individual case. It is worthwhile pointing out that the laboratories deal with anonymous samples and have no vested interest in the outcome. The laboratory's role is made more difficult by the fact that they are dealing with an untimed urine sample, so determining where a finding might be in a deliberate or inadvertent drug regime is not for the scientists, but should be part of the disciplinary process.

The role of an independent national organisation like UK Sport is to oversee the integrity of the testing programme and the collection, and to consider the standards of evidence being presented to the governing body. One hundred per cent of the documentation is scrutinised, to identify any issues or irregularities. Where an issue or irregularity in the process is identified, this is drawn to the attention of the governing body, which should be passing this information to the review panel, who will decide whether this affects the evidence of a case to answer.

Once the information is passed to the governing body, it is only the national organisation that could help to monitor the results management processes being followed by governing bodies. Independent scrutiny is needed to give confidence that a fair system is being followed. This helps to provide reassurance to others that findings are not being delayed to avoid an athlete being withdrawn on the eve of a major competition. Furthermore, if there is a need to dismiss inadequate evidence, there is an independent accountability for this decision. The appeal can either be followed by or replaced by an arbitration stage. Essentially, arbitration is final and binding, but that does not stop an athlete from resorting to law, if grounds can be identified.

In making a determination on whether the rules have been broken or not, it may be difficult to set aside the more subjective arguments that may be advanced. The personality or character of a national sporting hero is a difficult argument to counter. It is impossible to tell from that untimed urine sample whether the finding resulted from a deliberate or inadvertent administration of a prohibited substance. Applying the strict liability principle is tough, but fairer to the majority, and of course must be balanced by an appeal process and the opportunity for early reinstatement.

The IOC definition of doping does not refer specifically to performance enhancement, and some of the substances prohibited may not have an obvious performance justification. Some sports have been concerned about the misuse of drugs socially. Initially, that might not directly affect performance, but it could lead to a cycle of drug misuse that involves performance drugs. Social drugs can damage the reputation of a sport, so the argument that there is 'no perceived performance enhancement benefit' fails to take into account the role model responsibilities that come with being an elite athlete representing your country, as well as the responsibility you have towards your fellow athletes, sponsors and sport.

The athlete doth protest too much, methinks

The media circus that has surrounded some cases has done little to enhance the credibility of the anti-doping programme, and perhaps this has been deliberate. The Civil Procedure Rules 1998 should start to protect athletes and governing bodies from an entrepreneurial legal profession. The ambulance chasing mentality is evident even in the sports world. Criticisms levelled at the new discipline of sports law may have a point.

Public accountability has to be balanced with privacy in the process, so that an athlete who has not yet been confirmed as committing a doping offence is not unfairly identified. Yet the media is hungry to know the fate of its superstars, almost in disguised admiration of the achievements coupled with disbelief of the skill of the performance. Who couldn't have selected a better football team?

A new dimension that is urgently needed to maintain a fair and just process is reinstatement procedures. Every athlete who has been suspended for a period of time should have a formal rehabilitation and reinstatement programme to enable him or her to rejoin the sport and be accepted back. This remains a challenge for a sporting world that is not yet able to mount a more investigative approach to why the athlete tested positive and to consider the possible involvement, passive or active, of others in the athlete's decision.

CONCLUSION

The new World Anti-Doping Agency represents the most exciting development for the sporting world and for efforts to protect drug free sport. It is the much needed partnership of governments with sports organisations to achieve more by a co-ordinated approach. The discussions presently are centred on who will pay. There are likely to be more interested parties who could be investing in the health and safety system needed by sport than the governing bodies and governments. They would include sponsors, promoters, television companies and, of course, the pharmaceutical industry, from which the doping substances can originate. The athletes would appreciate their contributions to the development of a worldwide anti-doping movement.

However, if we were serious about eradicating drugs from sport, there are more drastic actions that could be considered. These actions would protect our athletes and their reputations, but is the sporting world really ready to use them? For example:

- urine and blood samples should be stored, and then we should await the technology being available to show that an athlete has competed drug free;
- athletes could be housed in a sterile environment for six months before a major event and nutrition and training controlled;
- athletes could submit their samples daily – these samples would be stored and a random selection be tested and validated by DNA analysis. If a drug is detected, the preceding samples could be submitted to determine how long the substance had been present;
- athletes who had been denied a medal or a place in a competition because of another athlete using drugs could be legally aided to challenge that athlete and claim loss of earnings, reputation and opportunity – provided that they also would produce the evidence that they competed drug free;
- lottery funding should not be available to athletes who have been found to have committed a doping offence;
- every event in the UK should be open to independent testing.

Ultimately, there are measures that will resolve the problems of doping in sport. However, there is a balance to be achieved; one that satisfies the various parties and their range of interests. The World Anti-Doping Agency represents the next step in consensus anti-doping measures. It promises to be a powerful and successful weapon in the fight against doping in sport.

CHAPTER 4

DRUGS, LAWS AND VERSAPAKS

Michael J Beloff QC

INTRODUCTION

If anyone doubted the corrosive effect that the drugs issue is having in modern sport, they should look at my professional diary. Between May 1998 and May 1999 – to take a sample year – I advised the two British weightlifters in litigation arising out of their expulsion from the Barcelona Olympics; I chaired a Court of Arbitration for Sport (CAS) Panel in Lausanne in the (unsuccessful) appeal of the Chinese swimmers tested positive at the Perth World Championships – an appeal against my judgment to the Swiss Federal Court of Appeal has been rejected; I sat on a CAS Panel in the cases of Michelle Smith, the Irish swimming multiple gold medallist from Atlanta and of Peter Korda, the Czech tennis star; I headed a UK Athletics Committee of Inquiry into the affair of Dougie Walker, the European 200 m champion; I argued cases for the International Amateur Athletic Federation (IAAF) in Monte Carlo against Mary Decker-Slaney and Dennis Mitchell; and – just to prove that the problem is not restricted to human competitors – I pronounced another CAS decision in the case of an owner who insisted on entering her horse in an international equestrian event although it had recently been treated with phenylbutazone. Nor is my experience atypical. In the recently published *Digest of Awards*[1] of the CAS, there is a special section on appeals concerning doping cases – the largest section in the book. The IAAF's casebook is entirely devoted to the subject.[2]

OBJECTS OF DOPING CONTROLS

The objects of doping control are clear. The essence of a sporting contest is that it should be fairly conducted, with the competitor's success or failure being the result of natural talents: speed, skill, endurance, tactical awareness –

---

1   Reeb, M (ed), *Digest of CAS Awards 1986–1998*, 1998, Berne: Staempfli Editions SA. This includes awards of the CAS's Ad Hoc Panel. See, generally, Beloff, M, Kerr, T and Demetriou, M, *Sports Law*, 1999, Oxford: Hart, Chapter 7.

2   See, also, Tarasti, L (ed), *Legal Solutions in International Doping Cases Awards 1985–1999*, 2000, Milan: IAAF Arbitration Panel.

honed, it may be, by instruction, training and body maintenance in its widest sense. The much used metaphor – a level playing field – derives from sport. The use of drugs violates all such notions of equality: the drug taker starts with an unfair advantage. Success becomes the product of the test tube, not the training track. The interests of innocent athletes need protection by punishment of the guilty.

FACTUAL ISSUES

Drugs cases raise a range of possible factual issues. Was the positive sample that of the athlete at all? In that context, was the chain of custody – transport, storage, and security – sound? Was the sample kept free, during storage and laboratory testing, from exposure to outside elements? Was the testing equipment properly functioning? Was the prohibited substance (if endogenous, that is, natural to the body), for example, testosterone, the result of, for example, hormonal change rather than external administration or injection? Was such substance (if exogenous, that is, unnatural to the body), the result of, for example, taking of a legitimate health or other food?[3] Did the athlete take the prohibited substance knowingly, recklessly or negligently?

INGREDIENTS OF OFFENCE

But drugs cases also raise a range of possible legal issues. Some legal issues are rule-specific. For example, did the test take place in circumstances authorised by the rules? This question was raised in the *Krabbe* case, where the rules of the German Federation inadequately failed to legitimise out-of-competition testing.[4] Alternatively, was the substance actually banned at all? This question was raised in respect of clenbuterol in the weightlifters' case and bromantan in the case of the Russian swimmers, Korneev and Gouliev, at the Atlanta Olympics.[5]

And it is self-evident that the precise elements of a doping offence, like any other offence, must be derived from a correct construction of the rules in play: primarily for the tribunal concerned, ultimately it may be for the courts.[6]

---

3   The long running saga of nandrolone, alleged, according to research by Professor Maugham of Aberdeen University, to be the product of an interaction of food supplements and strenuous exercise, focuses on this question.

4   IAAF disciplinary proceedings against *Katrin Krabbe* (1992) unreported, 28 June. See *op cit*, Tarasti, fn 2, p 125.

5   CAS Arbitration (Atlanta) No 003-4.

6   A working party of the IOC, on which I served, was charged with redefining the offence for IOC purposes.

JUDGE-PROOFING

In English law, judge-proofing is impossible, except in so far as it is permitted by the Arbitration Acts 1979 and 1996. The courts will ignore, as being contrary to public policy, efforts to exclude their role as interpreters of law. Lynskey J said, with reference to rules of the British Amateur Weight Lifting Association:

> The parties can, of course, make a tribunal or council the final arbiter on quotations of fact. They can leave questions of law to the decision of a tribunal, but they cannot make it the final arbiter on question of law.[7]

In England, they retain that role without relish. The courts have on many occasions said, in the words of Sir Nicholas Browne-Wilkinson VC:

> Sport would be better served if there was not running litigation at repeated intervals by people seeking to challenge the decisions of the regulating bodies.[8]

In other countries, immunisation from judicial supervision may be more easily achievable. The athlete's declaration at the Atlanta Olympics, undertaking to accept CAS's jurisdiction and abstain from resort to the courts, was never tested as to its validity.[9] I am personally aware of the doubts expressed as to the outcome had it been put to the test in Georgia, let alone elsewhere in the world. CAS's own awards are liable to challenge before the Swiss Federal Tribunal, but only if vitiated by obvious error of law or unfairness.[10]

RULES OF INTERPRETATION

In *USA Shooting and Quigley v Union Internationale de Tir*,[11] a CAS Panel has stated:

> The fight against doping is arduous, and it may require strict rules. But the rule makers and the rule appliers must begin by being strict with themselves. Regulations that may affect careers of dedicated athletes must be predictable. They must emanate from duly authorised bodies. They must be adopted in constitutionally proper ways. They should not be the product of an obscure process of accretion. Athletes and officials should not be confronted with a thicket of mutually qualifying or even contradictory rules that can be understood only on the basis of the *de facto* practice over the course of many years of a small of insiders.

---

7   *Baker v Jones* [1954] 2 All ER 553, p 558.

8   *Cowley v Heatley* (1986) *The Times*, 14 July.

9   The same question arose at the Sydney Olympics. See, now, *Raguz v Sullivan* (2000) unreported, 1 September, NSW Court of Appeal.

10 *Op cit*, Reeb, fn 1, Pt 8. See, also, *Wang v CAS* (1999) unreported, 31 March, Swiss Federal Tribunal, acquitting me, as Chairman of a CAS Panel, of any impropriety.

11 CAS 94/129. See *op cit*, Reeb, fn 1, p 187.

In my experience, rules of domestic or international federations tend to resemble the architecture of an ancient building: a wing added here, a loft there, a buttress elsewhere, without adequate consideration of whether the additional parts affect adversely the symmetry of the whole.[12] In *NWBA v IPC*, where the rules were silent on the definition of doping, the CAS commented adversely on such an example of 'drafting that engenders controversy'[13] and refused the IPC its costs.

And, in *Reel v Holder*, Lord Denning MR, in the Court of Appeal, said about the rules of the International Amateur Athletic Federation:

> One can argue to and fro on the interpretation of these rules. The people who drew them up would not possibly have envisaged all the problems which would have to be coped with in the future in regard to them. The courts have to reconcile all the various differences as best they can.[14]

The methods of interpretation of such rules are not necessarily those applicable to Acts of the legislature or of commercial documents. A more relaxed approach is required. Sports association rules should be construed purposively, not pedantically. In *Cowley v Heatley* (1986), a South African-born swimmer claimed that the Commonwealth Games Federation had misconstrued the word 'domicil' in their regulations and had unlawfully banned her from competing in the Commonwealth Games in Edinburgh. Sir Nicholas Browne-Wilkinson VC said:

> One had to look for the meaning of the word in that context; to inquire beyond the language and see what the circumstances were with reference to which the words were used, and the object appearing from those circumstances which the person using them had in view.[15]

And, given their quasi-penal consequences, doping rules should be construed *contra proferentem* in favour of the athlete.[16] This is especially so in cases of rules of strict liability.[17]

APPLICATION OF RULES OF INTERPRETATION

At the Nagano Olympics, Mr Ross Rebagliati, the gold medallist snowboard champion, was found to have traces of marijuana in his urine. However, the

---

12 See, however, the Anti-Doping Convention of the Council of Europe, Strasbourg, 16 November 1989.

13 CAS 95/122, p 10, para 35. See *op cit*, Reeb, fn 1, p 123.

14 *Reel v Holder* [1981] 3 All ER 321, p 325.

15 See above, fn 3.

16 Beale, H, *Chitty on Contracts*, 28th edn, 1999, London: Sweet & Maxwell, Vol 1, para 12-087.

17 *Halsbury's Laws of England*, 4th edn, 1991, London: Butterworths, Vol 44, para 14.56.

IOC Rules, on their true construction, treated the use of marijuana as doping only if there was an agreement between the IOC and the relevant sports federation to that effect, and there was in fact none.

The CAS Ad Hoc Panel recognised that it was neither a court of law nor a court of ethics, but a domestic tribunal applying a particular code. They said:

> In reaching our result, we do not suggest for a moment that the use of marijuana should be condoned, nor do we suggest that sports authorities are not entitled to exclude athletes found to use cannabis. But if sports authorities wish to add their own sanctions to those that are addicted by public authorities, they must do so in an explicit fashion. That has not been done here. Indeed, Mr Hodler expressly affirmed that FIS does not consider cannabis consumption as a doping offence and that although FIS discourages both alcohol and cannabis consumption it has never positively enacted specified prohibitions with respect to either. The Panel recognises that from an ethical and medical perspective, cannabis consumption is a matter of serious social concern. CAS is not, however, a criminal court and can neither promulgate nor apply penal laws. We must decide within the context of the law of sports, and cannot invent prohibitions or sanctions where none appear.[18]

In *Quigley*,[19] the CAS, applying Swiss law, overturned the decision of the UIT (the international shooters' union) to ban Mr Quigley for three months and to disqualify his team from victory in one of the shooting events of the 1994 Cairo World Cup. The UIT had accepted that Mr Quigley had not intended to take ephedrine and other banned substances present in certain medication prescribed for his bronchitis. But it acted on a misconstruction of the UIT's anti-doping rule which included a definition of doping that included reference to 'the aim of attaining an increase in performance'. The rule, therefore, required (unusually) *mens rea* in use of prohibited substances, not merely an intent to use, but an intent to use for a particular purpose. In the conventional sporting code, drugs offences are offences of strict liability.

An aquatic-asthmatic case, *Cullwick v FINA*,[20] concerned a New Zealand water polo player who tested positive for salbutamol at Dunkirk in July 1995 and appealed against a two year ban, again on the basis of ingestion by inhalation pursuant to medical necessity. The CAS considered Mr Cullwick's submission that prior notification to a relevant authority of the medical necessity to inhale salbutamol was a free standing obligation, but not a precondition of the swimmer's right to invoke the exception to the ban on salbutamol. But the submission was rejected in favour of a purposive construction which drew inspiration from the *Quigley* case. (An earlier case,

---

18 NAG OG/98/002. See *op cit*, Reeb, fn 1, p 479.

19 CAS 94/129. See *op cit*, Reeb, fn 1, p 187.

20 CAS 96/149, presided over by the author. See *op cit*, Reeb, fn 1, p 251.

Lehtinen v FINA,[21] was held distinguishable, in that there had been evidence in that case of prior written notification to the relevant authority by the athlete's doctor.)[22]

But the National Wheelchair Basketball Association of the US failed in its challenge to the decision of the predecessor body to the International Paralympic Committee to disallow the victory of the US basketball team over The Netherlands at the 1992 Barcelona Paralympic Games. One member of the US team took a painkiller containing a banned substance and tested positive immediately after the championship final. The CAS distinguished the *Quigley* case on the ground that the rules there in play created an offence of intention, while those applying in the case before it did not and 'no one subject to the [relevant] rules could come to the conclusion that they would excuse the inadvertent ingestion of banned substances'.[23] The CAS interpreted the relevant rules as creating strict liability even though, first, there was no explicit definition of doping at all, and, secondly, the rules provided only for sanctions in respect of those 'guilty of doping'.

STRICT LIABILITY

A more fundamental question arises, namely, whether a strict liability rule (which disables the athlete from providing any exculpatory explanation of the circumstances in which a substance was found in the body fluids), or even a rule which inverts the ordinary burden of proof, is fair or even lawful.[24]

The justification behind rules of strict liability is that otherwise, a coach and horses could be driven through the policy which underlies the rules – the absolute prohibition on the use of substances which give one competitor an unfair advantage over the other. To require the relevant sports body to establish *mens rea* would impose upon it a burden which it could not easily discharge, and which could lead to protracted, bitter and, ultimately, inconclusive hearings. 'Indeed, if for each case the sports bodies had to prove the nature of an act in order for it to be deemed an offence, the fight against doping would become virtually impossible.'[25]

---

21 CAS 95/142.

22 *Ibid*, pp 19 and 20, paras 5.7 and 5.9; evidencing the growth of an incipient body of precedent in the CAS jurisprudence.

23 *NWBA v IPC* CAS 95/122, p 9, para 32. See *op cit*, Reeb, fn 1, p 173.

24 See the valuable discussion in Young, RR, 'Problems with the definition of doping: does lack of fault or the absence of performance enhancing matter?' and 'Drug testing in sport, legal challenges and issues' (1999) 20 Queensland ULJ.

25 *Chagnaud v FINA* CAS 95/141, para 13.

Further, there can be no objection in principle from disqualifying anyone who has won a race with the aid of drugs, even though he, she or it was entirely innocent in the matter. The fact remains that the advantage has been gained – and, in objective terms, unfairly.

Different and more subtle problems arise when the long term future of the athlete or associate is concerned. The English Jockey Club Rules, for example, appear to appreciate that it may not be right to put a trainer's livelihood at risk if he has been the victim of some outside conspiracy (or, indeed, of accident). Rule 53(1)(i) makes the withdrawal of licence or permit from the trainer discretionary, even if it is established that the horse was doped; and, although placing the burden of proof upon the trainer, provides for a waiver of fine if it can be shown that the offending substance was not administered by him or someone for whom he is responsible, or not administered intentionally, and that he had taken 'all reasonable precautions to avoid a breach of this rule'.

In their original form, by contrast, the Rules of the IAAF did not even have this type of get-out clause. In the case of the Swiss athlete Sandra Gasser, who came third in the final of the women's 1,500 m in the World Championships in Rome, but in whose urine an anabolic steroid was found, it was argued that 'a rule which did not permit an athlete even to try and establish his or her moral innocence, either in resisting conviction or in mitigation of sentence, was unreasonable and unjustifiable'.[26] However, Scott J[27] concluded 'that in the circumstances the restraints were reasonable'.[28]

The factors that appear to have influenced his decision were, first, the difficulty of determining the validity of an explanation that the drug was ingested unknowingly; secondly, the importance to world athletics, both in the public interest and in the interest of the athletes themselves, that the practice of doping should be firmly dealt with; and, thirdly, the slowness with which the courts should interfere with the manner in which an association governing a particular branch of the sport administers the sport.

Under the *present* IAAF Rules (r 59.7), 'in exceptional circumstances athletes may apply to the Council for reinstatement before the IAAF period of ineligibility has expired'. It appears that the IAAF's legal advisers have been astute to ensure that they more easily defend, in future, any attack on the validity of their strict liability rules against doping.

In the series of cases decided by the CAS, the correct interpretation of anti-doping provisions has been debated; the principal issue has been whether particular rules under consideration create a 'strict liability' offence of

---

26 *Gasser v Stinson* (1988) unreported, 15 June, transcript paras 8F–G.

27 Now Lord Scott.

28 *Ibid,* para 40A.

ingesting a banned substance, or whether knowledge and/or intention to ingest the substance must additionally be proved. In such cases, the CAS considers that the general principle of law, *nulla poena sine culpa*, must not be applied too literally, reflecting the view that strict liability doping offences are not necessarily invalid on public policy grounds, since performance enhancing drugs confer an unfair advantage even if taken accidentally or without intent to gain advantage.

A *dictum* from *Quigley* exemplifies this policy:

> Furthermore, it appears to be a laudable policy objective not to repair an accidental unfairness to an individual by creating an *intentional* unfairness to the whole body of other competitors. This is what would happen if banned performance enhancing substances were tolerated when absorbed inadvertently. Moreover, it is likely that even intentional abuse would in many cases escape sanction for lack of proof of guilty intent. And it is certain that a requirement of intent would invite costly litigation that may well cripple federations – particularly those run on model budgets – in their fight against doping.

> For these reasons, the Panel would as a matter of principle be prepared to apply a strict liability test. The Panel is aware that arguments have been raised that a strict liability standard is unreasonable, and indeed contrary to natural justice, because it does not permit the accused to establish moral innocence. It has even been argued that it is an excessive restraint of trade. The Panel is unconvinced by such objections and considers that in principle the high objectives and practical necessities of the fight against doping amply justify the application of a strict liability standard.[29]

In application of this principle, the subjective elements of the case are not examined: the guilt of the athlete is presumed and she or he does not have the right to supply exculpatory evidence, save in relation to mitigation.[30]

A formidable case could be mounted that Scott J's decision and the CAS approach are wrong. It is not in issue that the rules constitute a restraint of trade. The only issue is as to the reasonableness or otherwise of the restraint. Why, it may be asked, should an athlete who is, say, the victim of a conspiracy by the rival camp, and who *unwittingly* takes drugs, find that, as a result, he or she is disqualified from the sport for ever, without means of redress?

The public law of the land in England provides a useful guidance. There are 'special reasons' upon which a court may refrain from disqualifying in respect of a drink-driving offence. In *Pugsley v Hunter*[31] it was held that, where a defendant can establish that his drink was laced, he did not know or

---

29 *Quigley v UIT* CAS 94/129, para 14; emphasis added. See *op cit*, Reeb, fn 1, p 187.

30 *Wang v FINA* CAS 98/208, para 535; *Cullwick v FINA* CAS 96/149, paras 6.5, 6.6.1; *op cit*, Reeb, fn 1, p 251; *Volkers v FINA* CAS 95/150, paras 40, 44; *Foschi v FINA* CAS 95/156, para 15.

31 (1973) RTR 284.

suspect that his drink was laced and, if his drink had not been laced, the alcohol level in his blood would not have exceeded the prescribed limit, then the court would be entitled to find special reasons.

I have always assumed that the IAAF has ruled that its rules create a strict liability doping offence.[32] But, at the International Symposium on Sports Law held in Berlin and Potsdam on 19 November 1997, Lauri Tarasti, a Justice of the Supreme Administrative Court of Finland and former Chairman of the Arbitration Panel of the IAAF, observed[33] that the principle *nulla poena sine culpa* was global, but subject to exceptions. He distinguished four types of doping offence under the IAAF rules: (1) presence of a prohibited substance; (2) use of a prohibited substance; (3) admission of use of a prohibited substance; and (4) failure or refusal to submit to doping control. He went on to state that, as to (3), no issue of liability arises; the case is determined by the admission. As to (2), use implies *mens rea*.[34] As to (4), mere refusal is sufficient, but could itself be the product only of intent or negligence.[35] As to (1), presence of the substance suffices; there is no need for the IAAF to prove that the drug has assisted performance. But, controversially, he said that presence indicates intent or negligence, so that, if there is no such intent or negligence, the offence is not committed.[36] However, I respectfully submit that Judge Tarasti was in error in his interpretation of rule (1). Presence is a question of pure fact; thus, an IAAF Panel dealing with the issue of presence stated without any misdirection that 'no mental element of intent or negligence has been taken into consideration'.[37]

HARD CASES

Nonetheless, the CAS, like Judge Tarasti, has sometimes been inclined to construe strict liability rules as if they contain a rebuttable presumption of

---

32 *Re Capobianco* (1997) unreported, 17 March. See *op cit*, Tarasti, fn 2, p 147.

33 See Tarasti, L, *Strict Liability in Doping Cases in the Light of Decisions made by the Arbitration Panel of the IAAF*, Conference Paper, 1997, and now *op cit*, Tarasti, fn 2.

34 See IAAF disciplinary proceedings against *Katrin Krabbe* (1992) unreported, 28 June. *Op cit*, Tarasti, fn 2, p 125.

35 See IAAF disciplinary proceedings against *John NI Gugi*. *Op cit*, Tarasti, fn 2, p 131.

36 This was Judge Tarasti's interpretation of the 1996 *Bevilacqua* case, concerning an Italian highjumper, where the Panel held that the athlete had 'not done enough to ensure that no prohibited substance has entered her body tissues or fluids': *op cit*, Tarasti, fn 2, p 143.

37 *Ibid, Re Capobianco*. However, Judge Tarasti's view has august support from a CAS Arbitrator, Denis Oswald; see his *Doping Sanctions: Guilty or Innocent*, FISA No 6, 1995, pp 2–3. New York sports attorney, A Wise, argues from a US perspective that strict liability rules are intrinsically illegal; see, eg, (1997) 1 *Defensor Legis* 119.

guilt arising from the presence in the body of a prohibited substance. Such was its conclusion in the case of a French swimmer, Mlle Chagnaud, who appealed against a two year ban imposed by the international federation, FINA, of which the French Swimming Federation was a member. The relevant anti-doping provision contained an explicit definition unmistakably couched in the language of strict liability.[38] The CAS approved the use of strict liability rules irrespective of any question of guilty intent.[39] Despite this, the CAS construed the rules in favour of the swimmer, relying on previous flexibility exercised by FINA in applying them. (There was evidence that FINA had previously allowed a swimmer to adduce exculpatory evidence disproving fault, deliberately ignoring the letter of its rules.) Accordingly, the CAS would have allowed Mlle Chagnaud to try to rebut the presumption of deliberate ingestion, but held on the facts that she had failed to do so. In *Chagnaud*, they stated, at para 17:

> The Panel considers that, generally speaking, the principle of presumption of the athlete's guilt may remain but, by way of compensation, the athlete must have the possibility of shifting the burden of proof by providing exculpatory evidence. The athlete will thus be allowed to demonstrate that he did not commit any fault intentionally or negligently.

They added, however, at para 14: 'Such a development is possibly only if the applicable rules allow it.'

The previous case which the CAS had in mind related to another swimmer, Samantha Riley. Ms Riley had escaped with a warning after testing positive for propoxyphene metabolite. FINA instead imposed a two year ban on her coach, a Mr Volkers, who admitted giving Ms Riley the analgesic painkiller which caused her positive test. The ban was then shortened to one year. Mr Volkers appealed against it. The CAS applied 'the rules of FINA and ... general principles of law', having heard citations of Swiss and Australian law in argument. It decided that the rule created strict liability for a coach as well as a swimmer, and dismissed Mr Volkers' appeal against FINA's finding of guilt.[40]

The decision in *Volkers* is difficult to square with that in *Chagnaud*. The former case is charitably seen as an interesting example of the effect which prior custom and practice may have on the correct interpretation of disciplinary rules. FINA's failure to discipline Ms Riley on the basis of strict liability was invoked in *Chagnaud* in support of a construction favourable to

---

38 See *Chagnaud v FINA* CAS 95/141, p 7, para 4: '... the identification of a banned substance ... in a competitor's urine or blood sample will constitute an offence ...'

39 Citing Dallèves, *Conférence Droit et Sport*, CAS 1993, p 26.

40 *Volkers v FINA* CAS 95/150.

the swimmer and at odds with the plain meaning of the words creating a strict liability offence. Similarly, in English law, the interpretation of contractual terms, including disciplinary rules, may be informed by past custom and practice, but only to the extent that the meaning of the words in question is unclear or ambiguous.[41] But I prefer to see *Riley* (and *Chagnaud*) as an example of the proposition that hard cases make bad law.

In my view, the reconciliation of interest of the sports world at large, and the athlete in particular, require disqualification from the event to be automatic, but further sanctions to depend upon degree of fault.

BURDEN OF PROOF

The next question which may arise is which party bears the onus of proving guilt, or of proving a particular factual point relevant to guilt. The starting point is the normal rule that a party asserting the existence of a particular fact bears the onus of proving that fact. But that rule may be modified or displaced by the effect of disciplinary rules creating presumptions or reversing the onus of proof on a particular issue, provided that the effect of any such modification is not to create a presumption of guilt.

Thus, in a doping case, the onus must be on the association bringing the case to prove the presence of a banned substance in the athlete's body. But the association's disciplinary rules may also require that ingestion of the substance occurred voluntarily and/or with intent to gain advantage, so that the case is not one of strict liability. In that event, the rules may also create a presumption that ingestion occurred voluntarily and with intent to gain advantage, arising on proof of the presence of the substance in the body, unless the athlete can show the contrary – for example by producing a witness who says he 'laced' the athlete's drink, or similar evidence.

English law does not find objectionable the placing on the accused of the onus of proving a specific factual defence.[42] Nor did the IAAF, in a recent interlocutory ruling in the case of *Decker-Slaney*.[43] I, too, consider that this approach aptly balances the scales of justice.

---

41 *Op cit*, Beale, fn 16, para 12-056/7.

42 Howard, M, *Phipson on Evidence*, 15th edn, 1999, London: Thomson Professional, paras 4–16.

43 Referred to in the final ruling in *Decker-Slaney* (1999) unreported, 25 April, transcript para 9; see *op cit*, Tarasti, fn 2, p 155. See, also, the IAAF ruling in *Merlene Ottey* (2000) unreported, 3 July, transcript para 16.

STANDARD OF PROOF

The CAS held in the Chinese swimmers cases that the standard of proof required of the regulator, FINA, is high: less than criminal standard, but more than the ordinary civil standard.[44] The Panel was content to adopt the test, set out in *Korneev and Gouliev v IOC*,[45] that ingredients must be established to the comfortable satisfaction of the court, bearing in mind the seriousness of the allegation made. To adopt a criminal standard (at any rate, where the disciplinary charge is not one of a criminal offence) is to confuse the public law of the State with the private law of an association.

The CAS went on, in *Korneev*, to reiterate the proposition that the more serious the allegation, the greater the degree of evidence required to achieve 'comfortable satisfaction'.[46]

Again, federation rules can provide their own standard. Under IAAF Rules, when testosterone is the prohibited substance, and testosterone/epitestosterone ratios or concentration 'so exceed the range of values normally found in humans as not to be consistent with normal endogenous production', the athlete has to prove 'by clear and convincing evidence that the abnormal ratio is attributable to pathological or physiological condition'.[47]

What standard of proof should be required of prosecutor and defendant where, under the rules, the burden shifts? In English criminal law, the defendant, in principle, has to make out of the defence only on the civil standard. But, in the case of the Chinese swimmers, where the issue arose – but did not fall to be decided – the Panel left the matter open:

> Whether the burden which lies upon the competitor can be discharged on the balance of probabilities or on the same standard of proof as lies upon the regulatory body initially which does not fall for decision in this case, it is clear that the submission of the Appellants that, notwithstanding the shifting of the burden, the sporting regulator is still obliged to eliminate all other possibilities must be rejected. Such a submission is consistent *neither* with the concept of a shifting burden *nor* with language of the provisions *nor* required by Swiss law.[48]

In my personal view, given that the rules are administered by domestic bodies, not stage agencies, there is a principled possibility that what is sauce

---

44 *Wang v FINA* CAS 98/208, 22 December 1998, para 5.6.
45 *Korneev and Russian NOC v IOC; Gouliev and Russian NOC v IOC*, reported in *Mealey's International Arbitration Report*, February 1997, pp 28–29.
46 *Ibid.*
47 IAAF Procedural Guidelines, Sched 1, Pt 1. See the IAAF Panel decision in *Merlene Ottey* (2000) unreported, 3 July, transcript para 16, creatively applying the same test to nandrolone, which is also said to be capable of endogenous production.
48 *Wang v FINA* CAS 98/208, para 5.1; emphasis added.

for the goose is sauce for the gander: the same standard of proof should be imposed on prosecution and defence.

THE BENEFIT OF THE DOUBT IN ACTION

In the controversial case of *Andrei Korneev*,[49] the Panel said:

> The ongoing fight against the use of drugs in sport would be severely hampered by there being an exclusive list of substances being the only substances whose use was prohibited. The court wishes to emphasise the overriding importance of the fight against doping in sports. Doping both threatens the integrity of competition and puts the health of athletes at risk. Whenever there is a proof that it has occurred, it is not to be tolerated.

> The intention and the effect of the Medical Code is to ban the use of stimulants. The listing of examples of stimulants is to assist those engaged in sport to be aware of the minimum range of banned substances and to put beyond doubt whether or not certain substances are prohibited or in some cases the level of dosage which is permissible.

> After carefully considering the evidence of Dr Holbrook and of Prof Segura we are of the view that the scientific evidence before us establishes that Bromantan may well be a stimulant within the meaning of the Medical Code but that the evidence before the court is not sufficient to establish that conclusion to the relevant and high degree of satisfaction necessary to support such a finding.

> The surrounding circumstances while suspicious do not form a basis for concluding, in the light of the scientific evidence, that bromantan is a stimulant. The surrounding circumstances, of themselves, are not evidence of the objective fact of the actual chemical composition and qualities of bromantan. They could be evidence of the belief of those using the substance but not of the correctness of that belief.

> While it may be that further study may establish that bromantan is a prohibited substance the totality of the material before us not allow us to reach that conclusion.

The CAS are loath to allow strict liability rules to operate unfairly so as to punish the innocent in a case where the rules themselves are unclear or their applicability to the facts of the case doubtful.

But doubts can sometimes be unreasonable. An accused athlete, Capobianco, has pointed to contaminated meat as the source of innocently ingested banned steroids in his body. Expert evidence had been deployed to support the assertion that unscrupulous meat producers sometimes illegally inject animals destined for slaughter with the very same banned steroids in order to increase the yield of meat from the animals. Scientists responsible for

---

49   CAS Arbitration (Atlanta), No 003-4.

testing samples taken from athletes accept that illegal contamination of this kind is not unknown, but regard the prospect of innocent contamination as infinitesimally small. Consequently, they discount, as did the IAAF tribunal, such a defence, even where meat of a type known to be susceptible to illegal contamination is shown to have been on the menu shortly before the test.[50] The issue remains a live one.[51] Another argument advanced in respect of female athletes is that an unnatural amount of testosterone can be the product of hormonal disorder; thus, in the US, the Olympic runner, Mary Decker-Slaney, was acquitted of a doping offence before the US Amateur Athletic Federation Panel on the basis of this defence. The claim was dismissed before the IAAF Panel in Monte Carlo, on the basis of inadequate factual or expert evidence.[52]

NATURE OF EVIDENCE

On what factual material may a sporting tribunal exercising punitive jurisdiction lawfully rely in support of a finding of guilt? In some cases, disciplinary tribunals have sought to make findings of guilt and impose penalties in consequence, on the basis of evidence whose nature and sufficiency is subsequently put in issue in a legal challenge before the courts.

The starting point here is the proposition that the disciplinary tribunal, like all domestic tribunals, must have some evidence before it supporting a finding of guilt, if such a finding is to be lawful; but that the weight to be placed on such evidence is a matter for the tribunal and not the court.[53] English law insists on autonomy of decision making for domestic tribunals, including those concerned with discipline in the sporting field, provided that the tribunal has some evidence before it to support its finding, and provided (as explained above) that it applies valid rules correctly interpreted.

Nor is such a tribunal bound by the strict rules of evidence which apply in English courts. The type of evidence which can come before sporting tribunals

---

50 *Re Capobianco* (1997) unreported, 17 March. See *op cit*, Tarasti, fn 2, p 147.

51 This resurfaced in the cases of *Meca-Medina* and *Madjan* (CAS 99/234–35), where enhanced nandrolone production was said to be the consequence of eating a Brazilian dish, sarapatell, made of boar's testicles. The case has been remitted for a fresh hearing in 2001 to consider further scientific evidence. See, also, *ITF v Korda* CAS 99/223/A, where the tennis player accused veal sauce on his pasta.

52 *Op cit*, Tarasti, fn 2, p 155. An IAAF Panel has held that an athlete is entitled to the benefit of the doubt where a metabolite of a prohibited substance could also come from an allowed substance, such as a contraceptive drug: see *Akpan* (1995) unreported, IAAF; *op cit*, Tarasti, fn 2, p 135.

53 *Dawkins v Antrobus* (1881) 17 Ch D 615 (CA), pp 626–28, *per* James LJ; pp 630, 633, *per* Brett LJ; pp 633–34, *per* Cotton LJ. *Faramus v Film Artistes Association* [1964] AC 925, pp 941–42, *per* Lord Evershed; pp 944–48, *per* Lords Hodson and Pearce. See, also, Josling, JF and Alexander, P, *The Law of Clubs*, 5th edn, 1984, London: Oyez, pp 32–33; *Lee v Showmen's Guild* [1952] 2 QB 329 (CA), pp 432–44, *per* Denning LJ.

is rarely constrained by the distinction between admissibility and relevance, familiar to English adjectival law. What is relevant is admissible, and vice versa. Direct evidence is weightier than indirect – but indirect evidence can be adduced. This has the consequence that a sporting disciplinary tribunal may accept hearsay evidence without the procedural requirements of the Civil Evidence Acts 1968 and 1995, and of rules of court.[54] Thus, the tribunal may generally receive evidence in written form without cross-examination, even in the case of expert evidence. However, the latitude allowed to such disciplinary tribunals is always qualified by the duty to act fairly. If the nature of evidence received and relied upon by the tribunal is such as to compromise the duty of fairness, the resulting decision could later be set aside in court; for example, where evidence relating to the scientific appropriateness of laboratory procedure in a doping case is given by a secretary at the laboratory with no scientific qualification.

Expert evidence is particularly important in doping cases. Any expert called on to give evidence before a sporting disciplinary tribunal should bear in mind the guidance given by Cresswell J in the English Commercial Court on the duties of an expert: to be, and be seen to be, independent; to provide an objective, unbiased opinion; to state the facts or assumptions on which that opinion is based; to volunteer material facts which detract from his opinion; to delineate clearly his area of expertise and identify any issue falling outside it; to distinguish between concluded opinions and provisional ones; and to communicate to the other side any change of view on a material point arising, for example from availability of new material.[55]

FAIR PROCEDURES

The courts have not been shy of interfering where the allegation is of a breach of the rules of natural justice. In the area of sport, the general rules of natural justice are adapted to the special elements of the matter in question.[56] The full panoply of a court hearing is not required; nor are technical rules of evidence adhered to. Those rules – so far as material – are few in number. The first is that both sides should be heard. Secondly, a person should be disqualified from determining any matter in which he may or may not fairly be suspected to be biased. In the composition of a tribunal, justice must not only be done, but be seen to be done. A person appearing against a party as an advocate in one matter cannot be an arbitrator where that same party is involved, even in

---

54 See RSC Ord 38.

55 *The Ikarian Reefer* [1993] 2 Lloyd's Rep 68 (reversed on appeal on an unrelated point).

56 *Russell v Duke of Norfolk* [1949] 1 All ER 109, p 118.

a completely separate matter.[57] There must be 'the absence of any appearance of presumption', ditto. However, an objection to an arbitrator must come from a party, not a co-arbitrator.[58] Thirdly, the person making a finding in the exercise of such a jurisdiction must base his decision upon evidence that has some probative value:[59]

> ... what is required by [this] ... is that the decision to make the finding must be based upon some material that tends logically to show the evidence of facts consistent with the finding, and for the reasoning supporting the finding, if it be disclosed, if not logically self-contradictory.

THE RIGHT TO BE HEARD

Violation of these elementary precepts is well known in the field of the decision of sports associations. In *Angus v British Judo Association*,[60] the Association decided to ban the judoka after he failed a drug test, without giving any opportunity to explain that a prohibited substance was found in a sinus decongestant which he was taking under a lawful medical prescription. The decision was set aside as clearly contrary to the rules of natural justice.

OTHER EXAMPLES

The CAS, however, has enlarged the doctrine of fairness beyond narrow rules and into the realm of more general principle.

In *Cooke v FEI*,[61] a urine test, which is scientifically more reliable than the blood test, disclosed that the horse had been injected with a prohibited substance. However, the owner had not been told of the negative blood test and had not requested a second test (as was her right). However, the co-existence of a negative blood test with a positive urine test did not, by itself, cast doubt on the validity of the urine test, since the veterinary regulations themselves recognised that a urine sample is superior to a blood sample for

---

57 *Celtic plc v UEFA* CAS 98/201. This referred to the author, who subsequently became the advocate for the party which had sought to have him appointed as arbitrator. Moreover, it has been held by an arbitrator (Ronald Walker QC) that someone who has adjudicated in a particular matter cannot be an advocate in the same matter at a later stage. (This also referred to the author.)

58 *Wang v FINA* CAS 98/208.

59 *Mahon v Air New Zealand* [1984] 1 AC 808, p 820G, *per* Lord Diplock.

60 (1984) *The Times*, 15 June.

61 CAS 98/184.

testing purposes.[62] The Panel (which I chaired) was, however, of the view that, had the appellant been informed of the existence of the negative blood test, more likely than not she would have asked for a confirmatory analysis. She could not be held to have waived her right to an analysis of the 'B' sample by failing to request one within 10 days when, because of the omission of the respondent, she was not given the material on which to exercise an informed choice. We were not prepared to speculate as to what such confirmatory analysis would have shown.

SANCTIONS

Disqualification is usually (and properly) mandatory. It would be unfair to other athletes to include in a ranking someone who had used artificial means of performance enhancement if the rules are sufficiently clear; this includes disqualification of a team where one individual only committed a doping offence.[63]

Disciplinary sanctions, for example, suspension, are additional. If the rules of the association permit discretion, the seriousness of the offence should reflect in the seriousness of the penalty. Subjective elements should be taken into account in each doping case.

The *lex mitior* involves applying the penalty range in force at the time of adjudication, if more benign than that in force at the time of the offence:[64]

> In the Panel's opinion, the principle whereby a criminal law applies so soon as it comes into force if it is more favourable to the accused is a fundamental principle of any democratic regime. It is established, for example, by Swiss law (Art 2, para 2 of the Penal Code) and by Italian law (Art 2 of the Penal Code).

> This principle applies to anti-doping regulations in view of the penal or at the very least disciplinary nature of the penalties that they allow to be imposed.

> By virtue of this principle, the body responsible for setting the punishment must enable the athlete convicted of doping to benefit from the new provisions, assumed to be less severe, even when the events in question occurred before they came into force.

---

62 Moreover, the respondent had produced expert testimony from two qualified persons, D Horpool and Professor McKellar, explaining why urine may be positive and blood negative, and why the positive test should be accepted.

63 *NWBA v IPC* CAS 95/122.

64 *Cullwick v FINA* CAS 96/149, para 6.4, citing and relying on the advisory opinion pronounced by the CAS and the request of the UCI and the Italian NOC in February 1995 (CAS 94/128, pp 48–49, para 33).

I note, too, that there is a live issue as to whether a life ban (or a ban which operated for an athlete's lifetime) might be an unlawful restraint of trade.[65]

CONCLUSION

As trading nations developed a *lex mercatoria*, so, little by little, a *lex sportiva* is in gestation. On the CAS Ad Hoc Panels in Atlanta in 1996 and Kuala Lumpur in 1998 on which I served, the Panel were obliged to apply, *inter alia*, 'general principles of law and the rules of law, the application of which it deems appropriate'.[66] Those general principles and rules are the common heritage of major systems of law, applied in a sporting context. And the CAS has injected sporting values into its decisions: the best man or woman should win; the integrity of the referee's decision should be respected; arbitrary discrimination is intolerable; procedures of governing bodies must be fair play in action. These values inform decisions on doping as in other cases. It is, alas, predictable that there will be more of the former than of the latter.

---

65 Eg, on 19 April 1999, Ben Johnson, stripped of his gold medal for the 100 m at the Seoul Olympics for a doping offence, was reinstated to sports eligibility in Canada. An independent adjudicator concluded that the lifetime ban imposed on Mr Johnson by Athletics Canada was excessive in the circumstances, partly on the basis that he had been misinformed at an earlier stage about his apparent rights.

66 The same applied to the Sydney Panel.

CHAPTER 5

THE FUNDAMENTAL RIGHTS OF ATHLETES IN DOPING TRIALS

JanWillem Soek

All international governing bodies have made the fight against the use of doping in their sports part of their policy. Athletes' bodies are more intensively tested for the presence of doping substances than ever before – both in and outside competition. The sports pages of the papers report almost on a daily basis about athletes who test positive. If analysis of an athlete's doping sample indicates that his body shows signs of the presence of substances which qualify as doping by his sports organisation, he will have to answer to disciplinary charges. After some time, the papers will report the outcome of the proceedings against him. As these usually take place behind closed doors, the actual proceedings themselves are seldom reported. Do the same norms of fair play apply in these proceedings as they do on the pitch? Can the accused player in these cases appeal to the same fundamental rights as apply in criminal law procedures, such as the right of *audi alteram partem*, or the right to be heard?

As doping trials show many similarities to criminal law procedures, the rights of the defendant in criminal law procedures will first be dealt with below. Secondly, the chapter will examine whether it is possible to claim those rights in the disciplinary proceedings of sports associations. Thirdly, the guarantees for a fair trial given by the international federations (IFs) will be discussed. Because a large number of federations have made violations of their doping regulations subject to strict liability for the athlete in question, making his position in doping trials different from that in which the sports organisation has to prove that he is guilty, attention will be paid to this type of liability. The chapter will examine whether an accused athlete may utilise the provisions of the Anti-Doping Convention of the Council of Europe (properly entitled the Council of Europe Convention Against Doping) and whether the Court of Arbitration for Sport may bring any influence to bear on IF policy in the framework of fundamental rights.

HUMAN RIGHTS TREATIES

Article 6 of the European Convention for the Protection of Human Rights and Fundamental Freedoms ('the Convention') and Art 14 of the International Covenant on Civil and Political Rights (ICCPR) represent the yardsticks of our civilisation. Although the rights laid down in these two Articles are only of a procedural character, this is in fact an illustration of the quality attained in the development of human rights since these rights were put into words by the philosophers of the era of Enlightenment. The rights contained therein aim to protect civilians against their governments. Their goal is guaranteeing a fair trial to everyone. These guarantees, fundamental though they may be, are, however, subject to an important restriction. They can only be invoked where the determination of civil rights and obligations as enjoyed by a person in connection with the soundness of the criminal charges brought against him is at stake. Pursuant to Art 6(1) of the Convention, the accused has a claim to a 'fair and public hearing within a reasonable time by an independent and impartial tribunal established by law'. Judgments must be announced publicly, unless other rights due to the accused in democratic society resist. Paragraph 3 of the Article provides a catalogue of minimum rights to which every person faced with criminal charges is entitled. The person charged must be informed promptly, in a language he understands, of the accusation against him. He must be given ample time for the preparation of his defence. He must be enabled to receive legal assistance and to examine witnesses under the same conditions as witnesses against him. Finally, Art 6(3) provides for the right to free interpretation if the accused is tried in a language foreign to him. The second paragraph of Art 6 contains the adage of the presumption of innocence until proven guilty according to law.

DISCIPLINARY LAW IN SPORT

The procedure described in the regulations of IFs, following the accusation of an athlete of a doping offence, is of a disciplinary character. A competent federation body shall examine whether the doping activities of the accused athlete actually fit the description of the doping offence as laid down in the regulations. If the body is convinced that this is the case, it may impose a sanction on the athlete in question. Sports organisations' disciplinary law operates in a field which is, on the one hand, bounded by the law of obligations voluntarily entered into and, on the other hand, by compulsory criminal law. The disciplinary law to which the top athlete who is accused of using doping is subjected is very close to criminal law. A top athlete is unable to exercise his chosen profession if he no longer holds the membership of a club and, through it, of the national federation, and, through that, of the IF. Apart from this aspect of the law of association, situations also occur in which an athlete who is not a member of any club can only enter competitions by entering into binding contracts. In this way, every sportsman wishing to exercise his profession or sport is subject to the disciplinary law governing his branch of sport, either because he is a club member or because he has contractually committed himself. This absence of the possibility to choose makes disciplinary sports law very like criminal law. The severity of the sanctions which may be imposed, once it has been proven beyond doubt that a doping offence was committed, also makes disciplinary sports law very similar to criminal law. Disciplinary law in sport is the disciplinary law of associations. Therefore, similar though they may be, this type of disciplinary law is not criminal law. Disciplinary law in sport may be designated 'pseudo-criminal law'. As opposed to disciplinary law based in formal legislation (such as medical disciplinary law and the disciplinary law to which notaries public are subject), it is entirely free from interference by government or parliament. It remains within the sphere of the freedom of association.

As a result of the fact that disciplinary sports law does not directly involve the State, this type of disciplinary law cannot be tested against the criteria set out by the Convention, nor by those of the ICCPR. Apart from the fact that Art 6 of the Convention speaks of a 'tribunal established by law' – which the disciplinary body of a sports organisation is not – and apart from the fact that the concept of jurisdiction with respect to such tribunals must be interpreted broadly, the Convention addresses the Contracting Parties through its Art 57, which states that 'any High Contracting Party shall furnish an explanation of the manner in which its internal law ensures the effective implementation of any provisions of the Convention'. Ratification of the Convention obliges a State to ensure the rights and freedoms intended in the Convention for everyone within its actual power and under its responsibility. The Convention only imposes obligations on States. The doctrine of so called horizontal, or third party, effect falls outside the scope of the Convention. Although the national legal order may endow the rights of Art 6 with horizontal effect, the Supreme Court of The Netherlands rejected this effect in 1990.

If a norm is of a statutory disciplinary law character, the European Court of Human Rights in Strasbourg has a supervisory task. This supervision is intended to prevent States from backing out of their Art 6 obligations by placing a norm in a disciplinary law framework. But disciplinary sports law is non-statutory and, if it does not contain the criteria of Art 6, States can in fact shirk their duties under the Convention. The Court decided on 8 June 1976[1] that, if sanctions are imposed which, measured by their severity, should be considered to be of a criminal law nature, the statutory disciplinary proceedings must be treated like criminal proceedings in the sense of Art 6. Although sanctions imposed as a result of doping offences may be severe, this does not, so to speak, turn the disciplinary sports proceedings into criminal proceedings. The authorities cannot force sports organisations to include the criteria of Art 6 in their doping regulations.

---

1   *Engel and Others v The Netherlands* (1976) 1 EHRR 647. Cf Harris, DJ, OnBoyle, M and Warbrick, C, *Law of the European Convention on Human Rights*, 1995, London: Butterworths, p 167 *et seq*; van Dijk, P and van Hoof, GJF, *Theory and Practice of the European Convention on Human Rights*, 1998, The Hague: Kluwer, p 409 *et seq*.

This paradox means that a national of a Contracting Party may legally invoke Art 6 criteria in proceedings in the realm of criminal law or statutory disciplinary law, but is unable to do so if subject to the disciplinary proceedings of his national or international sports federation. The law of association thus contributes to the fact that he may not claim rights which he is entitled to in cases outside that law. A sportsman answering to disciplinary charges in a doping trial may, with an eye to his defence, only appeal formally to those procedural rights which are given to him by the regulations of the sports organisation charging him.

Looking at doping regulations, it is apparent that international governing bodies, operating within the same civilisation which brought us Art 6 of the Convention and Art 14 of the ICCPR, lag behind in the development of that civilisation, as far as the rights of the accused are concerned. Fourteen Olympic international governing bodies do not guarantee any rights to the accused in doping procedures, while another 14 only list a few in their doping regulations. Only seven offer athletes the bulk of the rights contained in Art 6. It must, however, be noted that all international governing bodies have taken care to ensure that doping procedures may be brought before disciplinary bodies which supposedly operate impartially and independently of the international body. Some suspicion regarding this impartiality and independence is justified, though. Just recall the procedure that was followed during the 1988 Olympics in Seoul, in the doping case against Ben Johnson. During those Games, a medical commission of the International Amateur Athletic Federation (IAAF) acted both as judicial body and as the body determining the doping lists and, thereby, the offences.

Article 7 of Chapter 9 of the International Olympic Committee (IOC) Medical Code[2] stipulates that everyone has the right to be heard by the organ competent to impose sanctions. This right includes the right to be informed of the charges, to appear in person or through a representative, and to produce evidence. This last right, according to the Medical Code, also includes the right to examine witnesses and the right to a defence in writing. Part of the catalogue contained in Art 6 of the Convention may, thus, be found in Art 7. The Medical Code was in force until 1 January 2000. On that date, the Olympic Movement Anti-Doping Code entered into force. An odd situation now occurs, in that the provisions of Art 7 of the Medical Code have not been retained in the new Code even though the preamble expresses the wish on behalf of the Olympic movement 'to act in the best interests of athletes ... whose rights to justice must be safeguarded'. The IOC – perhaps due to the haste in which the new Code was drafted – has, thereby, stepped back in time.

---

2   Any individual, team or any other individual or legal entity has the right to be heard by the IOC organ competent for applying or recommending a measure or sanction to such individual, team or entity. The right to be heard includes the right to be acquainted with the charges; to appear personally; to be represented; to bring forward evidence, including witnesses; or to submit a defence in writing.

Article 2 of Chapter 2 of the new IOC Code contains a provision which upsets the balance between the parties in a doping trial even further. The provision presupposes that the accredited laboratories have conducted their analyses in accordance with current and adequate standards, as developed in scientific practice. This renders the position of the laboratory more exclusive than that of an expert witness in a criminal trial. The presumption may be challenged by showing 'convincing evidence to the contrary'. The laboratories are not *prima facie* obliged to show that the procedures have been conducted without deviating from their usual practice. The Code does not provide the defence with the right to inspect the full laboratory report. All this causes the accused athlete to be two points down before he has even touched the ball.[3]

THE VARIOUS FUNDAMENTAL RIGHTS

Only two international governing bodies grant the accused athlete the general right to a defence. The International Hockey Federation (FIH)[4] offers him 'every opportunity to defend the charges' and the International Archery Federation (FITA)[5] grants 'the accused person the right to defend him/herself'.

The right to be informed of the charges

This right, which is seemingly so obvious because, without it, athletes cannot defend themselves against charges they are not familiar with, is only contained in a limited number of anti-doping regulations. The new Olympic Movement Anti-Doping Code is completely silent on fundamental rights, but the old IOC Medical Code did stipulate that the athlete accused of doping had 'the right to be acquainted with the charges',[6] although it did not elaborate. This right was supposed to lay the foundations for equal treatment of parties to the proceedings. From the IOC rule, it does not follow that counsel for the defence is entitled to inspect all documents that the opposing party disposes of and on which it bases its accusation. The International Luge Federation (FIL) has integrally included the provision of the IOC Medical Code in its anti-doping regulations.[7] The IBF takes it one step further. According to its anti-

---

3 Metaphor of Morton-Hooper, A, 'Have we created a monster?', in *Drugs in Sport: A Time for Re-Evaluation?*, Symposium on Legal and Ethical Issues, Royal College of Physicians, 23 April 1999.

4 FIH Statutes and Bylaws, Art 22.1(a).

5 FITA Doping Control Procedures, Appendix 4, Art 11.5.

6 IOC MC, Ch 9, Art 6.

7 FIL International Luge Regulations, Artificial Track Supplement 4.

doping rules, every athlete who is suspected of doping must not only be informed in writing of the fact that the alleged offence has been taken into consideration, but must also be (albeit summarily) informed of the nature of the evidence obtained against him.[8] The FITA, too, has made similar provisions.[9] A number of international governing bodies again take it one step further, as far as disclosure of documents relevant to the athlete is concerned. The International Baseball Association (IBA) grants the athlete the right 'to consult the report of the preliminary investigations'.[10] The UCI entitles the athlete 'to take cognisance of the case file'.[11] Upon payment, each party can obtain copies of the file and, during the hearing, the file will, moreover, be available for inspection. Pursuant to FIH regulations, an accused athlete must not only be informed of the charges, but must also be given access 'to all relevant material in the possession or under the control of the FIH' and must be given 'every reasonable opportunity to defend the charges'.[12]

The right to appear in person/the right to be heard

In principle, it must first be possible to appear in person during proceedings before it is possible to be heard. Still, the IOC Medical Code treats this right as a corollary of the right to be heard.[13] The latter could be considered a step following that of the right to be informed of the charges. Provisions containing this right are, *inter alia*, laid down in the anti-doping regulations of the IAAF, International Canoe Federation (FIC), International Tennis Federation (ITF), International Ski Federation (FIS), Association of Tennis Professionals (ATP) and Women's Tennis Association (WTA) Tour.[14] The ITF adds thereto that, in case the athlete does not wish to appear in person, this will not restrain the Appeals Committee from proceeding with his case.[15]

The principle of *audi alteram partem* contains the athlete's right to act in his defence. Not only does this principle include the right to appear in person or through a representative, it also includes the right to submit evidence and the

---

8 IBF Disciplinary Regulations, Art 3.2.

9 FITA Doping Control Procedures, Appendix 4, Art 11: Disciplinary Procedures.

10 Anti-Doping Rules, Ch 11, Art 11.3.

11 UCI Cycling Regulations, Pt 14, Ch 7, Art 75.

12 FIH Statutes and Bylaws, Art 22.1(a).

13 IOC MC, Ch 9, Art 7.

14 IAAF Rules and Regulations, Div 3, r 61(5); FIC Doping Rules and Procedural Guidelines for Doping Control, r 5(3); ITF Bylaws, r 8; FIS Doping Rules, r 7.2; ATP/WTA Official Rulebook, Tennis Anti-Doping Programme, rr (L) 4, 5.

15 ITF Bylaws, r 8; ATP/WTA Official Rulebook, Tennis Anti-Doping Programme, r (L) 4.

right to examine witnesses and experts. If the athlete is unable to appear, he must be given the opportunity to defend himself in writing. Moreover, the principle must also be explained to include the athlete's right to deliver oral statements. All of these rights are contained in the IOC Medical Code.[16]

The IAAF and the FIC entitle athletes to a hearing before a competent panel prior to any decisions about their participation in competitions. This right is repeated in the summons. In case the athlete fails to return the form entitling him to a hearing within the allotted time, he is considered to have voluntarily forfeited this right.[17] The FINA, upholding a similar rule, allows the swimmer in question 28 days to request a hearing. If he does not respond, he will be deemed to have waived this right.[18]

Various international governing bodies have merely included the accused athlete's right to a hearing in their regulations.[19] The anti-doping regulations of the ITTF only list this rule in the part dealing with 'World and Olympic Title Competition'.[20] A rower or coxswain suspected of doping also has that right, and the relevant provision of the FISA adds thereto that sanctions may only be imposed after the right to be heard has been exercised within the time allotted.[21] The provisions of the ITU and the FIS concerning the right to be heard run parallel to that of the FISA.[22] The hearing described in the UCI Regulations is more or less obligatory. The national federation of a cyclist 'shall summon the rider to come and present his explanations and arguments'. The rider may, however, 'waive the right to be heard in which case the investigation shall be conducted in writing'.[23] In the proceedings described by the regulations of the IWF, 'the principles of natural justice will be observed'. These principles demand: '(a) the right to be heard by an unbiased committee, and (b) the right to be heard in answer to those charges.'[24] The FIH, too, demands of its subsidiary organs that the procedure be conducted fairly for all

---

16 See above, fn 2.

17 IAAF Rules and Regulations, Div 3, r 59(3) and Procedural Guidelines for Doping Control, 2, r 2.58. FIC Doping Rules, r 5, is r 59(3) of the IAAF Rules *verbatim*.

18 FINA Doping Control Rules, Art DC 8.7.

19 IBF Disciplinary Regulations, Art 3.1; FIBA Regulations Governing Doping Control, Art 6.6.2, para 4; UCI Cycling Regulations, Pt 14, Ch 1, Art 5; IBU Disciplinary Rules, Art 11.3 and Appendix 4.

20 ITTF Regulations for World and Olympic Title Competition, Art 4.3.1.4: 'A player accused of an infringement of the eligibility regulations shall have the right to request a hearing by the IOC Executive Board, whose decision shall be final.'

21 FISA Rules of Racing and Related Bylaws, Pt 7, r 83.

22 ITU Doping Control Rules and Procedural Guidelines, Arts 3.40 and 3.41. See, also, Art 5.2 and 5.5; FIS Doping Rules, r 5, para 2.

23 UCI Cycling Regulations, Pt 14, Ch 7, Art 69.

24 IWF Anti-Doping Policy, Art 15.8.

parties involved and that 'those parties' basic rights' are upheld. It must, among others, be safeguarded that the accused athlete 'is given every reasonable opportunity to defend the charges and to be heard'.[25] Pursuant to FIVB regulations, the right to a hearing is, on the one hand, not a firm right that athletes may claim: 'The FIVB Medical Commission recommends that, before a final decision is made on a particular case, a fair hearing be granted to the player (and possibly the other persons concerned).' On the other hand, if the results of a sample analysis only become known after the competition, the volleyball player is entitled to a hearing: 'In case the result is received after the competition, the players have the right to ask for a hearing to be organised or to send a confidential letter to the President of the FIVB Medical Commission, if they want circumstances and facts to be taken into consideration.'[26] More than any other IF, the FIVB has set out guidelines for the content of the hearing:

> Such hearing should take into consideration the circumstances (extenuating or not) and the known facts of the case. During the hearing, it is also recommended that the head of the accredited laboratory which reported the result be consulted. It may impinge on the athlete's rights if the hearing is planned at very short notice. The athlete must be given ample opportunity to prepare his defence. The right to be heard may also be impinged upon if the hearing takes place at a location disadvantageous to the athlete or at a disadvantageous time of day. Here it must also be noted that the combined time and place may be right for the athlete, but not for possible witnesses and experts.

The right to representation

The right to be heard also includes the right to representation, according to the IOC Medical Code.[27] The FIL rule is identical in this regard to that of the IOC.[28] In various anti-doping regulations, this provision (apart from other rights that the athlete may claim) is found. In some instances, it is expressly stipulated by whom – and at whose expense – the athlete may be represented.[29]

---

25 FIH Statutes and Bylaws, Art 22.1.
26 FIVB Medical Regulations, 2; FIVB Anti-Doping Control Regulations, Art 2.6.6.
27 See above, fn 2.
28 FIL International Luge Regulations, Artificial Track Supplement 4, Ch 7, Art 7.
29 IBF Disciplinary Regulations, Art 3.4; IBA Anti-Doping Rules, Ch 11, Art 11.3; UCI Cycling Regulations, Pt 14, Ch 7, Art 77; FIG Medical Regulations, Art 3.1(c); IWF Anti-Doping Policy, Art 15.10; ATP/WTA Official Rulebook, Tennis Anti-Doping Programme, r (L) 5.

The right to submit evidence

According to the IOC Medical Code, the right to be heard includes the right to submit evidence.[30] A small number of IFs grant this right in so many words to athletes in doping trials.[31] It is not stipulated how much freedom the doping panel has in relation to the application of the law of evidence, nor is the panel's freedom with regard to issues of admissibility and weighing of evidence recorded. Can the panel itself deal with an incident involving false evidence, or should a civil court be called in?

Reversal of the burden of proof

The IOC Medical Code guaranteed the athlete the right to submit evidence, but this fact alone did not also guarantee equality between him and the IOC in the doping trial. Not only did the IOC hold a trump card with the positive results of doping analyses, but this card was also hidden by the law of evidence. The Medical Code presupposed that the laboratory performed the tests in accordance with the highest scientific norms. The results of analyses were therefore always considered to be scientifically correct.[32] It was also considered to be a given that the laboratory did its testing in accordance with current and adequate standards of care. The same went for the way in which the laboratory stored samples. Only suspicions regarding the standard of care could be countered by evidence to the contrary. The laboratories were not *prima facie* obliged to show that the procedures were conducted without deviating from the usual practice.[33] The Code did not provide the defence with the right to inspect the full laboratory report. Through these provisions, the position of the laboratory – and, indirectly, that of the IOC – was more or less endowed with evidentiary immunity. The two provisions on the position of the laboratory in the IOC Medical Code are repeated in the Olympic Movement Anti-Doping Code, condensed into one provision. Now, laboratories are presupposed to have performed tests and stored samples in accordance with current and acceptable norms of scientific practice. This presumption may again be countered, this time by 'convincing evidence to the

---

30 See above, fn 2.

31 UCI Cycling Regulations, Pt 14, C Art 74; FIH Statutes and Bylaws, Art 22.1(a)(iii); FIH Doping Policy, Art 10.3; FIL International Luge Regulations, Artificial Track Supplement 4, Ch 7, Art 7; ATP/WTA Official Rulebook, Tennis Anti-Doping Programme, r (L) 6.

32 IOC MC, Ch 10, Art 2. Cf FINA Doping Control Rules, DC 8; FIL Medical Code, Supplement 4, Ch VIII, Arts II and III.

33 IOC MC, Ch 10, Art 3.

contrary'.[34] Again, the laboratories are not *prima facie* obliged to show that the procedures were conducted without deviating from the usual practice.[35] Although the Anti-Doping Code does not grant the athlete accused of using doping the right to submit evidence, it does grant him this right where the functioning of the laboratories is concerned.

Distribution of the burden of proof with regard to strict liability

At the moment, the anti-doping regulations of international governing bodies feature two kinds of descriptions of the doping offence: those establishing fault liability and those establishing strict liability. The first kind *in abstracto* formulates human behaviour, which – because it is disapproved of – is prohibited. If the athlete's actions correspond to the abstract behaviour described, this does not automatically lead to a conviction. First, it must be proven that the athlete's will, at the moment he succumbed to the undesirable behaviour, was directed at that particular behaviour. An example of a description of a doping offence establishing fault liability is provided by the FIFA Regulations:

> Doping is any attempt by a player ... to enhance his mental and physical performance unnaturally or to treat ailments or injury when this is medically unjustified for the sole purpose of taking part in a competition ...[36]

This type of description of the doping offence has the shortcoming that, in many cases, it is hard to prove that any blame attaches to the athlete with regard to his actions. In order to find a way out of these evidentiary problems caused by fault liability, a number of international governing bodies have resorted to describing the doping offence in terms of strict liability. In this second kind of description, the athlete's actions are no longer the focus of attention, but the actual condition of his body at the moment that it was tested for doping. An example of this type of description may be found in the IAAF Regulations:

> The offence of doping takes place when either:
>
> (i) a prohibited substance is found to be present within an athlete's body tissue or fluids; or
>
> (ii) an athlete uses or takes advantage of a prohibited technique.[37]

---

34 'Convincing evidence to the contrary' is an ambivalent concept. On the one hand, it could mean that not all evidence to the contrary is acceptable, but only that which convinces the disciplinary body; on the other hand, it could mean that evidence, which may not be hard, would still suffice if it could establish the benefit of the doubt in favour of the athlete.

35 IOC MC, Ch 3, Art 2. Oddly enough, this Article, like those of the Medical Code mentioned before, is contained in a chapter dealing with the appeal.

36 Doping Control Regulations for FIFA Competitions (except for FIFA World Cup), r 1.

37 IAAF Rules and Regulations, r 55, para 2.

Fifteen other Olympic IFs, as well as the IOC, ATP and WTA, use descriptions of the doping offence establishing strict liability.[38] Through the switch from fault to strict liability, the centre of attention in the description of the doping offence has moved from human actions to the establishment of facts; in other words, from the unlawful act to its consequences. In several doping cases brought before the CAS for resolution, the tribunal has shown itself to be a proponent of strict liability and has thereby rejected the principle of *nulla poena sine culpa*. When a doping offence establishes strict liability, it is no longer necessary to show the relationship between the sanction and the will directed at the offence (that is, wilful intent).[39] The strict liability principle does not, however, free the sports organisation concerned from the duty to show that a doping offence was committed.[40] One of the arguments in favour of accepting strict liability was that, without it, the sports organisations could find themselves bankrupted as a result of costly procedures. Furthermore, the CAS considers it to be prudent policy not to repair the secondary injustice suffered by a few through creating a deliberate injustice, suffered by all athletes collectively. This is what would happen if non-intentional use of prohibited substances was allowed. The collective comes before the individual. On the basis of the wording of the descriptions of the doping offence establishing strict liability, and on the basis of the CAS judgment in this respect, it may be concluded that the accused athlete in doping proceedings has found himself in an extremely disadvantageous position, as far as the evidence that a doping offence was committed is concerned. There are no opportunities left for him to prove his innocence. Misleading labelling, unsound medical advice ... these are all of no avail to him.

---

38 IOC MC, Ch 1, Art 4; FISA Rules of Racing and Related Bylaws, Pt 7, r 80, ss 1(1), 1.2, 2; IBF Competition Regulations, Art 23.1; FIC Doping Rules, r 1, para 4; FIG Technical Regulations, Ch 11, reg 11.1; IWF Anti-Doping Policy, 5, 5.1; IHF Anti-Doping Regulations, 1; FIH Doping Policy, 1; FINA Doping Control Rules, DC 1.2; IBU Anti-Doping, Blood Test and Gender Verification Rules, 1; ISF Doping Control and Testing (as Established by the ISF Medical and Doping Commission), rr 1.0, 1.1; WTF Competition Rules, Art 4, para 3.1; ITF Tennis Anti-Doping Programme, r (C) 2; ITU Doping Control Rules and Procedural Guidelines, 2, 2.2, 2.6; ISAF Regulations 1998, Medical Code (Old 17), rr 1.2, 1.2.1; FIS Doping Rules, 1, 3; ATP/WTA Official Rulebook, Tennis Anti-Doping Programme, r (C) 1.

39 'The principal offence of doping consists merely of the finding of the presence of a prohibited substance in an athlete's body tissue or fluids. The rule does not provide that an athlete must have taken the substance deliberately. It creates an offence of strict liability in that the athlete's intent is completely irrelevant.' Gay, M, in a speech during the International Symposium on Sport and Law, Monte Carlo, 1991.

40 Cf *Wang v Fina* CAS 98/208.

The bulk of doping cases heard by the CAS centred around the question of whether or not the athlete had intentionally ingested a prohibited substance, which the body is unable to produce on its own. In a case decided by the CAS in August 1999,[41] the issue arose as to whether the athlete had actually used a prohibited substance. When the sample was analysed, a substance was found which did in fact feature on the doping list, but which could also have been produced by the body itself. The CAS considered that, in case a sports organisation chooses to sanction the consequences of the unlawful act rather than the unlawful act itself, the causal link between that unlawful act and its consequences must be entirely clear and undisputed. In civil law, regarding unlawful acts, there is no general suspicion of a causal link between the unlawful act and its consequences. Even in cases of unlimited liability, requiring no evidence of guilt, the causal link between actions and consequences remains an issue that has to be proven by the party claiming the liability. Bearing in mind the disciplinary (pseudo-criminal) law character of anti-doping hearings and sanctions, the CAS Panel judged it unacceptable to interpret the strict liability rule more stringently against persons subject to that liability, such as accused athletes, than is generally done in civil law, where the concept has its roots. The existence of a causal link between the unlawful act and its consequences therefore remains an issue that has to be proven by the party basing its arguments on said consequences. The strict liability rule rules out the sports organisation's need to prove that the athlete is guilty of the presence of a prohibited substance in his body; it does not, however, rule out the organisation's duty to prove that such presence is the result of use by the athlete.

Once the use of doping has been convincingly shown, according to the doctrine developed by the CAS, a second stage is reached, in which the burden of proof is shifted.[42] The athlete is yet given the opportunity to show that he is not, or not entirely, guilty of the offence. During this stage of the proceedings, only the severity of the sanction to be imposed as measured against the principle of proportionality is at stake, at least in so far as the federation in question uses a system of flexible sanctioning.

Application of the strict liability principle, according to the doctrine developed by the CAS, may not result in the automatic imposition of a

---

41 *In re Bernhard v ITU* CAS 98/222.

42 See CAS 98/208: 'If the presence of a prohibited substance is established to the high degree of satisfaction required by the seriousness of the allegation, then the burden shifts to the competitor to show why, in case of a diuretic, the maximum sanction should not be imposed. The Panel repeats that, under the new FINA rules, it is only at the level of *sanction*, not of finding of innocence or guilt, that the concept of shifting burden becomes relevant at all. And it is only at this juncture, too, that questions of intent become relevant.' Emphasis added.

sanction following the positive results of sample analyses.[43] Although, as it may seem, the critical element of doping procedures has shifted from the prohibited act to its consequences, the sports organisation remains under an obligation to show the causal link between the act and the established facts. The application of the principle may be of great influence on the legal position of the accused athlete and his right to a defence, but it does not completely eliminate this right. The athlete is still entitled to rebut the sports organisation's allegations of doping by producing evidence to the contrary. If substances were found in the athlete's sample which medical science is convinced can never be produced by the human body itself, the athlete will have a hard time proving the contrary. If, however, substances were found which may, according to medical science, also be produced naturally by the human body, the chances of the evidence succeeding are very real. If the sports organisation has proved beyond a doubt that a doping offence was committed, the doping trial enters the second stage, during which the relationship between the seriousness of the offence (absence of wilful intent, the fact that only minute amounts of the prohibited substance were found, etc) and the sanction to be imposed is dealt with. Here, however, there is the problem that most international governing bodies make use of fixed sanctions.

Against those propagating the strict liability principle (usually based on the conviction that, without its application, the fight against the use of doping in sports cannot be fought), the argument has been made that sanctioning athletes without entering into the issue of their guilt is unacceptable.[44] The opinions of proponents and opponents are much divided. The middle course which has to be found in order to find a way out of the stalemate could possibly take the shape of using a provision which the FISA has laid down in its doping regulations: 'The presence of such a substance in the urine or in the blood of a rower or of a coxswain shall constitute a rebuttable presumption of voluntary use.'[45]

---

43 Various Olympic IFs, namely, the IAAF, IBF, IBU, ISF, WTF, ISU and FIS, which uphold the strict liability principle, have not recognised the CAS's jurisdiction. The doping panels of those organisations do not need to worry about any causal link between finding the doping substances in the athlete's sample and the unlawful doping activities of that athlete.

44 See, *inter alia*, Lob, J, 'Dopage, responsabilité objective ("strict liability") et de quelques autres questions' (1999) 12(95) Schweizerische Juristen Zeitung 272.

45 FISA Rules of Racing and Related Bylaws, Pt 7, r 80.

The right to call witnesses and/or experts

The anti-doping regulations of some international governing bodies contain the athlete's right to call witnesses and/or experts.[46] The doping panels of these federations are obliged to hear the witnesses and experts called by the defence. It is not stipulated whether all such requests for hearing witnesses and experts for the defence must be granted. The proceedings could be unnecessarily dragged out if, after a first witness hearing, a second would be requested. The anti-doping regulations usually do not contain guidelines about the manner in which hearings should be conducted. The only exception is contained in the regulations of the IWF. In appeal proceedings, all parties are entitled not only to call witnesses, but also to examine and cross-examine them.[47] It is possible to have witnesses and experts brought forward by the defence examined by the panel as a whole, but it is also conceivable that they are heard by one panel member only. The doping regulations do not contain any provisions about the costs involved in hearings.

The FIG anti-doping regulations not only stipulate that those who have rendered judgment in the first instance may no longer participate in the FIG Executive Committee which considers the appeal, but also which categories of persons may be heard by the Committee as witnesses at the athlete's request.[48]

The right to conduct the doping trial in writing

The anti-doping regulations of a large number of IFs contain provisions enabling the athlete involved in doping proceedings to handle the case in writing. 'The right to be heard includes the right ... to submit a defence in writing,' says the IOC Medical Code.[49] Usually, this right is not considered a corollary, but an independent right.[50] The ITF, ATP and WTA also provide for the possibility to conclude the case merely on the basis of the case file. This,

---

46 IBA Anti Doping Rules, Art 11.3; UCI Cycling Regulations, Pt 14, Ch 7, Art 77; IWF Anti-Doping Policy, Art 15.10; FIL International Luge Regulations, Artificial Track Supplement 4, Ch 7, Art 7.

47 IWF Anti-Doping Policy, Art 15.10(a).

48 Medical Regulations, Art 3.1: 'The Committee will, if so required by the appealing competitor, hear the parties (the gymnast, a representative of his/her Federation, a representative of the laboratory, a representative of the FIG Medical Commission).'

49 IOC MC, Ch 9, Art 7.

50 IAAF Rules and Regulations, Div 2, r 23(8); IBF Disciplinary Regulations, Art 3.3; IBA Anti-Doping Rules, Ch 11, Art 11.3; FIG Medical Regulations, Art 3.1(c); IWF Anti-Doping Policy, Art 15.9; FIH Doping Policy, Art 10.2; FIL International Luge Regulations, Artificial Track Supplement 4, Ch 7, Art 7.

however, does not set aside the obligation of the Appeals Committee to organise a hearing, although the athlete concerned, or his representative, need not be present at it. In order to reach a verdict, the committee may consider all written statements.[51]

Listing the number of IFs that have laid down certain fundamental rights in their regulations may provide some insight into the situation of fundamental rights in the disciplinary law concerning doping. On the other hand, looking at the data from a negative perspective, and so listing the number of IFs which have not provided for certain fundamental rights, gives an even more disconcerting view of the reality of that situation. The right to be informed of the charges is *not* contained in the regulation of 29 of the 35 Olympic IFs. The same number has no provisions made for the right to appear in person; 17 do not contain the right to be heard; 22 lack the right of representation; 30, the right to submit evidence; and another 30, the right to hear witnesses and/or experts; while 26 fail to provide for the right to a written defence. The UCI is the only IF to grant the accused athlete the right of having the last word.[52] The right to a motivated judgment is not offered by any doping regulation. If an athlete is to be informed at all of the charges against him, the corresponding provision does not include the requirement that this shall be done in a language that the athlete understands. The Art 6 right of granting the suspect the time needed for preparing his defence does not feature in the regulations either.

THE ANTI-DOPING CONVENTION OF THE COUNCIL OF EUROPE AND FUNDAMENTAL RIGHTS

States party to this Convention[53] have bound themselves to elicit from their sports organisations the start of harmonisation of (among others) their respective disciplinary proceedings, 'applying agreed international principles of natural justice and ensuring respect for the fundamental rights of suspected sportsmen and sportswomen; these principles will include: ... the right of such persons to a fair hearing and to be assisted or represented ...'.[54] We have to conclude that the obligation of the contracting parties to urge their national federations to show respect for the athlete's fundamental rights has still had

---

51 ITF Bylaws, 8; ATP/WTA Official Rulebook, Tennis Anti-Doping Programme, r (L) 5.

52 UCI Cycling Regulations, Pt 14, Ch 7, Art 77: 'Each party shall be heard as well as any witnesses and experts summoned. The rider or license-holder shall be entitled to the last word.'

53 Council of Europe Convention Against Doping, Strasbourg, 16 November 1989.

54 *Ibid*, Art 7, para 2(d).

little effect. Neither national authorities nor, moreover, their national federations have any influence on the policy of the respective IFs. The national federations apparently find themselves in the difficult position of having to serve two masters. In an advisory opinion, answering the question of which doping regulations have to be applied (those of the international or the national federation), the CAS considered the following: 'A national federation confronted both with the internal legislation of its country and the International Federation's regulations is obliged to interpret and apply these provisions in the light of the principles of the Council of Europe Convention Against Doping.'[55] This opinion carries with it the risk that the regulations of an international governing body have to be interpreted differently, in accordance with the scope of the Council of Europe Convention, which has only a regional effect.

THE CAS AND FUNDAMENTAL RIGHTS

The CAS can bring a positive influence to bear on the development of fundamental rights in disciplinary sports law. The tribunal is not a disciplinary body, but a court of arbitration, which must formally take its cue from Swiss arbitration laws. Other than in the area of disciplinary sports law, Art 6 of the Convention is applicable to arbitrations based in national legislation if a case has not been fairly and impartially decided because the decision was prepared without recourse to fundamental principles of law. Swiss arbitration laws should cover such cases. If, for example, the principle of *audi alteram partem* was violated or the judgment was based on a document produced by one of the parties on which the other party was not heard, the judgment would go against public order. In such a case, it would not be necessary also to appeal to Art 6 of the Convention. Apart from this, the CAS could promote the application of the provisions of the Anti-Doping Convention of the Council of Europe containing rules for upholding respect for the fundamental rights of athletes accused of doping. However, the contribution that the CAS could make to the development of fundamental rights with the international governing bodies affiliated with it must not be overestimated. The CAS does not adjudge the merits of decisions that are appealed before it, nor does it apply a marginal test to such decisions. As a rule, it deals with cases *de novo*. Only by taking into account the procedural rights of the parties on the basis of binding arbitration laws or 'the elementary rules of natural justice and due process' may the CAS serve as an example to governing bodies not taking these rights into account. The CAS's influence is

---

55 Advisory Opinion CAS 93/109, 31 August 1994; Reeb, M (ed), *Digest of CAS Awards 1986–1998*, 1998, Berne: Staempfli Editions SA, p 475.

also limited, in that only half of the Olympic federations allow for the possibility to appeal their doping decisions before the CAS.[56]

A FAIR TRIAL CHARTER

The athlete facing doping charges is, in many cases, unable to invoke the rules of procedural fairness, unlike his fellow citizens in proceedings before governmental bodies, if the regulations of the IF in force in his particular branch of sport do not provide these. This may be different only in doping proceedings started by a national federation of a country which is a party to a treaty like the Anti-Doping Convention of the Council of Europe.[57] Internationally organised sport will itself have to come up with regulations to fill this void in order to remain in step with the developments in civilisation – a civilisation that the sport itself is part of. The Olympic movement could draw up a general charter containing the rights of Art 6 of the Convention. Such a charter would need the signatures of all IFs which are part of the Olympic movement. A second option is broadening the functional scope of Art 6 of the Convention and Art 14 of the ICCPR so that they would also apply to the area of non-statutory disciplinary law. The first option mentioned is to be preferred, though, because fair trial regulations would thus be given a broader international effect than through a treaty which may not be in force for all countries concerned (like the ICCPR) or only has a regional effect (like the Convention).

---

56 Apart from the IOC, 17 Olympic IFs and the ATP and WTA have recognised the jurisdiction of the CAS: FISA Rules of Racing and Related Bylaws, bylaw to rr 80–83, Arts 10.1, 10.3; IBA Statutes, Ch 8, Art 69 and Anti-Doping Rules, Ch 12, Art 12.1; FIBA Regulations Governing Doping Control, Arts 6.5, 6.6.2(7); UCI Cycling Regulations, Pt 14 and Anti-Doping Examination Regulations, Ch 7, Art 81; FEI Code of Conduct, Ch 6, Art 1023(8); FIG Medical Regulations, Art 3.1(d); IWF Anti-Doping Policy, 16; IHF Bylaws, 10, Art 37; FIH Statutes and Bylaws, Art 21, paras 1, 2, 3; FINA Doping Control Rules, DC 8.9 and Guidelines for Doping Control, Pt 1; ITF Bylaws, 8; Tennis Anti-Doping Programme, r 5, para 3; ISSF Anti-Doping Regulations, regs 9.1, 9.3; ITU Doping Control Rules and Procedural Guidelines, rr 5.10, 5.11; ISAF Regulations 1998, Medical Code (Old 17), r 3.9; IHF Statutes, D, 46; WCF Constitution, 9, Art 34(a); FIL International Luge Regulations, Artificial Track Supplement 4, Ch 8, Arts 1, 7; ATP/WTA Official Rulebook, N, 2(a).

57 Council of Europe Convention Against Doping, Explanatory Report, 69: 'Article 7.2.d implies that sports organisations should adapt – or if necessary, adopt – regulations which would give expression to the concept of natural justice, or due process. The principles to be followed are those set down in, for example, the International Covenant on Civil and Political Rights of the United Nations (1960) and, for the Member States of the Council of Europe, in the Convention for the Protection of Human Rights and Fundamental Freedoms (1950), or in the procedures adopted by the IOC.'

CHAPTER 6

A SNORT AND A PUFF: RECREATIONAL DRUGS AND DISCIPLINE IN PROFESSIONAL SPORT

Roger Welch

INTRODUCTION

In the world of sport, most of the discussion concerning the use of drugs by participants focuses on their use for performance enhancement. However, the realisation that professional sportsmen,[1] along with countless other members of their generation(s), from all walks of life, might use drugs for purely recreational purposes became part of the public domain in the summer of 1986. This was the year in which national hero Ian Botham was banned from test match cricket as a result of a conviction for the possession of cannabis. It is worth recording that Botham did return for the final test of the summer against New Zealand. He took the wicket of Bruce Edgar with his first ball, and then went on to overtake Dennis Lillee's record of 355 test wickets. Whether Ian Botham ever consumed cannabis after his conviction is unknown (and is no one else's business). However, the incident does suggest that the use of mind altering drugs might not necessarily impair sporting performance at the highest level.

This point is central to the main propositions contained in this chapter, which is that it is necessary to differentiate between recreational and performance enhancing drugs, and to question whether regulatory bodies should have the power to impose bans and/or fines on sportsmen for consuming drugs of the recreational variety. In seeking to classify in which category a particular drug should be placed, it is accepted that some drugs might fall into both. It is assumed that it is non-contentious that drugs such as cannabis, LSD and ecstasy are used only for recreational purposes, and that hard drugs such as heroin and crack cocaine are not going to assist the sportsman on the field of play.[2] On the other hand, there would appear to be no purpose to steroid-based drugs other than performance enhancement.

---

1 References to sportsmen (or sportsman) are not intended to imply gender bias, but to reflect the fact that participants in the professional team sports with which this chapter is generally concerned are men.

2 Arguably, an extreme example of a regulatory body taking disciplinary action is provided by the fining of snooker players for smoking cannabis. See Everton, C, 'Wayward Hunter's pot proves expensive' (1998) *The Guardian*, 15 April. Given the mildly hallucinogenic qualities of cannabis, it is difficult to see how the drug could assist in the potting of relatively small, different coloured balls.

Amphetamines and cocaine can arguably be placed in both categories, as they are artificial stimulants. For the purposes of this chapter, they will be treated as purely recreational drugs. It is contended that such stimulants do not increase the fitness levels of professional footballers, rugby players or cricketers and the like, but are sufficiently disorientating to affect precision timing and judgment. Thus, if anything, their use prior to or during a competitive match will have a deleterious effect on a player's performance.

The common factor between the drugs listed above is, of course, that their possession and use are contrary to the criminal law. Equally obviously, the difference between these drugs and the drug that many professional sportsmen publicly consume, that is, alcohol, is that the latter is both a legal commodity and traditionally an integral part of male sporting culture. Therefore, it could simply be argued that, in prohibiting the use of recreational drugs, sporting bodies are doing no more than protecting the reputation of the sport concerned by upholding the criminal law.

It is thus freely admitted that this chapter is written from a (Left) libertarian perspective that the State and the law should have no role in regulating the private behaviour of individuals where the harm inflicted, if any, is against the self. It is the view of this author that the possession of drugs for personal use, even the more overtly obnoxious ones such as heroin and crack cocaine, should, at the very least, be decriminalised, if not legalised altogether. For this author, the use of recreational drugs and the consumption of alcohol by professional sportsmen are viewed as similar forms of social behaviour. This chapter also unashamedly locates professional sport as constituting part of the entertainment industry, and thus regards it as appropriate to draw comparisons with other areas of popular culture that the industry both reflects and generates.

However, whilst it is argued that regulatory bodies should not be empowered to discipline players for using drugs for recreational purposes, it is believed that clubs, as employers, and the supporters of clubs, as the paying public, do have legitimate concerns in ensuring that the off-field behaviour of a player does not adversely affect his performance on the field of play. This chapter will thus include analysis and discussion of the legal and social bases for clubs dismissing players for having taken drugs.

THE BASIS FOR DISCIPLINARY ACTION?

We can identify a number of reasons why regulatory bodies might want to discipline players who have tested positive for drugs. One reason is cheating. It has been argued that players should be able to decide for themselves whether they wish to incur the risks to their health associated with the side effects of many performance enhancing drugs, and that it should be a matter of individual choice whether aids to performance are used or rejected.[3] Whilst I am not unsympathetic to this perspective, it seems reasonable that, where rules prohibiting performance enhancing drugs are in place, regulatory bodies should be able to enforce them. Sports participants who knowingly break the rules are seeking an unfair advantage over their opponents and are thus, in a word, cheating.

It is acknowledged that recent high profile cases do suggest that there are inherent problems with drug testing, and that is possible for banned substances to be taken unintentionally through the consumption of medicines or even foodstuffs.[4] However, this chapter is not so much concerned with the fairness or otherwise of punishing sportsmen and women for having consumed a performance enhancing substance as with the fairness of punishing sports participants for using drugs as part of their recreational activities. As argued above, typically, such drugs are anything but performance enhancing, and the issue of cheating does not arise from their use.

There are reasons for prohibiting the use of drugs which can be perceived as relating to both performance enhancing and recreational drugs. These are located in notions of bringing a sport into disrepute, and the status of the professional sportsman as role model – in particular, for the young. It is in this context that the debate over the use of drugs by sports professionals connects with wider debates over the legal regulation of drug use. It is certainly questionable why regulatory bodies in sport should have any role to play in acting as moral guardians in society. The extent to which young people look to their sporting heroes as role models in any capacity beyond how they play the game concerned is also questionable. Moreover, the fact that a sportsman uses drugs will usually only become public knowledge as a result of a random drug test by a regulatory body, or as the result of the bringing of a criminal prosecution.

The use of drugs is not part of sporting culture in the way that is the case with, for example, sections of the music industry, where, ironically perhaps, mind altering drugs are performance enhancing, but their use is hardly regarded as cheating. For example, the drug influences on *Sergeant Pepper* have always been obvious, but there appears to have been no criticism of what many regard (albeit not this lifelong Beatles fan) as the finest rock album of all time which is based on the notion that its creators were cheating by virtue of their copious and self-proclaimed use of marijuana and acid during the period of its recording. Indeed, such an allegation does not appear to have been made

---

3   For various perspectives on this issue see Gardiner, S, Felix, A, James, M, Welch, R and O'Leary, J, *Sports Law*, 1998, London: Cavendish Publishing, pp 161–69. See, also, Eassom, S, 'Drugs and ethics' (2000) 3(2) Sports Law Bulletin 2.

4   See, eg, the ongoing controversy surrounding the drug nandrolone. For discussion see O'Leary, J, 'Drugs update: nandrolone' (2000) 3(2) Sports Law Bulletin 11.

about any top musician who is a self-confessed drug user, be we talking about this author's personal hero, John Lennon, or his contemporary admirers, the Gallagher brothers.

Moreover, based on empirical evidence, which is either purely anecdotal or reflects personal experience, it was the case with youth in the 1960s and 1970s that musicians were much more influential on lifestyle choices than, say, any member of the 1966 World Cup squad, or, indeed, in the latter decade, Ian Botham. It seems reasonable to assume that this is still the case with young people today. It also begs the question whether footballers have any wish to be role models in the way they conduct their private lives, or whether we, the public, have any right to hold them up as such.

Thus, it is contended that the taking of disciplinary action by regulatory bodies against professional sportsmen for taking recreational drugs cannot be justified by reference to combating cheating, or by bringing the sport into disrepute through committing criminal offences and/or constituting a negative role model. Indeed, players who have been found guilty of, or have confessed to, domestic violence, or who have been convicted for driving under the influence of drink or for assault, have generally not been faced with any disciplinary action by the appropriate disciplinary body. This is not to argue that they should have been. However, it is contended that, for many people, these offences are regarded as being more serious in nature than the consumption of illegal recreational drugs.

There are arguments that drugs impair the fitness of a player, but, as will be argued below, this is generally more an issue of concern for the club, as an employer, and its supporters than for regulatory bodies. Arguably, the exception to this is where a player's judgment is so affected by drugs that he constitutes a danger to others on the field of play. There is certainly a case for disciplinary action by regulatory bodies if such circumstances are established, but, then again, this would not appear to be a common problem and is not qualitatively different from a player taking to the field of play in an intoxicated condition. I am not aware of any occasion where a professional sportsman has been disciplined for having consumed alcohol prior to a competitive match. A club might choose not to field a player in such a condition, but that is a separate issue.

There are now a fair number of examples of sportsmen who have been punished by sporting bodies and/or clubs or, at worst, found their careers terminated as a result of having been found guilty of drug use. Equally, there have been examples of clubs adopting a sympathetic or even supportive approach. Compare and contrast employer responses to the following incidents: the alcoholism of Tony Adams and Paul Merson and the latter's addiction to cocaine and gambling; the short bans imposed on Chris Armstrong and Lee Bowyer for smoking cannabis; the dismissal of Craig Whittington for the same offence; the dismissal of Roger Stanislaus for using cocaine; the termination of the cricketer Ed Giddins' contract for the same offence.

More recently, Barnsley FC decided to take no further action against Dean Jones, who received a three month ban from the Football Association (FA) for taking an amphetamine-based substance. According to the player, he had been using the substance to stay awake in a nightclub. On the other hand, at around the same time, Charlton Athletic FC dismissed Jamie Stuart after testing positive for cocaine and marijuana. Also, consider as examples of club leniency, where drugs are not involved, the decisions by Chelsea FC and Manchester United FC not to impose club penalties on Dennis Wise and Eric Cantona after their respective convictions for assault.

Where players' careers have been lost or put in jeopardy, it would generally appear to have been the case that employer decisions have been taken primarily by reference to moral stances rather than fitness issues. It may never be known whether the same decisions would have been reached if the players had been subjected to confidential tests carried out by the clubs themselves which did not generate media coverage. It is the view of this author that clubs should consider taking disciplinary action against players whose private conduct affects their performance on the field of play, as this can have negative consequences for both the club and its supporters. Equally, where off-field conduct appears to have no impact on a player's capability to perform to the best of his abilities in a competitive match, it is argued that such behaviour is the player's own concern. Certainly, there should be no distinction drawn between 'clubbing' or 'partying' involving the consumption of large amounts of alcohol and participating in the same activities with the assistance of recreational drugs. However, the legal constraints on clubs as employers dismissing players in such circumstances will now be considered.

PLAYERS' CONTRACTS AND WRONGFUL DISMISSAL

There are clauses in players' contracts of employment which can clearly be related to the consumption of recreational drugs and, indeed, alcohol. For example, the Football League Contract includes the following:

Clause 2   The Player agrees to play to the best of his ability in all football matches in which he is selected to play for the Club and to attend at any reasonable place for the purpose of training ...

Clause 5   The Player agrees to observe the Rules of the Club at all times. The Club and the Player shall observe and be subject to the Rules and Regulations of the Football Association and the Football League. In the case of conflict such Rules and Regulations shall take precedence over this Agreement and the Rules of the Club.

Clause 7 ... The Player shall at all times have due regard for the necessity of his maintaining a high standard of physical fitness and agrees not to indulge in any sport, activity or practice that might endanger such fitness ...

Clause 13 ... The Player may, save as otherwise mutually agreed and subject to the overriding obligation not to bring the game of Association Football into disrepute ...

Similar provisions to the above can be found in the standard Contract for Professional Cricketers and the England and Wales Cricket Board's (formerly the Test and County Cricket Board (TCCB)) Rules and Regulations. Of particular interest, in both football and cricket, is the catch all offence of 'bringing the sport into disrepute'. Clearly, this can relate to the notion of sports professional as a role model – particularly for the young – in promoting a healthy, fit, and even moral lifestyle, and to bans imposed by regulatory bodies for drug taking activities.

Players' contracts are generally for a fixed term – normally for at least one year. Summary dismissal before that time has expired is *prima facie* a breach of contract and, thus, a wrongful dismissal by the employer, unless the employee is guilty of gross misconduct. For this to be the case, the employee must be in breach of a term – express or implied – which is at the root of the contract. Disobedience of a lawful and reasonable instruction by the employer *may* constitute gross misconduct. It is clear[5] that there is no standard test for ascertaining whether misconduct is gross. The circumstances of the case must be taken into account in determining whether or not the employee has committed a repudiatory breach of contract. Only if this is the case is the employer justified in treating the contract as at an end. From a contractual perspective, the dismissal is simply the employer communicating to the employee that the latter's breach has discharged the employer from his obligations under the contract, and that the employer has consequently elected to regard the contract as terminated.

It cannot be concluded that a player who takes recreational drugs must be guilty of a repudiatory breach of contract. Individual circumstances will have to be taken into account on a case by case basis. As is the case with unfair dismissal law (see below, pp 83–88), clubs deciding to dismiss will be in a stronger position if their disciplinary rules specify that drug taking constitutes gross misconduct and, subject to any individual mitigating circumstances, they are consistent in treating drug use as grounds for summary dismissal. With respect to incidents listed above, Roger Stanislaus was clearly regarded by Leyton Orient as being guilty of gross misconduct once he had been found guilty by the FA of having been tested positive for cocaine. A similar view was taken by Sussex CCC with respect to Ed Giddins. However, interestingly,

---

5   Contrast the cases of *Laws v London Chronicle Ltd* [1959] 2 ALL ER 285; *Wilson v Racher* [1974] IRLR 114; and *Pepper v Webb* [1969] 2 All ER 216.

Sussex claimed that it had not dismissed Giddins. His contract was deemed to have terminated automatically as a result of the cancellation of his registration by the TCCB.

The legal basis for this conclusion was not put to the test. Clause 2(c) of the Cricketers' Contract provides: '... this Agreement will terminate immediately if the Board cancels or terminates the registration of the Cricketer by the Club.' Thus, it might have been possible to argue that Giddins' contract was frustrated. A term of imprisonment can frustrate a contract of employment. Arguably, a ban for a lengthy period could be considered analogous, on the basis that the club has been deprived of a player's services by the decision of an external agency. On the other hand, any termination of an employment contract by the employer is a dismissal and, in the author's opinion, this is what happened in Giddins' case. Case law has established that the courts will not permit a dismissal to be disguised as termination of the contract through mutual agreement.[6] Certainly, it cannot be argued that an employee's behaviour is such that he can be regarded as having dismissed himself.[7]

REMEDIES FOR WRONGFUL DISMISSAL

The normal remedy for a wrongful dismissal, that is, a dismissal in breach of contract, is damages for actual financial loss suffered. In the case of fixed term contracts, this will, subject to the normal duty of mitigation, be loss of earnings for the period of time that the contract had left to run. Therefore, in professional sport, there is an obvious potential for the awarding of high levels of damages.

Now that behaviour by professional sports participants – both on and off the field of play – has become an issue of national interest or concern, it is perhaps only a matter of time before a player who has been dismissed summarily for taking drugs brings an action for wrongful dismissal. However, as was the case with Ed Giddins (who was signed to play for Warwickshire once he had served his ban), the issue might be effectively resolved by a rival club employing the player who has been dismissed. If nothing else, this shows that clubs, who may regard themselves as occupying the moral high ground, are upholding their own standards rather than standards observed within the sport as a whole.[8]

---

6   See *Tracey v Zest Equipment Co* [1982] IRLR 268 and, in particular, the Court of Appeal decision in *Igbo v Johnson Matthey Chemicals Ltd* [1986] IRLR 215.

7   *London Transport Executive v Clarke* [1981] ICR 355 (CA).

8   See (1996) *The Guardian*, 1 November, for a discussion of the Ed Giddins affair and the fact that, once Sussex terminated his contract, he was approached by 10 of the 17 other first class counties. The report also suggests that it was the general view of his fellow professionals that, in sporting terms, he had done nothing wrong. See, also, O'Gorman, T, 'Ed Giddins v TCCB' (1997) 5(1) Sport and the Law J 23.

It is a fundamental legal principle that courts will not compel performance of a contract of employment or any contract which involves the provision of personal services. Ever since the actress Bette Davis sought to break her contract with her film studio,[9] it has been clear that this principle applies to the entertainment industry. However, this case revealed the potential for injunctions to be granted to restrain a breach of contract. In more recent times, this has become an issue where injunctions have been sought to restrain dismissals in breach of disciplinary procedures contained in the employment contract.

In orthodox contract law, the victim of a repudiatory breach of contract is not obliged to treat the contract as at an end. The injured party has a choice and, thus, can elect to treat the contract as continuing to exist. If an employee is dismissed in breach of procedures contained in the employment contract, it has been accepted in a number of cases that the employee can seek an injunction to prevent the dismissal from taking effect until and if contract-based procedures are observed.

In *Dietman v Brent LBC*,[10] the High Court confirmed that an injunction could be so granted if:

(a) the plaintiff (now claimant) acts quickly, as otherwise the employee will be deemed to have accepted the termination of the contract;

(b) mutual trust and confidence have not been destroyed;

(c) damages are inadequate. This might be the case if the dismissed employee could show that, were he allowed to plead his case at a hearing, the employer might decide against dismissal.

Both professional footballers and cricketers have contractual rights of appeal against dismissal to the appropriate authorities. Thus, there remains the possibility, given the issues at stake, that, if a player was dismissed in breach of contractual procedures for drug taking, he might seek an injunction to restrain that dismissal from taking effect. The major stumbling block to securing this remedy, particularly if there was clear evidence that the player was 'guilty', would be an argument by the club that its trust and confidence in the player had been destroyed by his behaviour.

---

9   *Warner Brothers Pictures Inc v Nelson* [1937] KB 209.

10 [1987] IRLR 259. However, in *Boyo v Lambeth LBC* [1995] IRLR 50, the Court of Appeal indicated support for the more restrictive view that a dismissal, even in breach of contract-based procedures, automatically terminates the contract of employment. Were this position to be endorsed by the House of Lords, then even as a theoretical possibility injunctions would cease to be available, and the only remedy would be damages for wrongful dismissal.

However, in the case of cricketers' and footballers' contracts, this might include the length of time for which the player would still have been employed if the dismissal had not occurred until after contractual procedures had been followed. In this case, even if a player was guilty of gross misconduct, he would be entitled to some compensation on the basis that his dismissal was procedurally wrongful.

UNFAIR DISMISSAL AND THE RANGE
OF REASONABLE RESPONSES

A player with at least one year's continuous employment is eligible to claim unfair dismissal. Such a claim is independent of any claim for wrongful dismissal and can be presented to an employment tribunal even if the dismissal does not constitute a breach of the player's contract. Such claims are likely to prove more attractive even to relatively highly paid employees, such as professional sportsmen, now that the statutory maximum for compensatory awards has been raised to £50,000. Moreover, although such orders are rarely granted, tribunals are empowered to order an employee's reinstatement (a failure by the employer to comply will result in the employee's compensation being increased).

Under s 98(1) of the Employment Rights Act 1996, it is for the employer to show (a) the reason for the dismissal, and (b) that it is a potentially fair reason falling within sub-s (2), such as incapability or misconduct. 'Capability' may be assessed by reference to an employee's skill, aptitude, health or any other physical or mental quality. This can clearly relate to the impairment of fitness through the use of alcohol and/or drugs.

Where the employer has fulfilled the requirements of s 98(1) and (2), then, under s 98(4), the determination of the question whether the dismissal is fair or unfair depends on:

(a) whether, in the circumstances (including the size and administrative resources of the employer' s undertaking), the employer acted reasonably or unreasonably in treating it as a sufficient reason for dismissing the employee; and

(b) shall be determined in accordance with equity and the substantial merits of the case.

The decision as to the fairness of the dismissal is for the tribunal to make. The burden of proof is neutral. However, as a point of law, it is of primary importance that a tribunal does not substitute its views for that of the reasonable employer. Employers may operate within a range of reasonable responses. Only if a dismissal is outside this range will it be unfair.[11]

A clear explanation of this test was provided by Browne-Wilkinson P:

> ... (1) the starting point must be the words [of the section] themselves; (2) in applying the section an [employment] tribunal must consider the reasonableness of the employer's conduct, not simply whether they (the members of the [employment] tribunal) consider the dismissal to be fair; (3) in

---

11 This test was approved by the Court of Appeal in a number of cases, including *British Leyland (UK) Ltd v Swift* [1981] IRLR 91.

judging the reasonableness of the employer's conduct an [employment] tribunal must not substitute its decision as to what was the right course to adopt for that of the employer; (4) in many (though not all) cases there is a band of reasonable responses to the employee's conduct within which one employer might reasonably take one view, another quite reasonably take another; (5) the function of the [employment] tribunal, as an industrial jury, is to determine whether in the particular circumstances of each case the decision to dismiss the employee fell within the band of reasonable responses which a reasonable employer might have adopted. If the dismissal falls within the band, the dismissal is fair; if the dismissal falls outside the band, it is unfair.[12]

Thus, it is clear that a dismissal may be reasonable, even if a particular tribunal regards it as harsh, if it can be shown that other employers, particularly those in the same line of business, would regard dismissal as an appropriate penalty. The essential questions are: who constitutes the reasonable employer, and what stance will this elusive person take in response to misconduct, etc, on the part of an employee? The answers are no clearer in sport than in any other field of employment. This is shown by the quite different reactions of football clubs to the use of drugs by their players – particularly those deemed recreational in nature and consumed in a social, not sporting, context. Consistency of treatment by an employer is an important factor in determining whether a dismissal is fair. Of particular interest here is the dismissal of Jamie Stuart by Charlton Athletic FC. At the times of their respective bans, both Chris Armstrong and Lee Bowyer were Charlton players. Again, with respect to Ed Giddins, it is interesting to note that Sussex was very much in the minority of county cricket clubs who appeared to view Giddins' alleged use of cocaine as grounds for treating his contract as terminated.[13]

It is, perhaps, significant that, in identifying cases where clubs have taken a lenient approach, all the names which immediately spring to mind are 'star' footballers. The fates of Roger Stanislaus and Craig Whittington, as examples, suggest that journeymen players and/or players in the lower divisions are more likely to find their careers terminated if found guilty of taking recreational drugs. This will, perhaps, particularly be the case if a player's absence through suspension and/or imprisonment had significant repercussions for the fortunes and/or finances of the club concerned. Conversely, in the case of the 'star', a club may well regard it as worthwhile to wait for the player to be available once more for team selection. Essentially, is it within the range of reasonable responses for a club to adopt a policy of 'the greater the "star", the greater the latitude that will be given'?

It can certainly be argued that, as is the case with employers in general, the range of reasonable responses test essentially works in favour of clubs

12 *Iceland Frozen Foods Ltd v Jones* [1982] IRLR 439, p 442.
13 See above, fn 8.

successfully defending decisions to dismiss as fair. It is, therefore, important to comment that the days of the test's applicability may be numbered. In July 1999, in the case of *Haddon*, the Employment Appeal Tribunal (EAT), under the leadership of the outgoing President, Morison J, characterised the range of reasonable responses test as an unhelpful 'mantra' and an unwarranted 'embellishment' on the words contained in s 98(4) of the Employment Rights Act 1996. The EAT argued that, in practice, the test only permits a finding that a dismissal is substantively unfair where the decision to dismiss is so perverse that no reasonable employer could have reached it.[14]

The facts of the case itself vividly illustrate the practical consequences of declining to invoke the 'mantra'. Haddon was instructed to attend a ceremony which had been organised to present him with a good service award. This function was to take place towards the end of his shift, but he was told that he would have to return to work after it had finished, as there was a staff shortage. However, alcohol was provided with the buffet meal, and it was company policy that employees should not return to work if they had been drinking. On this basis, Haddon went home at the end of the function. He was dismissed for gross disobedience. The tribunal found this dismissal to be 'harsh in the extreme', but nevertheless within the range of reasonable responses. Thus, unwillingly, the tribunal found the dismissal to be fair. In declining to apply the range of reasonable responses test, the EAT felt able to reverse this decision.

Since *Haddon*, a different EAT has supported the view that it is for a tribunal to decide whether or not a dismissal is reasonable in all the circumstances.[15] To complicate matters, most recently, yet another, differently constituted, EAT has ruled that the EAT has no authority to rule that the test is wrong, as this effectively means that it is overruling decisions of the Court of Appeal.[16] However, in adopting this position, the EAT acknowledged that tribunals should not be restricted to regarding dismissals as unreasonable only in circumstances where the employer's decision could be considered perverse. It remains to be seen whether the Court of Appeal, or, if necessary, the House of Lords, will approve the bold step taken by the EAT in *Haddon*, and confirm that the test will no longer have a role to play in unfair dismissal law.[17]

Were such a development to occur, then all employers, including clubs, will have to be more careful in ensuring that they are not being over harsh, as well as inconsistent, in deciding to dismiss employees for behaviour which is essentially part of an employee's private life. Clubs would probably need to specify in their own rules that the taking of recreational drugs is regarded as

---

14 *Haddon v Van de Bergh Foods Ltd* [1999] IRLR 672.

15 *Wilson v Ethicon Ltd* [2000] IRLR 4.

16 *Midland Bank plc v Madden* (2000) EAT/1107/98.

17 Since this chapter was originally conceived, the Court of Appeal confirmed in *Madden and The Port Office v Foley* (2000) unreported, 31 July, that tribunals must apply the range of reasonable responses test. See IDS Brief 672, November 2000.

gross misconduct, particularly by reference to a player's fitness, and act consistently in treating such conduct as grounds for dismissal. Leniency towards a 'star' player could well render unfair any subsequent dismissals of players perceived as less important to the club's fortunes on the field of play. Clubs wishing to take the harder line with players, in the context of drug taking, might also be in a stronger position if the impairment of fitness through consumption of alcohol is designated as constituting gross misconduct.

PROCEDURAL FAIRNESS

In defending a claim of unfair dismissal, an employer also has to show that it has acted reasonably with respect to the procedures which have been followed prior to the decision to dismiss. Model procedures are provided by the 1998 Advisory, Conciliation and Arbitration Service (ACAS) *Code of Practice on Disciplinary Practices and Procedures in Employment.*[18] In particular, employers should conduct appropriate investigations, convene formal hearings and provide for appropriate rights of appeal.

If an appropriate investigation does establish that it is reasonable to view an employee as guilty of dishonesty, a dismissal will stand as fair even if, by the time of the tribunal hearing, the employee's innocence has been established.[19] In the context of a positive drugs test, it might well be the case that, by the time of the tribunal hearing, new medical evidence, not available to an employer at the time of dismissal, reveals that the test was in some way flawed. The potentially unreliable nature of such testing has been illustrated by a number of high profile cases, such as those concerning Diane Modahl and Linford Christie. These cases also reveal the considerable negative consequences that drug testing can have for a sports participant's reputation and future career. The tests in these two cases, of course, relate to allegations of cheating, and the problem of a banned drug, such as nandrolone,[20] being contained in a medicine is not going to apply to recreational drugs. However, there is still room for reasonable doubt in the latter context, be it with regard to a flawed urine test,[21] or a drink being spiked,[22] or passive smoking at a party.[23]

---

18 These procedures are not new and date from the original ACAS *Code* adopted in 1977.
19 See *British Home Stores v Burchell* [1978] IRLR 379.
20 Eg, the ongoing problems faced by Linford Christie despite the fact that he has been cleared by UK Athletics. See above, fn 4.
21 See discussion of *Modahl v BAF Ltd* in (1999) 2(5) Sports Law Bulletin 6.
22 This was the defence pleaded by Ed Giddins.
23 This was the defence successfully pleaded by skateboarder Ross Rebagliati.

As shown by the above, it will generally be the sport's regulatory bodies who carry drug testing and hold hearings prior to imposing a penalty on a participant. Although drug tests are not foolproof, an employing club will almost certainly be acting reasonably if it does not conduct an investigation of its own but reaches a decision based on the investigation conducted by the regulatory body. Arguably, however, the reasonable club would still convene a hearing before reaching any decision to terminate the player's contract. Again, by way of contrast, we can consider the position taken by Sussex CCC that the finding of the TCCB that Ed Giddins had taken cocaine automatically terminated his contract of employment, and thus further procedures by the club were superfluous. It is, therefore, possible that a decision to dismiss may well be based on the actions of the relevant regulatory body alone. On this basis, it is useful to discuss the legal status of the ACAS *Code*.

This continues to be one of the trickiest problems of the law on unfair dismissal. It is clear that the *Code* is not law and that, therefore, a failure to follow its provisions does not in itself render a dismissal unfair. In *Polkey*,[24] the Law Lords emphasised that a reasonable employer will normally abide by the *Code*. However, the judgments also emphasised that, despite failing to follow the *Code*, an employer could still be regarded as acting reasonably as adherence to the *Code* could, in appropriate circumstances, be considered futile or useless. In such circumstances, despite procedural deficiencies, a dismissal could still be fair. It seems clear from cases decided since *Polkey* that the issue of procedure is to be considered within the overall context of the range of reasonable responses test.

For example, in *Mathewson*,[25] a dental laboratory assistant confessed to his employer that his late return to work after lunch was due to his arrest by the police for the possession of cannabis. He was dismissed 'on the spot'. The confession meant that there were no further facts to be investigated. The purposes of a formal hearing include the challenging of evidence through the employee giving his version of the facts and the cross-examination of witnesses, and any pleas of mitigation that the employee should be given the opportunity to present. As the employee was clearly guilty of being a user of cannabis, and there were not (in the employer's view, could not be) any mitigating circumstances, it was reasonable to view the following of the *Code* as futile. The only question to be determined was whether the substantive reason for the dismissal was within the range of reasonable responses. If so, then (as the EAT indeed decided) the dismissal was fair.

This case has clear repercussions for sports participants who use prohibited and/or illegal drugs. Once a regulatory body has conducted its own investigation and hearing, it might well be the case that the employing

---

24 *Polkey v AE Dayton Services Ltd* [1987] 3 ALL ER 974.
25 *Mathewson v Wilson Dental Laboratory* [1988] IRLR 512.

club need not initiate further procedures prior to reaching a decision to dismiss. The sole question would then be whether the substantive basis of the dismissal is within the range of reasonable responses. Alternatively, it could (should) be argued that a player should still be permitted to plead his side of the case. This is because factors such as past loyalty to the club or personal problems may not be the concern of the regulatory body but should be the concern of the reasonable employer. This is particularly the case if, in the past, a club has shown leniency or, indeed, as was the case with Arsenal and Paul Merson, has been supportive of the problems the player is seeking to overcome. There will also be cases, as illustrated by the Lawrence Dallaglio affair,[26] where clubs will have to be very careful in ensuring that they carry out their own investigations before reaching any decision to dismiss. In similar circumstances, if a player was dismissed without proper procedures being followed, then such a dismissal would surely be unfair, and this would be the case even if, at a later date, the allegations were shown to be true.

Another major aspect of the *Code* is providing rights of internal appeal to an employee against a dismissal. Professional footballers and cricketers have *contractual* rights of appeal – ultimately, to panels established by the relevant regulatory bodies. Normally, a refusal to permit a contractual right of appeal will be considered unreasonable and, therefore, the dismissal must be unfair.[27] However, again, this is not automatic, as the issue of whether an appeal should be permitted remains within the range of reasonable responses.[28]

CONCLUSIONS

The central conclusion of this chapter is that a clear line of demarcation should be drawn between drugs which are considered performance enhancing and those which should more properly be considered as recreational. Whilst there are clearly problems, both practical and philosophical, in banning sports participants for taking the former, it is contended that consumption of the latter should cease to be the concern of regulatory bodies. Such bodies did not come into existence to act as moral watchdogs, and it is clearly debatable whether, today, such bodies are in touch with public opinion and, thus, the opinion of many of those who pay money to view particular sports. For example, with respect to the Dallaglio affair, there was discussion whether, even had the allegations proved to be true, Dallaglio's career should have

---

26 Dallaglio was dropped by the English Rugby Union side in the wake of allegations from the *News of the World*, 23 May 1999, that Dallaglio had boasted of taking and selling a variety of recreational drugs. These allegations were not substantiated, and Dallaglio has resumed his international career.

27 *Stoker v Lancashire CC* [1992] IRLR 75.

28 *Westminster CC v Cabaj* [1996] IRLR 399.

been jeopardised for simply doing what many other individuals do, or have done at some time in their lives.[29] (And this was with respect to rugby, where, arguably, the followers of the game are more conservative in their moral outlook than is the case with football fans, where the links with other forms of popular culture are much more overt. Take, for example, the number of musicians and actors who appear as guests on Sky's *Soccer AM* programme on a Saturday.) It is also the case that regulatory bodies, along, it seems, with politicians, ignore the increasingly widespread view, particularly amongst those who reached adulthood in the 1960s or during the decades since then, that some or all drugs should be legalised, or their possession at least decriminalised.[30]

It is acknowledged that there is a basis for clubs, as employers, deciding to take disciplinary action, up to and including dismissal against players, where it is established that they have been taking drugs for recreational purposes. However, again, it is contended this should not be by reference to notions of upholding moral standards, nor requiring professional sportsmen to be role models for the young, as far as moral behaviour is concerned, but by reference to maintaining maximum fitness during the season of play. In this context, it can thus be argued that whatever position a particular club holds on drugs, it should also hold this same position on alcohol. Moreover, what players get up to out of season should not be the concern of their clubs, unless it can be shown to have a negative impact on a player's longer term fitness.

Even this position might be considered illiberal given the alcohol fuelled culture with which English professional football has traditionally been associated. However, the times they are a changing, and more and more clubs are introducing fitness regimes which cover every part of a player's life – not just the 24 hours prior to a competitive match. Losing the right to abuse one's body, at least during the competitive season, is perhaps the price that contemporary sportsmen can be required to pay in return for salaries that are often in excess of those earned by the large majority of their fans.

It is important, from the perspective of both natural justice and clubs protecting themselves from successful litigation, that clubs who view the taking of drugs as a serious disciplinary offence make this clear in their rules of conduct. Similarly, clubs should be consistent in their treatment of players – 'star' and 'journeyman' alike. Clubs should follow full procedures, particularly if they are contract-based, prior to taking any decision of a disciplinary nature. On the other hand, latitude should be shown where it is

---

29 See Freedland, J, 'Across that white line' (1999) *The Guardian*, 26 May; Reeves, R, 'Free the cocaine two' (1999) *The Observer Review*, 27 August.

30 The extent to which attitudes towards the consumption of recreational drugs has changed over recent decades is perhaps encapsulated by the call on the Government, by the Editor of *The Daily Telegraph*, to draw up plans for the legalisation of cannabis, and the call by *The Daily Mail* for a 'rational and mature debate'. See Arlidge, J, 'A taboo goes up in smoke' (2000) *The Observer*, 2 April.

clear that a player's use of drugs is in response to wider and deeper problems of a personal nature.[31] This last point will become rather more pertinent, in law, if and when the range of reasonable responses test is abolished, and a tribunal can consider a particular dismissal to be harsh by reference to all the circumstances of a case, and thus unfair. Finally, it should be clarified that, in the author's view, as a long suffering football fan rather than as an employment lawyer, players should not find that their careers are in jeopardy just because they have had the occasional 'puff' or 'snort' on a Saturday night (unless, of course, they are playing the following day).

---

31 It seems bizarre to this author that there was some discussion by the FA over whether it should investigate allegations that Stan Collymore had taken drugs whilst he was in a clinic for treatment of serious depression. See (1999) *The Guardian Sport*, 24 May.

CHAPTER 7

'SAY IT AIN'T SO, MO.'[1]
INTERNATIONAL PERFORMERS' PERCEPTIONS
OF DRUG USE AND THE DIANE MODAHL AFFAIR

David McArdle

INTRODUCTION

> It might be wondered, in passing, whether some recent developments in
> sporting practices such as doping ... are not in part an effect of the revolution
> which I have too rapidly sketched. Sport ... has become, through television, a
> mass spectacle, transmitted far beyond the circle of present or past
> 'practitioners' to a public very imperfectly equipped with the specific
> competence needed to decipher it adequately. The 'connoisseur' has schemes
> of perception and appreciation which enable him to see what the layman
> cannot see; to perceive a necessity where the outsider sees only violence and
> confusion.[2]

This chapter analyses the reactions of a small group of elite level athletes to
sports governing bodies' attempts to proscribe the use of performance
enhancing substances in athletic competition. The research interviews were
carried out shortly after Diane Modahl, the British 800 m runner, tested
positive for testosterone at the European Championships in the summer of
1994. In March 1995, Modahl was exonerated after her legal advisers
discovered fundamental flaws in the procedures used by the testing
authorities; these interviews were carried out between October 1994 and
February 1995 – that is, after Modahl was banned but before she was
reinstated. Accordingly, the research process was particularly concerned with
the extent to which interviewees' attitudes had been shaped by their
perceptions of Modahl's experiences. The paper reveals that most of the
interviewees radically altered their views on performance enhancing
substances and the broader issues of the science and morality of drug testing
in the wake of Modahl's case. The opinion that the science of drug testing is

---

1   In 1919, baseball star 'Shoeless' Joe Jackson of the Chicago Black Sox was implicated
     in a plot to throw the World Series. In 1921, he was acquitted of match fixing charges
     by a Chicago jury, but was banned for life by the Baseball Commissioner. Legend has
     it that at some stage in the affair Shoeless Joe was accosted by an all-American small
     boy, who looked him in the eye and pleaded, 'Say it ain't so, Joe. Say it ain't so'.
     Shoeless looked down upon the boy and, with tears in his eyes, said, 'I'm sorry son,
     I'm afraid it is'.

     Like all the best sports stories, this one is a myth. The conversation with the (sm)all-
     American boy never took place. And Shoeless didn't help throw the World Series: see
     members.aol.com/stealth792/shoeless/shoeless.html.

2   Bourdieu, P, 'Sport and social class' (1978) 17 Social Science Information 819, p 829.

not as watertight as the governing bodies would have the media, the public and the athletes believe was widely held among those competing at the highest levels in this particular sport.

A POTTED HISTORY OF DRUG TESTING

Given that the International Olympic Committee's (IOC's) stance on drug use, and the attempts by it and other governing bodies to address the issue, have developed over the past 40 years or so, it might be presumed that the concept of doping is a recent phenomenon, fuelled by late 20th century pharmacology. This is categorically not the case. Donohoe and Johnson[3] discuss the use of drugs by ancient Greek Olympians and by participants in medieval jousts and those who were 'playing their prize'.[4] However, it was not until the death of a Norwegian cyclist in 1960, growing evidence of drug use among footballers in North America and the appearance of unfeasibly muscular Eastern European women such as Irine and Tamara Press that drug testing was introduced. With that in mind, it is worth noting that the Press sisters were almost certainly genuine intersex cases rather than the result of systematic doping policies or, as was widely believed at the time, men pretending to be women in order to compete in women's events. Although Simpson *et al* remark that 'the possibility that men may masquerade as women in women's events was widely discussed in the early 1960s',[5] in approximately 30 years of sex testing at athletic events, no case of masquerading men was ever documented. The real consequence has been the exposure of subjects with disorders of human intersex to publicity and ridicule.[6] The history of sex testing is even more dishonourable than the history of drug testing.

'[S]tarting about 1960, the modern techniques of analytical chemistry, especially chromatography, provided the possibility to detect more and more dope agents or their metabolites in biological fluids, preferably in urine.'[7] However, the IOC's Medical Commission was not established until after the

---

3   Donohue, T and Johnson, N, *Foul Play: Drug Abuse in Sports*, 1986, Oxford: Blackwell.

4   Birley, D, *Sport and the Making of Britain*, 1993, Manchester: Manchester UP.

5   Simpson, J *et al*, 'Medical examination for health of all athletes replacing the need for gender verification in international sports' (1992) 267 J American Medical Association 850.

6   See De La Chappelle, A, 'The use and misuse of sex chromatin screening' (1986) 256 J American Medical Association 1920; Hay, E, 'Sex determination in putative female athletes' (1972) 221 J American Medical Association 998; Hood-Williams, J, 'Sexing the athletes' (1995) 12 Sociology of Sport J 290; Sakamoto, H *et al*, 'Femininity control at the XXth Universiad in Kobe, Japan' (1988) 9 International J Sports Medicine 193.

7   Donike, M *et al*, 'Dope analysis', in Bellotti, P *et al* (eds), *IAAF World Symposium on Drug Use in Sport*, 1988, London: IAAF.

death, partly as a consequence of amphetamine use, of British cyclist Tommy Simpson at that year's Tour de France. Until that time, there was little agreement on which substances should be banned[8] and, until the various sporting organisations came together under the Olympic Medical Commission's umbrella, national governments were responsible for legislating against drug use if they saw fit to do so – ironically, France (and Belgium) had already taken measures back in 1965. These first forays into drug testing were couched in terms of ensuring the health and well being of the athletes rather than with sporting 'morality' and fair play, but the apparent emergence of widespread and State sponsored doping practices in the 1970s and 1980s heralded a change in emphasis. However, the returns from the Olympic Games that followed the introduction of widespread random testing but preceded the collapse of Communism would appear to give the impression that only a small minority of athletes were engaged in doping practices. Of course, this was not ever the case – sports administrators were less than candid about the extent of drug use for fear of the damage that such openness would cause to a multi-billion dollar industry.[9] For the record, Dubin noted that, in the 1976 Olympics in Montreal, only six positives were recorded from 275 tests. No positives were recorded from 1,500 tests at Moscow in 1980. Los Angeles, 1984, saw 17 positives from the same number of tests and Seoul, 1988, yielded 30 out of 1,500, although Jennings[10] asserts that, at Seoul, over 40 positive tests were shredded by IOC officials. Of course, one of the test results that were allowed into the public domain was that of the Canadian scapegoat Ben Johnson.[11] And, even though no positive tests were recorded from Moscow, those 1980 Games stand out as the first occasion when the widespread misuse of testosterone became evident.

---

8   Ferstle, J, 'Evolution and politics of drug testing', in Yesalis, C (ed), *Anabolic Steroids in Sport and Exercise*, 1993, Champaign, Ill: Human Kinetics.

9   *On the Line: Drug Testing*, BBC 2 broadcast, 22 August 1994; Simson, V and Jennings, A, *The Lords of the Rings: Power, Money and Drugs in the Modern Olympics*, 1992, London: Simon & Schuster.

10   Jennings, A, 'Methods used by investigative reporters', unpublished paper presented at the North American Society for the Sociology of Sport Annual Conference, Savannah, GA, November 1994.

11   Giving evidence to the Dubin Inquiry (Dubin, C, *Commission of Inquiry into the Use of Drugs and Banned Practices Intended to Increase Athletic Performance*, 1990, Ottawa: Canadian Government Publishing Centre), British Olympic Committee Chairman Sir Arthur Gold asserted that 'only the careless and ill-advised get caught ... Many, many more athletes than those actually testing positive have taken advantage of banned substances and practices'. Johnson, a cocksure but semi-literate Jamaican immigrant, had the misfortune to come along just as the IOC decided that it needed to make an example of somebody with a high profile. The Ben Johnson affair was nothing more than the high-tech lynching of an uppity Black.

TESTOSTERONE

A brief word about the benefits of testosterone as a performance enhancing substance might be appropriate at this stage. Proscribed anabolic-androgenic agents such as clenbuterol and dehydroepiandrosterone (DHEA) are merely synthetic forms of testosterone and, as such, they possess testosterone's properties and share its capacity to facilitate the development of muscle mass, and aid recovery from injury in particular. Testosterone and these synthetic forms are, as the proper name of the latter indicates, both anabolic (that is, they assist in the building of tissue) and androgenic (that is, they promote the development of 'masculine characteristics' such as a deep voice and facial hair). Thus far, it has not been possible to develop a steroid which is anabolic but not androgenic, and 'one of the main medical uses of androgenic-anabolic steroids has been to treat problems associated with male development at puberty and thereby restore normal male secondary characteristics'.[12]

In the 1970s and 1980s, athletes increasingly substituted testosterone for androgenic-anabolic steroids because it was virtually impossible for the testing authorities to distinguish between naturally occurring testosterone and exogenous testosterone. Houlihan[13] states that 'at the 1980 Olympic Games as many as two-thirds of all random urine samples contained abnormal levels of testosterone'. If these figures are anywhere near accurate,[14] it suggests that innumerable[15] athletes were using testosterone with impunity, and almost certainly under the guidance and connivance of coaches and physicians.

The phrase 'male hormone', widely used in relation to testosterone, is a misnomer because testosterone is produced naturally by both sexes, although in women and pre-pubescent males the amount produced is a fraction of that produced by adult males. In both sexes and across all ages, the norm is for the body to produce one part testosterone to one part of its isomer – another naturally occurring hormone called epitestosterone. Significant variations from the 1:1 ratio give rise to the suspicion that the ratio has changed as a consequence of the ingestion of exogenous testosterone. Consequently,

---

12 Houlihan, B, *Dying to Win: Doping in Sport and the Development of an Anti-Doping Policy*, 1999, Strasbourg: Council of Europe, p 70.

13 *Ibid*, p 71.

14 Regrettably, Professor Houlihan is unable to provide readers with the source of this information.

15 Athletes from the US and elsewhere were prohibited from competing in the 1980 Olympics following the Soviet Union's invasion of Afghanistan in 1979 (on the legality of that ban in the US see *De Frantz v US Olympic Committee* 492 F Supp 1181 (1980)). While there were certainly State-sponsored doping programmes in the former Communist countries, it would be wrong to suggest that athletes in Western Europe and North America were less prone to drug use than their Eastern bloc counterparts. Accordingly, one ought to be wary of assuming that Professor Houlihan's astonishing figures would have been markedly different had Western athletes been present in Moscow.

epitestosterone is on the IOC's list of banned 'masking agents' because athletes can ingest it in an attempt to maintain the 1:1 ratio and thereby disguise their ingestion of testosterone.

The IOC believes a doping offence may have been committed if the ratio of testosterone to epitestosterone rises above 4:1.[16] Ben Johnson's ratio was 10:1 when he tested positive at the Seoul Olympics in 1988.[17] When the results of Diane Modahl's sample were made public in September 1994, it was revealed that her ratio was an incredible and unprecedented 42:1. But it soon became apparent that all was not as it appeared.

SITTING COMFORTABLY? THE DIANE MODAHL STORY

On 18 June 1994, the then Commonwealth Games 800 m champion Diane Modahl was selected to give a urine sample under the International Amateur Athletic Federation's (IAAF's) in-competition testing programme after finishing second at a prestigious European Championship meeting in Lisbon, Portugal. In accordance with IAAF procedure, her sample was transported to an accredited laboratory in Lisbon, where it was split into two vials, labelled 'A' sample and 'B' sample respectively.

The 'A sample' was tested for the presence of those substances that have been banned by the IAAF because they are deemed to have performance enhancing properties. In mid-August 1994 (over two months after the sample was taken), it was announced that Modahl's 'A' sample had tested positive for the 'male hormone', testosterone. On 30 August, her 'B' sample was opened and tested in the presence of her coach/husband Vincente Modahl and drug experts from the IOC, the British Athletic Federation (BAF) and the IAAF. The 'B' sample also tested positive. The result was communicated to Modahl, who at that time was competing in the Commonwealth Games in Vancouver; 48 hours later, the IAAF announced that, in accordance with their normal procedures, she would be suspended pending the outcome of any appeal.

Medical opinion at the time was that Modahl had either injected herself with testosterone almost immediately before racing, or she was gravely ill. A rare form of ovarian cancer could *possibly* cause the body to secrete such high levels of the hormone, it was suggested. Medical experts also believed two other, less serious, medical conditions (namely, 5-Alpha reductase and polycycstic ovary syndrome) could have had the same effect on her

---

16 Sports Council, *Doping Control*, 1993, London: Sports Council.
17 *Op cit*, Dubin, fn 11.

testosterone levels.[18] Extensive medical tests found nothing untoward, however. It appeared to be a case of an ill-advised athlete taking a big risk by using a banned substance just before a competition, believing that they had successfully masked their use of the proscribed substance or that they would be able to convince the authorities that nothing untoward had happened.

But disquiet was expressed as soon as the result of the 'A' sample test had been made public. Many athletes and commentators simply refused to countenance the possibility that Modahl, of all people, would ever contemplate using performance enhancing substances. Diane Modahl was (and remains) a person of deep religious conviction. Although a profound religious belief does not mean a particular athlete is incapable of cheating (Hansie Cronje is a devout Christian as well), many individuals who would come within Bourdieu's category of 'ill-equipped laymen' would have reasonably concluded that, 'if Modahl's on drugs, they must all be at it'. More pertinently, even a spokesman from the BAF was quoted as saying 'there is something odd about the whole business of Diane's test, but no one seems to know what it is'.[19] The possibility of illness had been discounted, however, and at this stage there were no grounds for suggesting that the sample had been switched or tampered with.

On the day after the 'B' sample test result was announced, a statement from Modahl's lawyers said that it was 'apparent that there had been material changes to the characteristics of the sample between 18 June and 30 August. This raises serious questions as to the compliance with IAAF guidelines in relation to the storage and treatment of samples pending analysis'.[20] In response to this statement, an IAAF spokesman admitted that one of the doping experts present at the testing of the 'B' sample had noted changes to the composition of the urine as soon as the vial was opened. The IAAF spokesman merely said that these changes could be ascribed to the passage of time. So far as Modahl's lawyers were concerned, though, the changes indicated the sample had actually degraded while in storage. In any event (said the lawyers), the IAAF could not use a degraded sample as evidence that an athlete had taken testosterone in order to enhance her performance and expect that a subsequent ban would be upheld. If necessary, they would take the governing bodies to court and argue that they had breached their own procedures regarding sample storage. They would also invite the court to hold that the enormous amount of testosterone present in the sample could have been a consequence of the laboratory's failure to store the sample properly, rather than the result of a doping offence.

---

18 *On the line: The Modahl Affair*, BBC 2 broadcast, 3 February 1996.

19 *Ibid*.

20 See (1994) *The Guardian*, 1 September, p 21.

In December 1994, Modahl exercised her right to appeal against her suspension before a panel convened under the auspices of the BAF, the (now defunct) governing body for track and field athletics in Great Britain. In accordance with her lawyers' earlier statement, the basis of her appeal was that improper storage of her sample by the testing laboratory in Lisbon had caused her urine sample to degrade, resulting in the unprecedentedly high testosterone reading. Personnel from the testing laboratory admitted that, far from the sample being refrigerated for the whole period between collection and testing, as required under the IAAF's own regulations, it had been stored for the first 48 hours in direct sunlight at temperatures of up to 80° Fahrenheit.

Despite being presented with this evidence, the BAF panel rejected Modahl's appeal. After hearing from five independent endocrinologists, the panel accepted there had been serious flaws in the testing procedure at the Lisbon laboratory. But, under the IAAF's regulations, the burden of proof fell on Modahl to provide a satisfactory explanation for the extraordinarily high level of testosterone in her sample. That burden had not been satisfactorily discharged, they said. A four year ban (the mandatory penalty under IAAF rules for a first offence of testing positive for testosterone) was imposed.

However, the BAF's regulations gave Modahl another right of appeal. In July 1995, she exercised that right before a specially constituted BAF appeal panel, which, to widespread surprise, found in her favour after a two day hearing. The appeal panel decided the unsuitable conditions in which the sample had been stored probably caused bacterial infection in the urine. This infection could have caused the sample to degrade, which may in turn have given rise to a false result. Worse, the incompetence of the Lisbon testing laboratory in failing to store the sample correctly had been compounded because the documents that would have proved that the sample had been kept securely were missing. The panel decided Modahl had no case to answer, and her four year ban was overturned.

The IAAF expressed its 'surprise' at the appeal panel's decision and emphasised that the final decision on Modahl's eligibility to compete rested with it, as the world governing body, rather than with a domestic federation. The IAAF announced that it would appeal against the appeal panel's decision before the IAAF's own Arbitration Panel. But, in March 1996, the 27 member IAAF Council decided to drop the case on the advice of its Doping Commission Chairman, Professor Arne Ljungqvist. Like the BAF appeal panel, Ljungqvist felt that the manifest failures in the testing procedure regarding sample storage and the loss of paperwork had effectively relieved Modahl of any obligation to provide an explanation for her testosterone levels. The athlete immediately launched legal proceedings against the BAF (the body that was effectively responsible for exonerating her), claiming a total of £960,000 in damages, legal fees and loss of earnings as a result of the four year ban that the BAF had imposed on her back in December 1994.

In June 1996, the BAF applied to strike out the statement of claim under RSC Ord 18 r 19, on the ground that it disclosed no cause of action. Modahl's statement of claim contained allegations that fell into two broad categories: first, that two members of the Disciplinary Committee had been biased against her; and, secondly, that the charge was brought in breach of the rules because the laboratory which tested her urine sample was not officially accredited. At first instance, Popplewell J dismissed the summons to strike out and ordered that both sets of allegations proceed to trial. The Court of Appeal upheld this decision on the bias point, but it allowed the appeal on the accreditation point and said that, on this issue, Modahl had no arguable case. Accordingly, the BAF was only required to answer allegations of bias. Modahl's appearance in the House of Lords in July 1999 was an appeal against this ruling. In the interim, however,[21] the BAF was placed in administration, with debts approaching £2 million – £800,000 of which was in respect of costs that had been incurred in the *Modahl* case thus far.[22]

The House of Lords hearing[23] was expected to last for two days. In the event, it was over before lunch on the first, and the Court of Appeal's decision was upheld. Counsel for Modahl had argued that, although the laboratory in Lisbon where the urine sample was tested was indeed on the IOC's list of accredited laboratories, it was not really 'accredited' because its premises had been moved without either the IOC or the IAAF being informed. Accordingly, counsel argued, in banning Modahl, the BAF had acted upon a result from a laboratory that was not accredited and, as such, had breached the terms of the contract between it (the BAF) and Modahl. Counsel opined that the terms of this contract meant, in Lord Hoffmann's words, that 'the only evidence which could justify the BAF in suspending her or initiating disciplinary proceedings for the offence of having a prohibited substance in her body was a positive result from an accredited laboratory'.[24] Lord Hoffmann, giving the judgment of the court, was not convinced:

> The IOC has procedures for the regular checking of accredited laboratories and a removal to less suitable premises could well be a ground for the IOC revoking an accreditation. The same might be true of changes in personnel or equipment. But I find it hard to see why such matters should *ipso facto* nullify the accreditation without any act on the part of the IOC.[25]

---

21 Specifically, in October 1997.

22 In accountants' parlance, Modahl is a contingent liability rather than a creditor of the BAF. However, at the time of the House of Lords hearing, over 100 athletes were among the creditors and were owed sums of between £2,500 and £75,000 by the BAF; debts which cannot be settled until the *Modahl* case is over. See Nichols, P, 'Athletes still wait on Modahl' (1999) *The Guardian*, 20 July, p 28.

23 *Modahl v BAF Ltd* (1999) 22 July (HL), available at www.parliament.the-stationery-office.co.uk/pa/ld199899/ldjudgmt/jd990722/modahl.

24 *Ibid*.

25 *Ibid*.

There was 'no allegation that the BAF knew or ought to have known that [the Portuguese laboratory] was not an accredited laboratory' and, in suspending Modahl, the BAF was 'simply carrying out its duties under IAAF rules'.[26] Accordingly, the Court of Appeal's ruling that this part of the statement of claim should be struck out was upheld.

At the time of writing, then, Modahl still has a ground for action on the basis that two members of the original BAF disciplinary panel which banned her for four years was biased against her. However, given that, in June 1999, Modahl's legal aid was withdrawn, it may be that a sensible offer from the BAF's administrators would see this long running saga brought to a close. In that case, a number of talented British athletes – including Ashia Hansen, Jamie Baulch and Mark Richardson – will see at least some of the money owed to them.

DRUGS, SPORT AND THE BIGGER PICTURE

The whole question of drug use in sport was being widely debated when the Diane Modahl story broke. The use of anabolic steroids was particularly high on the agenda, and those in favour of tougher penalties for their possession were lobbying for amendments to the Misuse of Drugs Act 1971. This Act empowers Parliament to proscribe the possession of substances designated as 'controlled drugs'. The penalties for unlawful possession of a controlled drug include fines and/or imprisonment, depending upon the relative harmfulness of the drug in question. Class A drugs (for example, heroin and cocaine) can attract unlimited fines, seizure of assets and/or life imprisonment. The possession of Class B or Class C substances now attracts maximum penalties of fines of £2,500 and £1,000 respectively (the penalties were amended by the Criminal Justice and Public Order Act 1994). In 1996, the Government reclassified anabolic steroids as a Class C drug under the 1971 Act through the Misuse of Drugs Act 1971 (Modification) Order 1996.[27] This came into force in early 1997 and makes the unlawful possession of anabolic steroids punishable by a fine of up to £1,000.

The use of illegal drugs is always a high profile issue and this was particularly the case in late 1995, following the death of Leah Betts, a 17 year old who died after using the dance drug, Ecstasy. The newspapers' acknowledged tendency to adopt a sensationalist approach to drug issues by taking worst case scenarios such as drug-induced death or violent behaviour and portraying them as the norm[28] was much to the fore in the days and

---

26 *Modahl v BAF Ltd* (1999) 22 July (HL).

27 SI 1996/1300.

28 Redhead, S, *Unpopular Cultures: The Birth of Law and Popular Culture*, 1995, Manchester: Manchester UP.

weeks after Leah Betts died. This approach was also evident in the news media's reporting of the Zoe Warwick case (see below, p 104), her illness and subsequent death being portrayed as a situation that could befall any anabolic steroid user rather than as an isolated and avoidable tragedy that was a consequence of one athlete using drugs in isolation without the support and advice of peers, coaches and physicians.

In the light of the Diane Modahl case, a number of interviews with various competitors from other sports – undertaken as part of a separate research project carried out by the author at that time – invariably turned to the topic of drug use. In the course of those conversations, it became apparent that most of those athletes believed that anabolic steroids were usually taken in measured doses and under medical supervision rather than in uncontrolled quantities by athletes acting of their own volition, as Zoe Warwick had done. Those athletes also felt that the damaging side effects the media associated with such substances, such as high blood pressure, testicular cancer, liver damage and uncontrollable aggression, were short term and reversible – assuming that their occurrence could be ascribed to the use of those drugs at all. A definitive link remained unproven, they thought.

It would probably be unwise to attach too much credence to those conversations, which had, after all, arisen from interviews on an entirely different subject. The best that can be said of them is that they provided a modicum of anecdotal evidence that a small group of international competitors had a standpoint on drugs which was at odds with the one being peddled by the newspapers and sports governing bodies at that time. But, whereas the media's anti-drug stance in particular proved to be instrumental in securing changes to the laws on anabolic steroids, nobody seemed too interested in what the athletes had to say about it.

This state of affairs provoked consideration of the effect of media representations of drug matters. The media's role and Parliament's response to it appeared to be a classic case of moral panic,[29] in which 'deviant behaviour' (in this context, cheating in sport by using performance enhancing substances) eventually resulted in the application of rules and sanctions against the 'offenders'. The media and other 'moral agents' successfully influenced the public's and the Government's attitudes towards the issue to such an extent that it precipitated changes to the law. A moral crusade had created moral panic, where 'a condition, episode, person or group of persons emerges to become defined as a threat to societal values and interests'.[30] The Modahl saga lent itself easily to the cause of those who wanted to 'do something' about drugs in sport:

---

29   Cohen, S, *Folk Devils and Moral Panics*, 1980, London: Robertson.
30   *Ibid*, p 9.

> We consider (doping) to be the most shameful abuse of the Olympic ideal: we call for the life ban of offending athletes; we call for the life ban of coaches and so called doctors who administer this evil.[31]

Modahl's exoneration came too late to influence the debate, for her case had been cited as the latest in a series of inglorious episodes that necessitated the introduction of stricter laws to deal with drugs in sport. By the time her ban was lifted, the machinery of justice had already ground into motion. Accordingly, a direct link can be made between her positive, but worthless, test for testosterone and the hue and cry that led to a change in the legal status of anabolic steroids.

The irony is that the people at whom the legislation was primarily aimed – elite athletes – are probably the group of potential users to whom steroid use poses the least risk of long term damage. Drug use by athletes occurs in a controlled environment. This means the damaging side effects associated with prolonged and unregulated use is delayed or prevented in athletes.[32] Other subcultures had far more to lose than the athletes did. The main users of steroids (and whose use of them is less likely to be controlled by coaches or physicians) are bodybuilders and gay men who subscribe to a particular gym-and-clubbing culture. Increased use among straight adolescent males who want to look the part in pubs and clubs has also been documented.[33] Health care professionals feared these individuals were particularly prone to the health risks associated with steroid use. And these were the groups whose unregulated use of anabolic steroids was likely to increase as a result of the 'panic laws'[34] that the Diane Modahl affair precipitated. The fear was that their use would be pushed underground, beyond the reach of education programmes and wiser counsel.

DRUG USE AND ELITE LEVEL COMPETITORS

This research with international fencers was motivated in part by a desire to find out whether those other athletes' views were shared by competitors who were not household names and who, far from making money from their sport, incur a great deal of expense for the privilege of competing internationally. These athletes are in a similar position to those who lost out financially because of the BAF's inability to pay the moneys owed to them. They hardly ever appear on television, their sport is not a popular one and the media

---

31 Sebastian Coe, quoted in *op cit*, Donohue and Johnson, fn 3, p 1.

32 Cashmore, E, *Making Sense of Sport*, 2nd edn, 1996, London: Routledge.

33 Lowther, J, 'Anabolic steroid use: law and practice', unpublished paper presented at the Socio-Legal Studies Association Annual Conference, Manchester, 1998.

34 *Op cit*, Redhead, fn 28.

usually paid them no heed. During the Great Steroid Debate, their views were certainly not solicited.

Interviews were preferred over other methods of data collection because the emphasis of this project was on understanding the perspective of those who were likely to have had experience of the drug testing regime. Moreover, opinions were likely to be influenced by the media, the governing bodies and other 'moral entrepreneurs' rather than through their own involvement with proscribed substances. Indeed, as an interview sample, this group seemed to possess characteristics of both the 'connoisseurs' and the 'laymen' that Bourdieu wrote about. While the methodology used would probably be formally categorised as a 'standardised open-ended interview', much of what occurred was decidedly unstructured. As such, it accorded with Sanger's[35] description of the unstructured interview as one that allows for 'tactical opportunism'. Although all subjects were asked the same questions in the same order, the structure of the interviews was flexible enough to allow those responses that seemed worth pursuing to be explored in more depth than those which turned out to be less interesting or important than one might have anticipated.

Fencing is very much an 'amateur sport' and has a reputation (not completely undeserved) of being the domain of the public schools and the public school educated elite. Its status as an Olympic sport is under threat because of its perceived lack of television appeal, and, despite attempts to make it more TV-friendly (alterations to the scoring system, the use of see-through masks), it will, sooner rather than later, be axed in favour of beach volleyball, tennis and mountain biking. It has had a few scandalous incidents over the years, which have involved tampering with clothing or equipment in an attempt to make sure 'on target' hits do not register. And, although there is anecdotal evidence of fencers taking proscribed substances to help recovery from injury, it does not have a reputation as a drug user's sport. A number of those interviewed said this was because fencers had yet to discover a drug that actually improved their performance rather than because they had adopted the moral high ground.

This research was carried out between December 1995 and March 1996. It involved face to face semi-structured 'snowball' interviews with 12 international fencers (six men, six women) who were at that time competing internationally in one of the three fencing disciplines (foil, épée, sabre). They had all competed in either the Olympic Games, the Commonwealth Games or the World Championships. Several had competed in two of those tournaments, and one had competed in all three.

---

35 Sanger, J, *The Compleat Observer: A Field Research Guide to Observation*, 1996, Sussex: Falmer.

The interviews lasted for between 45 minutes and one hour and covered various issues that had become pertinent in the wake of the Diane Modahl case and the attendant moral panic surrounding drug use. They concentrated initially on the athletes' knowledge of which substances were banned and the reasons for them being banned, but the nature of the interview process provided scope for discussion of their perceptions of the science behind drug testing, the banning of recreational drugs and the role of the governing bodies. Questions were also asked about their confidence in the accuracy of drug tests and the sources of information that had been influential in shaping their opinions. Some of those interviewed sought guarantees of anonymity in the event of the results being published, hence the absence in what follows of the use of codes or initials which could conceivably result in an athlete being identified by their peers or members of the governing body.

The research had its roots in Fuller and LaFountain's survey[36] of anabolic steroid use amongst 50 male college students, all of whom were admitted steroid users and who participated in (grid-iron) football, weightlifting, bodybuilding or wrestling. Fuller and LaFountain concentrated on whether those athletes regarded the use of steroids as 'cheating' the ramifications of breaking the law by buying steroids on the black market and the health risks associated with their use. Most of those surveyed by Fuller and LaFountain were unconcerned about the 'criminality' of their activities. They thought of it as a 'victimless crime', believed that serious athletes had to use them in order to be competitive nationally or internationally and said the success of other athletes was usually attributable to drug use. They were unconcerned about the health risks, were remarkably ill-informed about the possible side effects of anabolic steroid use and regarded their bodies as machines that had to be manipulated to achieve the desired results. Any concerns they may have had were dismissed as secondary to the commitment required of a dedicated athlete. It was just another form of sacrifice:

> I get a lot of fun and enjoyment from powerlifting. It gives me a chance to achieve for myself and I do all I can to make my body stronger. I don't use (recreational) drugs or drink or smoke and if my coach says steroids will make me stronger I will use them.[37]

Of course, the fundamental differences between this group and the fencers were that the fencers were not admitted drug users and they would not have been expected to mount a strong defence of drug use in their (ostensibly drug free) sport. But, given that governing bodies, the Sports Council and the testing authorities have taken steps to inform athletes of the official line in drug use, it was salutary to discover that the only notable similarity was both groups' alarmingly confused views about the supposed physical effects of

---

36 Fuller, R and LaFountain, J, 'Performance-enhancing drug use in college athletics: a different form of drug abuse' [1987] Adolescence 115.

37 *Ibid*, p 119.

anabolic steroid use. The fencers were able to speak vaguely about 'assisting recovery from injury' and 'helping you to train longer'. Only one of them was able to give information about the side effects which reflected that provided by bodies like the Sports Council and the sport's governing body in the UK, the Amateur Fencing Association (AFA):

> Steroids are bad for you. They can be killers if you over-use them, can give you terrible liver and heart problems. They really do damage your mind and body – and not enough athletes know that.[38]

In the months preceding these interviews, the British newspapers had reported the plight of Zoe Warwick, a former champion shot putter and javelin thrower whose body had been wrecked by prolonged, excessive and unregulated steroid abuse and who committed suicide at the age of 34. A Coroner's inquest had found that an inability to deal with the consequences of prolonged and excessive anabolic steroid use had contributed to the breakdown of her mental health and to the decision to take her own life. Warwick had suffered major liver and pancreatic problems, stomach haemorrhages, hearing impairment, skin rashes and hair and teeth loss as a result of her steroid abuse.[39] But the fencers were unaware of Zoe Warwick and several other high profile steroid cases of the time, and knew very little about the side effects associated with steroid over-use. Typical responses were:

> Anything I know about anabolic steroids comes from the newspapers. They promote muscle bulk and allow quicker recovery from injury, but I don't know what they do to you.

> Well, the information document from the Sports Council says 'in women they deepen the voice and cause facial hair'! I know they're supposed to have much more serious side effects [than that], but I don't really know what.

One might think that, if an athlete is not exposed to steroids and has no intention of using them, there is no reason why she should be aware of the risks, and that merely knowing they can be dangerously harmful is the only knowledge an athlete needs. But the organisations responsible for informing athletes about drugs ought to be concerned if their awareness raising campaigns have as little effect in other sports as they appear to have had in fencing. Disconcertingly, they lacked faith in the 'official' sources of information and preferred to seek other athletes', doctors' or pharmacists' advice as necessary. Their primary source of information on drugs was the newspaper reports, although, as a group, they were sceptical about the veracity of such information:

---

38 McArdle, D, 'Governing bodies', unpublished PhD thesis, Manchester Metropolitan University, September 1996. All extracts in the remainder of the chapter are taken from this work.

39 Jones, S, 'When dying to win can mean precisely that' (1994) *Observer Sport*, 25 September, p 9.

> I want to see more information about what drug use actually means in terms of the health risks and what their effects are. I don't want to read ... ill-informed sensationalism.

> The layman's perception of drugs – and I'm very much a layman because I only know about fencing – is clouded and shaped by what is said in the press.

Significantly, only one of the 12 interviewees said that her opinions had been formed by sources other than media reports, and she was also dismissive of the information offered by the Sports Council and the sport's governing body. She had given a lot of thought to media coverage and had changed her views as a result of a personal cynicism that pre-dated the Modahl affair. Other fencers' lack of awareness was similarly compounded by a distinct distrust of their national governing body, its members being regarded as arrogant and incompetent:

> Until a few years ago I took the official line and was influenced by what the newspapers said about it just being a few rotten apples, or about a few sports having a really big problem. Then I started using the gym at Crystal Palace, where a lot of the [track] athletes go when they're recovering from injury, and where people do and say a lot of things. My change of heart stemmed from talking to other athletes and actually seeing what goes on.

> I don't ever try to get information from AFA. They're a bunch of amateurs who have been there far too long and don't respond to change. They've got an attitude problem and they aren't receptive to new ideas. Do you want me to go on? I could *diss* the AFA for hours.

> The AFA is run by lawyers, and you just can't deal with them.

Of course, it does not necessarily follow that this group's troubled relationship with their governing body is replicated in other sports. And the officials at the AFA would probably have their own explanations for this apparent antagonism. A concern that may be replicated elsewhere was the fencers' marked lack of faith in the drug testing regime in general and especially in the scientific rationale that underpinned it. None of those interviewed expressed confidence in the testing procedure, and without prompting they all mentioned Modahl as the main reason for their lack of confidence. Some of those interviewed had scientific backgrounds, and their views were particularly illuminating:

> I don't have confidence in the biology of it. Storage, identifying the elements present and making sure they don't degrade all present problems. The more hands it goes through, the more problems there are.

> The technology is there but it's still in its infancy, and if things have gone wrong I doubt the testers would back down because they don't want to be seen to have made a mistake. That would destroy any credibility the testing procedure still has.

Those who did not have scientific backgrounds also had reservations about the testing procedures, although their concerns were not to do with the scientific basis so much as with more general concerns about sample security:

> The Diane Modahl case didn't make me feel confident about the procedure. There were a lot of questions unanswered about her case: the levels of security over her sample – you can't say for certain that it was her sample. Until you can be confident that the sample you give is properly looked after and the system is foolproof, people will always be sceptical.

> It's not necessarily the testers' fault but there are so many hands through which samples pass. I think corruption is rife in sport. There have been cases of tampering with samples and I think swapping a negative sample for a positive one could conceivably happen.

One of the most striking issues to emerge from this research was the extent to which those interviewed had real fears about testing positive for what might be regarded as 'peripheral' banned substances. Failing tests for testosterone or anabolic steroids was accepted as something that could possibly happen, but it was regarded as so remote a possibility that (with one exception) it was not a major cause for concern among the group. Their fears about being tested positive for caffeine and codeine were far greater. Although most (but not all) of the interviewees were aware that these substances were banned, they were not happy with that state of affairs. They resented the banning of over-the-counter cold remedies that contained codeine. The reasons for them being banned as potential performance enhancers were regarded as unconvincing and unnecessary:

> I think there should be more of a balance between sports regulations and the law of the land. Over-the-counter drugs should be allowed. If the law doesn't say 'it's dangerous and you can't take it', why should sport be different?

> In order to be taken seriously (the testing authorities) need to be able to distinguish between accidentally overdosing on coffee, say, and taking caffeine tablets to boost your performance. If they can't make that distinction, why should the athletes suffer?

Similar concerns were expressed about cannabis being banned. Four of those interviewed supported testing for cannabis on the grounds that it was an illegal drug. The others believed that unless a substance had performance enhancing qualities it was neither the responsibility of the testing authorities to look for it, nor for the governing body to penalise athletes for using it:

> With recreational drugs there may be peer pressure to take them or whatever, but there's no question of 'succeeding' or 'not succeeding'[40] as a result of that choice. The analogy with performance enhancers just doesn't arise. The two are very different.

---

40 The interviewee made hand gestures to indicate that s/he was placing quotation marks around 'succeeding' and 'not succeeding'.

> I don't agree with testing for cannabis, because it's not as if it improves your performance. I don't see why sport should be concerned with things that aren't performance enhancers. It's just an example of sporting morality, setting the right example to the kids.

The group's attitudes to drug use and drug testing were underpinned by a profound cynicism of the commercialism and financial imperatives of modern sport, and especially the extent to which money dominated the Olympics and other major events:

> Once you have an activity that brings in money it's not just about sport any more and it's in everyone's interests for the players to look good. They won't cut their own throats by accusing their elite performers of taking drugs.

> Because financially (catching drug users) isn't in the organisers' interests they turn a blind eye in most cases.

But, despite cynicism and distrust over drug testing, the consensus was that giving athletes the freedom to take performance enhancing substances if they chose to was something that ought to be resisted, especially if those substances could be proved to have damaging side effects. The fencers were of the opinion that a rational, coherent and scientifically valid testing policy had yet to be developed, and the system that did exist had been undermined by the perceived corruption of international sport. They appeared to favour a regime which reflected the original ideals of drug testing – protecting the health of athletes:

> Some people don't want to ruin their internal organs for the sake of knocking 0.1 second off their time, and they shouldn't feel forced into doing so in order to be able to compete with others.

Similarly, the fencers felt that drug use was not something that was carried out secretly, in isolation. Influence from coaches and physicians, the peer pressure of the 'locker room culture' and (in particular) the financial rewards available in some sports could conspire to make drug use an attractive proposition:

> I'm not saying I feel sorry for athletes who get caught, but it's become such a ridiculous situation. Really what you are saying is 'take this and you might make the team. If you don't, it's bye-bye'.

> The opportunities are certainly there, for anyone with talent who is trying to make a breakthrough. If your coach or someone says 'you should take this', that's a great incentive.

CONCLUSION

Those who support the drug testing policies as presently constituted might take heart from surveys like these. One can argue that the views of these athletes are evidence of an unnecessary cynicism and stem from a fundamental lack of knowledge that can be rectified by the more effective use of educational programmes. That may well be the case, especially if one agrees that it is ultimately the athlete's responsibility to find out which substances are proscribed and to know what side effects, if any, those substances may have. But this survey indicated far more than a mere lack of awareness of banned substances. The fencers' scepticism about the science of drug testing, their perception of hypocrisy and incompetence among the governing bodies and their cynicism about the way in which testing programmes are couched in terms of 'cheating' rather than addressing legitimate health concerns are unlikely to be eased by more drug awareness campaigns.

The effect of the Diane Modahl case on these athletes cannot be overstated. For some, it had heralded a fundamental shift in perceptions, while for others it merely reinforced a pre-existing lack of faith in the whole testing procedure. Not one of those interviewed expressed much faith in the testing regime. Until the athletes' fears of double standards, dodgy science and flawed reasoning are adequately addressed, questions such as how many athletes are actually using drugs, whether sports should test for recreational drugs and what penalties should be imposed on users are rendered irrelevant. The fencers thought the governing bodies and the testing authorities needed to provide definitive scientific evidence as to the efficacy of their procedures to the athletes' satisfaction (as opposed to the satisfaction of the media and other moral agents) if drug testing was to regain any vestige of credibility.

If exhortations of fair play mean little to elite level performers, it would be pointless to use such arguments to justify banning the possession and supply of anabolic steroids under the Misuse of Drugs Act 1971. So far as the fencers were concerned, the only possible justifications for bans would be on health protection grounds. Banning substances because their use was 'unfair' seemed indefensible. Banning them if they were shown to be harmful had more merit, but this had to be backed up by more effective education and health awareness programmes that have moved away from reliance on the 'cheating' argument. So far as this sport was concerned, those at the sharp end – the individuals who compete internationally and who are likely to be tested – lacked confidence in the procedure and science of drugs testing and in the organisations who carried it out.

Many of the fencers' comments might be wrong or ill-conceived, but if their perceptions are replicated in other sports, rebuilding British athletes' trust and confidence in the wake of the Diane Modahl affair is likely to be a very long process indeed.

CHAPTER 8

RUNNING SCARED: AN ATHLETE LAWYER'S VIEW OF THE DOPING REGIME

Andy Curtis

INTRODUCTION

The debate in the changing rooms surrounding drugs testing and the prohibition regime has increased due to the large number of recent high profile cases of positive tests for nandrolone. Despite there having been 343 cases worldwide in the past year at time of writing,[1] there is statistical evidence that there has been no real increase in their number, and these figures also show that athletics has a lower incident rate than other sports. Nevertheless, athletes feel under pressure as there is a theoretical possibility that athletes who have not intentionally taken nandrolone may still fail a test due to innocently ingesting it through a food supplement or by natural production of the substance within their body. Hopefully, answers to such theoretical possibilities will become known once the currently running inquiries of both the International Amateur Athletics Federation (IAAF) and the Fédération Internationale de Football Association (FIFA) have been completed. However, these cases throw up issues of wider concern which deserve further comment.

The aim of this chapter is to show how the drugs regime affects an athlete in everyday life, focusing upon the need to be on guard at all times against innocent ingestion of banned substances and the need to rely on third parties in order to do this. It will also explain my experiences of drug tests, fears of failing a test and how claims that all exceptional performances must be drug enhanced should be viewed. The chapter will then analyse some of the rationales that are used to explain the drugs regime, and explain how an athlete views these rationales. I shall investigate the possibility of importing some degree of intention, recklessness or negligence into the offence, but conclude that the strict liability nature needs to remain. The chapter concludes by making suggestions which should lead to a decrease in athletes innocently ingesting banned substances, leaving only those athletes with a greater degree of culpability than at present guilty of an offence.

The main thrust of the argument is that greater education is needed for athletes and officials alike, that regulation of the supplements market is

---

1   (2000) *Athletics Weekly*, 23 February.

required and that a separate independent agency should be given the task of carrying out the doping regime. Athletes must be supported by UK Athletics to challenge any questionable scientific theory behind testing procedures. Those procedures of inquiry must be altered so as to try the scientific evidence in public, taking an inquisitorial approach, with safeguards to protect an athlete who could be found innocent, and that the IAAF should look at the rationality of suspending athletes for their failed tests.

The practical implications of the drugs regime for elite international athletes

Doping is not simply an issue of whether an athlete wishes to take performance enhancing drugs or not. In addition, it is necessary to consider a real fear from the athlete's perspective, namely, the unwitting ingestion of a prohibited substance. Athletes who would never dream of taking banned substances have to be on guard against innocently ingesting substances that appear on a governing body's banned list. Innocent ingestion of a prohibited substance for an athlete is most likely to occur when taking a preparation, either licensed or not, for an ailment, injury or to improve recovery or performance. We, as elite level athletes, are issued with up to date lists of prohibited substances, lists of substances that are permitted, and telephone numbers to ring with any queries. However, just like the training programmes that we undertake, it is much harder to carry out in practice than it is in theory.

Although everybody who participates in any field of activity has their ability to do so restricted by an illness such as the common cold, it is especially true if your field of activity is professional sport. This is so much so that Frank Dick[2] has stated that we as a nation lose 25% of our medal potential in athletics every year due to illness and injury. Although I find it difficult to concentrate when suffering from a common cold (resulting in the quantity and quality of my work suffering), I can still produce work. However, my athletic training and racing is often reduced to zero by the onset of a cold.

Although there are competing views within the sport as to the amount of training which should be undertaken whilst suffering from such as the common cold, many athletes do no training at all when struck down by the slightest illness. I subscribe to the view that training whilst having a cold reduces the recovery time and thus allows me to return to full good quality training quicker than if I attempted to continue training with the cold. In my experience, it also lessens the harm which I do to myself in two senses. First, it prevents a cold turning into a heavy cold, and secondly, it prevents a diminution in my training capacity, that is, it appears that, by taking a week

---

2   Quoted in Grayson, E, *Sport and the Law*, 1994, London: Butterworths, p 194.

off training, I return after that week in a stronger and fitter state than if I had trained through the cold. However, if I had been able to train through that period in a fully fit state, my fitness and strength levels would have increased, and thus this is important time lost which cannot be regained. Many coaches share this view. I was once prevented from training at a national squad training weekend by a senior national coach as, according to him, several athletes over the years had succumbed to multiple stress syndrome. This is a condition which, according to him, means that the body cannot cope with the extra strain and pressure put on it by an athlete's training programme when already in a state of stress (through a heavy cold, for example).

The story is the same for injuries as for illnesses. If we, as athletes, sustain an injury, depending upon what type of injury it is, it can prevent us from training. Most often, however, the injuries that we most usually sustain are minor recurring injuries which, although negatively affecting performance, do not prevent us from training or competing. In fact, it is very rare to talk to an elite athlete who is not carrying some kind of injury. If injuries, major or minor, can be prevented, however, it allows us to train at full capacity, assisting our training and hence our final performances at championships. It also saves large amounts of money and time spent at the physiotherapists. Therefore, as prevention is better than cure for both illness and injury, there is an immense pressure on athletes to take whatever legal substances they are allowed in order to prevent an illness or injury from occurring, and many of those are substances which aid recovery between sessions. A healthy diet and periods of rest are often the best natural methods of doing this, but athletes take whatever admissible help is available in order to get the best out of their bodies. Therefore, supplements are used in order to add the vital legal substances which aid the prevention of illnesses and injuries.

It is the common cold, in my experience, that is the greatest and most common threat to an athlete's training programme. Interestingly, although many of my fellow athletes report high incidence of what may be called minor or low level illnesses such as the common cold, they do not seem to be too susceptible to higher level illnesses, such as influenza. An athlete's increased susceptibility to colds can be illustrated by the experience of one of the country's top blind marathon runners, who reports that he has not had a cold in the three years since he retired from the sport, despite being previously plagued by them.

I have used a variety of products in adopting this strategy of prevention, but even the most simple of preventative methods throw up dilemmas for professional athletes. The current supplement that is recommended by the nutritional advisor[3] to the British Olympic Association (BOA) is glutamine, a substance naturally occurring within the human body which is essential to the

---

3   Griffiths, J, nutritional seminar, Manchester, May 1999.

immune system. Its use prevents or lessens the body's susceptibility to illness, especially from upper respiratory tract viruses, such as the common cold. The body is most at threat from these viral infections when it is in a run down state, such as when an athlete is in the middle of an extremely heavy period of training. It is a fact of athletics that the majority of an athlete's hardest training occurs in the winter months, as this is when the foundations for the forthcoming season are laid. This, of course, is also the time when the incidence of illnesses such as the common cold and influenza is at its highest. Therefore, a supplement such as glutamine appears to be an essential part of an holistic approach to training. Many of our top able bodied athletes agree with this view, and I was told by one of our top female distance runners in Seville at the IAAF World Championships in 1999 that if she runs out of her glutamine supply, she succumbs to a cold almost immediately.

However, this is one of the products which is possibly linked with the recent nandrolone cases[4] and therefore it frightens me to think that I could be metabolising my own batch of nandrolone. A possibility that seems to have some validity is that a number of these products have substances in them that are not listed in the ingredients. Despite taking the precaution of purchasing a product from a reputable company, I still have niggling doubts as to whether I could be ingesting nandrolone or other such substances innocently. However, I still take this product, as my governing body permits the substance. Despite fears regarding adulteration, an athlete must cross his or her fingers and decide which substances he or she will take.

My greatest fears regarding adulteration of products comes from the health foods market, as I tend to use alternative health food remedies to prevent colds. One book recommended such products as vitamins, garlic, zinc lozenges, etc. However, although all these looked to be *prima facie* 'legal', there was a substance present in one of the products called echinacea, which I had never heard of, and I thought it could possibly be a similar substance to ginseng which has previously landed athletes in trouble. I checked my drugs guide, and nothing was mentioned of any of the items being either 'legal' or 'illegal', so I rang the Drugs Helpline at the Sports Council and asked if echinacea was a prohibited substance. The official told me that it was only possible to inform me as to the legality of licensed substances. Although this seemed to me to be passing the buck, I thought I would be able to get a better response for substances such as zinc or vitamin C with riboflavoids, but, again, the response was the same. They would not even tell me if vitamin C in an unadulterated form was a legally permissible substance.

I can understand that the governing body does not want to create a situation in which they could be found liable for any advice given on these

---

4   Mark Richardson reports taking this on the morning of his urine test: (2000) *Athletics Weekly*, 23 February.

unlicensed products. However, their advice that I took such products as a simple vitamin C tablet 'at my own risk' was, to me, taking the fear of potential legal action too far. The official's statement that these products could contain other substances not listed was correct, but to be unable to tell me if an unadulterated product was legal or not appears to me to set severe limits on the ability of the body to fulfil its function. As a result, I no longer take any health food supplements, apart from the glutamine. I am compromising my health just to increase the chance of me staying 'clean'.

If I were to rely upon the listed ingredients on the product and then innocently ingested a prohibited substance, I would be banned.[5] If I tried to take action against the manufacturers for negligence, I would only have a case if it had caused me physical harm, for instance, if I was allergic to a substance which caused me an allergic reaction. The only financial remedy I would have against them would be in contract, possibly for instance in misrepresentation which would get my money back for the product, but no consequential loss. Therefore, I protected myself by writing to the manufacturers stating my concerns, asking if any other substances could enter the product, and what the consequences would be if I ingested a prohibited substance in their product, for example, loss of income, etc. They wrote a letter back confirming that the list of ingredients was a true representation of what was present in the substance and that no other unlisted substances were present in the product. Thereby, I had created a *Hedley Byrne*[6] type scenario. If I had failed a drug test for a substance which could later be shown to be in the product I would have an action against the manufacturer for negligence if that statement had been untrue and I had relied upon it to my detriment. However, due to the strict liability nature of the test, I would still be banned.

I also take supplements to prevent injuries. The supplement I use is glucosamine, a naturally occurring substance found in the connective tissues of the body, such as tendons, and therefore it helps to repair these tissues. But again, despite it being recommended by the BOA, I face the same dilemma as with glutamine, that there could be extra substances in these products. I also take the latest super supplement, creatin, which is taken by the majority of athletes that I know. Creatin is a substance naturally occurring in the body and is used in the body's adenosinetriphosphate cycle, the cycle which converts potential energy into actual energy to power the body's muscles. Creatin phosphates are used in the first six to seven seconds of this cycle. By increasing the body's intake of the substance, there will be more of this energy store and thus more training can be undertaken and recovery time improved.

---

5   The exception to this being if I was lucky enough to fail the test at a championships such as the Olympics, as happened to Linford Christie in 1988, as the IOC rules appear to be not as draconian as those of the IAAF. He did not receive a ban, as he had innocently ingested this through a ginseng product.

6   *Hedley Byrne & Co Ltd v Heller & Partners Ltd* [1964] 2 All ER 565.

The advice from the BOA is that, due to the requirements of the discipline, sprinters such as myself should be using this product to aid recovery, training and final performance. Additionally, there were no reported disadvantages to taking it, apart from a slight body weight increase. However, a national senior coach informed me that it was the consensus of opinion, at a 400 m coaches seminar which he attended, that this product led to an increase in injuries and attacks of cramped muscles in training sessions, and thus many coaches advised their athletes not to take it. This leaves an athlete in a quandary: do they believe and follow the advice of their personal coach, the person who works with them every day and is responsible for training them to their peak, or a qualified nutritionist who is the expert in the science behind the product?

Although I have only taken the 'approved' substances, not all athletes are as discerning. Many take anything which promises to improve your performances, and my experience shows that most athletes believe, or at least are more interested in, the manufacturers' marketing than the advice offered by the BOA. There has been much debate surrounding such supplements following the recent nandrolone cases, and this has focused on the safety of these products, their possible regulation and tests as to their usefulness. Barnes[7] summed up the situation nicely when he stated that, with these supplements, 'they are not medicines, they are not licensed, they are not controlled, you don't always know quite what you are getting'. Goodbody[8] reported in a similar vein that the Government, in January 2000, had commissioned an inquiry into these supplements, which concluded that 'users of inadequately labelled products are at risk of unknowingly ingesting a banned substance'. However, how are we to know if they are inadequately labelled? The report continued: 'We recommend that the sports community maintains a high level of awareness of the possible hazards of using some nutritional supplements and herbal preparations.' This has led to calls for regulation of this supplements market. David Hemery, the president of UK Athletics, has stated: 'We would like Government support to accredit the makers so that we can get some kind of validity check. At the same time there needs to be a high level of education globally into the effect of these products and how much they help.'[9] Such testing of the products for prohibited substances will provide greater protection for athletes than written assurances. The latter point regarding effectiveness of the products highlights my earlier point regarding dispute as to whether these supplements actually work, as regulation would surely involve wild claims made by manufacturers having to be substantiated. This, in my opinion, would benefit my training and well being, but how likely is it to occur?

---

7   Barnes, S, 'Obsession that drives athletes over the edge' (2000) The Times, 9 February, p 54.

8   Goodbody, J, 'Moorcroft calls for supplement testing' (2000) The Times, 10 February.

9   (2000) Athletics Weekly, 23 February.

My preferred option would be to situate such regulatory powers within a central body such as the Sports Council, who could finance it by holding back a proportion of each sports allocation of finance. Birkinshaw notes[10] that regulation of the pharmaceutical industry before 1968 was basically voluntary, but most drug manufacturers complied, as their largest customer was the NHS. Therefore, as the supplements manufacturers' largest customers are likely to be sportsmen and women, it would suggest that a similar voluntary form of regulation might well work in the supplements market.

It suggested that a strategy of creating a list of approved supplements should be developed with tests being carried out for prohibited substances and effectiveness. Those found to be both legal and beneficial would appear on the top list, with those just found to be legal, but with no scientifically proved benefit, being listed separately. Products that have failed legality tests could also be listed separately, with manufacturers given the chance to amend the situation. Testing for legality should be carried out on a continuous random basis, whilst effectiveness would be a once only test. Such lists could then be provided to athletes, or posted on the internet, which would allow for speedy updates, especially if a product listed as legal fails a test at a later date. Clearly, this would rely a lot on athletes sticking to the advice given. If they did not, and took an unapproved supplement which led to a failed drugs test, then it would truly be their own fault and they would be deserving of punishment. This need not be limited to the performance enhancing supplements such as creatin, protein drinks or energy drinks, but could be extended to health care products for general health purposes. It would give athletes both better protection and greater choice in the products they could legally use, safe in the knowledge that they have been tested.

Athletes must be on their guard at all times, whatever the product or foodstuff they intake. This is illustrated by a recent example brought to my attention by an international athlete. He informed me that the consumption of a high-caffeine energy drink, popular in night clubs and discos, could lead to a failed drugs test. This shocked me greatly, as we as athletes are only warned to be careful with pharmaceutical products, especially over the counter remedies. It highlights just how cautious an athlete has to be in everyday life. Although I have not been warned officially about this from any administrator or sports official, rumours within the sport of athletics are rife with tales of athletes using this energy drink to aid their training.

Although many of my assertions regarding medical and nutritional theory may be queried, or even completely disputed, by a medical practitioner or nutritionist, it illustrates a very important point. Athletes such as myself are not medical practitioners or even competent in any field of health care, and thus, we have to rely on advice from a variety of sources regarding our

---

10 Birkinshaw, P, *Government by Moonlight: The Hybrid Parts of the State*, 1990, London: Unwin Hyman.

medical well being. Coaches, administrators, fellow athletes, physiotherapists and medical practitioners often put forward contrasting advice to the athletes with whom they work, and thus, we are left confused and bewildered by the dilemma of what to do when we are ill, or whether to take the latest 'legal' food or health supplement. More emphasis should be put into the education side of the drugs regime, and this of course would be aided by my suggested regulation strategy which would rely heavily on athlete involvement in sticking to the provided lists of recommended and safe supplements.

This call for education is also echoed in an Editorial in *Athletics Weekly*.[11] It confirms fears that all resources have been put into the testing side of the drug regime, rather than education. Money needs to be invested in teaching athletes ways of minimising the possible risk of unintentional ingestion through these means. This could probably best be achieved by including an education programme within an athlete's agreement with both UK Athletics and the Sports Council in order to benefit from the lottery money available to athletes in our position.

When the preventative approach fails, an athlete is left with no alternative but to seek out a cure for the illness. There are several aids for an athlete in this quest. First, there is a drug helpline at the Sports Council, which can be used to confirm that a substance is permitted. However, an answer is very rarely given immediately and, in my experience, it can often be later the same day or even the next day before an answer is provided. This is of little help when an athlete is suffering with severe toothache or a splitting headache. Secondly, athletes are issued with a guide to drugs and prohibited and permitted substances. Therefore, once struck down by an illness, an athlete merely has to wade their way through this medical guide to find something that is permitted to take for their condition. However, many athletes have said to me that they find the guide confusing, especially since they are not confident with this medical terminology. Many resort to taking this guide with them to a medical practitioner for their advice. On the one occasion when I produced this guide to a locum general practitioner, he stated that he did not have time to look through my guide and that I should take the script to the dispensary and then check the substance myself. On doing so, I found that it was prohibited, and thus had to make a new appointment later that week. The next time that I was suffering from an illness I took this guide with me to a pharmacist, who was more helpful.

Tales abound of unintentional breaches of the drug procedures. A fellow blind athlete always took Lemsip powders to combat colds. He knew that the doping regulations permitted only paracetamol, but he had asked a sighted friend to check the ingredients and was informed that it contained only paracetamol. To confirm this, he rang the drug helpline at the Sports Council

---

11   (2000) *Athletics Weekly,* 23 February.

and asked if this product was permitted. The official asked what the product contained and he relayed the information as it had been told to him. He was told the product was permitted. He had, thus, relied on this for many years, often singing its virtues in assisting with a cold. Imagine his surprise, then, when he subsequently visited a pharmacist and was told that Lemsip was on the banned list.

He immediately confessed to the governing body, who told him to contact the chief medical officer for athletics, who immediately told him that they were indeed banned, but that they had a 'clearing time' of only a couple of days and, thus, he had nothing to worry about. However, I could not help but think about what would have happened to him, or to any other of us blind athletes, if in such a scenario a random out-of-competition drugs test had been carried out.

Ironically, this was an unnecessary worry, as we were recently informed that we were not, at present, subject to the rigours of random out-of-competition drugs testing. This was news to all of us who had believed that there was no distinction between disabled and able bodied athletes in this respect.

Despite winning 22 international medals in nine years of competition as a blind athlete, I have yet to undergo a drugs test. The nearest I have come to having to provide a sample was at the European Blind Athletic Championships in Lisbon 1999. There were three occasions when I thought I would have to undergo this ordeal. The first came after winning my 100 m semi-final, when an official approached me, handed me a piece of paper and told me that I was required for a random sample, but this turned out to be a case of mistaken identity. The second and third times were following gold medal winning performances in both the 200 m and the 400 m. Under the usual procedures, the first in every final and one random athlete from the other finalists are required to give samples, but this procedure was not followed for reasons which were never made clear. I am still awaiting my first drugs test.

I fear failing a drugs test for several reasons, and this fear has been heightened by the recent questionable nandrolone cases. The first is the shame that it would bring upon me and anybody associated with my performances, a stigma which seems to attach regardless of an end finding of guilt or innocence. Secondly, it would prevent me from taking part in the sport that I love. This would be especially difficult for a disabled person to accept, as there are limited areas where a disabled person is allowed to compete on a level playing field and feel good about oneself and one's contribution to society generally. Thirdly, it would mean the loss of my income, which would affect my wife and children. Fourthly, it may affect my ability to secure employment, as it would be seen as a black mark against my name, a drug offence being a serious matter in whatever walk of life. In recent months, Linford Christie has been prevented from coaching athletes at State run facilities in Australia, so presumably he would not be eligible for a State supported coaching role in Australia because of his nandrolone offence.

Other athletes who are tested regularly appear more relaxed. If they are taking prohibited substances, and thus running the risk of detection, then their demeanour hides it well. The time I have spent both training and socialising with disabled and able bodied world class athletes has not been fraught with the kind of tension you might associate with people who are trying to hide the fact that they are guilty of an offence which could result in their expulsion from the sport they love. I conclude that they either do not take drugs, or have come to terms with the fact that they have to do this to compete on a level playing field with those who do. For my part, I believe, and hope, that the former is true.

The 'he must be on drugs' comment is, in my opinion, too often espoused without foundation. It is based purely on the performance itself. In my athletic experience, I have formulated a view that there are different performance planes on which athletes perform, depending upon the ultimate capacity of their bodies. Different athletes have different muscle types, different bone structures, different capacities to handle lactic acid, etc, but this has been clearly illustrated to me through my experiences. I perform at the top level of my sport, and thus possess a much more athletic body than many of my blind counterparts, but through previously competing as a county standard sighted athlete I am aware that many local county and area standard athletes possess even greater ability and athletic capacity than I. This was often illustrated by these athletes completing the same training session as me and, despite exerting similar levels of effort, they could run faster for longer, and complete more repetitions than I, and not even suffer the same level of pain as I did. This left a feeling in me that they were not human, that they must be doing something different to me, or that they were 'taking something' which I was not. The truth was simply that their bodies were more suited for the athletic disciplines that we were undertaking.

By extrapolation, and also by experiencing the training sessions which athletes were undertaking at the IAAF World Athletic Championships 1999 in Seville, it is clear to me that this is the same scenario that many top flight able bodied athletes find themselves in when a competitor, for no distinguishable reason, produces a far superior performance. The calls of 'drug cheat', in my opinion, can be explained when coming from those who have never competed in the sport, as this stratification of athletic capacity can only be appreciated when you experience it first hand. When the calls come from ex-athletes or ex-coaches, it does not surprise me either, as training techniques, medical care, facilities, etc, evolve to much greater levels of performance, whilst at the same time the human race is evolving, with records historically being lowered generation by generation. If the calls are made by fellow competitors, it is also quite understandable, as athletes do not like to acknowledge that they are not the best at what they do; the attitude is usually that they did not train hard enough or the training programme was wrong, or they ran a tactically bad race. Accepting that an outstanding performance by a competitor is legal involves an acknowledgment that your rival is better than you – which is one thing we are trained not even to entertain as a thought process. This will also be the same for current coaches. I feel that more people would see the situation in a similar light if they, too, viewed it from the internal viewpoint of an athlete. Accusers need educating.

There are, broadly, two reasons for prohibiting the use of certain substances, namely, paternalism (the idea that governing bodies must protect the health of their participants) and cheating. However, I prefer to view this debate as one about the rules of the sport. The rules of all sports have laid down that certain substances are prohibited and others are allowable, regardless of how rational and logically coherent the basis for this is, and to me these rules are no different from rules which state that an athlete must not step outside his or her lane in a sprint race, or that a 16 lb shot should be put and not a 15 lb shot.

Athletes usually focus upon the issue of unfair advantage. From the athlete's internal viewpoint, I would like to see those athletes who break the rules by intentionally taking performance enhancing drugs as listed in the governing bodies' regulations receive the severest of sanctions. Those athletes who enhance their performances by taking such substances unintentionally should receive lesser sanctions. However, as the rules currently stand, a lack of intent is not a defence under IAAF rules, which, like all strict liability offences, denies the fundamental right to show a lack of fault, knowledge or intent. This state of affairs is at odds with how individuals are treated on the running track as athletes and how they are treated in everyday life as a member of the public. This is illustrated by the parliamentary defence in criminal drugs cases, as under s 28(3)(e)(1) of the Misuse of Drugs Act 1971, any accused person shall be acquitted of a drug offence 'if he proves that he neither believed nor suspected nor had reason to suspect that the substance or product in question was a controlled drug'.

This provides, for many athletes, our greatest fear – that our food or drinks could be tampered with. We closely guard our water bottles at training tracks and competition warm up areas, but it is not possible to run whilst holding a bottle and, therefore, a malicious rival could tamper with them if the opportunity arises. The governing body would respond that if my bottle was tampered with at a warm up track, it would be my fault and I would deserve to be banned. It is my responsibility to ensure that I leave my bottle with an official whilst I complete my warm up runs, and to ensure that any bottles whose seals had been broken are thrown away.

However, on several occasions at major championships I have asked team officials to watch my bottles whilst I was running, only to return to find that the official had wandered off somewhere on other business. I am told that this would not happen at an able bodied major championship, as each athlete has an official assigned to him or her. However, I have competed at a major able bodied championship[12] and the official to whom I was assigned also had several other athletes in his charge, and therefore there were severe limitations on his ability to cope.

From an athlete's perspective, this approach seems rather harsh. Culpability could be apportioned if the athlete had relied upon someone they had chosen negligently or recklessly, but, in the case of team officials, these conditions are imposed upon us. To suggest it is the athlete's own fault is to me somewhat tenuous and totally against how similar incidents in wider society would be viewed. The victim of date rape where drugs are used is not blamed for ingesting the drug unintentionally.

However, in defence of the current regime, a requirement of intent would be difficult to implement, as athletes would always be able to find somebody who would admit to tampering with their bottles – a parent, friend or partner, for instance. This third party could not be subject to any sanctions from the governing body, unless they themselves were an athlete or coach. They may be deterred from providing such an escape route for the athlete, however, if the governing body or the police could take action against them. It must be possible to find suitable ways of deterring such third parties from coming forward to save an athlete's career. This could take the form of a criminal offence of administering a noxious substance, or the tort of interference with a subsisting contract between the athlete and the governing body, a term of which is not to take prohibited drugs.

Equally, I believe it would be possible to import a *mens rea* element into the drug regulations of sports, although such procedures are unlikely to be applied uniformly around the world. It could be possible if all inquiries were heard by the IAAF itself, but they are not inclined to do so, preferring member countries to undertake inquiries themselves. This last point is the major stumbling block to a more informed legal approach to a finding of culpability, and for this reason the strict liability nature of the regulations has been adopted by the IAAF.

As, in practice, strict liability seems to be the only suitable global rule to adopt, how can we prevent innocent parties from being found guilty? My preferred option is to adopt a strategy of education in conjunction with regulation of the supplements market. There must be a separate drug agency, the adoption of an inquisitorial rather than an adversarial approach in inquiries, and more open and transparent inquiry procedures.

There are several reasons why a separate drug agency is to be favoured. The first comes from a perceived credibility in decisions made by this new

12   The 1999 IAAF World Athletics Championships in Seville.

body as opposed to those made by UK Athletics at present. This is evident from the recent nandrolone cases, where decisions in the cases of Doug Walker and Linford Christie suggest a conflict of approach between UK Athletics and the IAAF.

The second is more justice for athletes. The only way to challenge a positive finding in a sample, other than the procedures followed, is, as Scott J stated,[13] to question the scientific validity of the test. This happened successfully in the *Diane Modahl* case,[14] where she was able to show that the substance could have been present due to another reason. But this leaves justice open to only those athletes who can afford to challenge the scientific validity of the tests and the expense that this incurs. This cannot be justified. As asserted by Armstrong[15] and the Dubin Commission,[16] in order to have a fair right of appeal, an athlete should be in a position to test the scientific validity of the test. David Moorcroft, the Chief Executive of UK Athletics, has stated[17] that the 25% of UK Athletics' budget which is not accounted for in advance and which is currently spent on doping issues would be saved if this function were passed on to an agency. This could then be put into place to support athletes who fail a test and wish to challenge the scientific evidence.

A third reason could be that the new body could have its remit extended to include a sport agency role. It could then be responsible for overseeing how sport is run throughout the nation, co-ordinating action and education programmes, having the financial power to fight or settle court actions, such as Modahl's, which brought down a federation, and oversee increasing accountability, transparency and fairness throughout sport in general.

Regardless of which body carries out the inquiries into positive tests, there are several issues that need addressing. In the *Modahl* case, the approach taken by the British Athletic Federation's doping panel was an adversarial approach, with the panel being judge and prosecutor. An inquisitorial approach is to be preferred. Doping hearings are conducted behind closed doors. This is not good for transparency and accountability, and leaves athletes like me questioning what exactly is going on in these inquiries. There is also an issue surrounding the IAAF's approach to naming athletes who have not been found guilty of an offence, such as Mike Edwards. Moorcroft stated: 'If an athlete is judged not guilty, should the case ever be brought into the public

---

13 *Gasser v Stinson* (1988) unreported, 15 June, *per* Scott J, quoted in *op cit*, Grayson, fn 2, p 214.

14 As reported in Gardiner S, Felix, A, James, M, Welch, R and O'Leary, J, *Sports Law*, 1998, London: Cavendish Publishing, p 188.

15 Quoted in *op cit*, Grayson, fn 2, p 215.

16 Dubin C, *Commission of Inquiry into the Use of Drugs and Banned Practices Intended to Increase Athletic Performance*, 1990, Ottawa, Canadian Government Publishing Centre, quoted in *op cit*, Grayson, fn 2, p 213.

17 (2000) *Athletics Weekly*, 23 February.

domain? We believe not.'[18] However, if it was a criminal trial, then after a person is accused, they are named and face a trial in public where the evidence is heard. This has led to a suggestion[19] that, after the 'B' sample tests positive, the athlete should be named and the evidence tried in public to improve transparency and bring the issues into the open. This would hopefully show the basis for their decisions to be rational and supportable, and thus counter criticisms that UK Athletics appear to be soft on drug cheats and letting down clean athletes.[20] We should also explore the possibility any testimony required from the athlete, or any person who would lead to an identification of the athlete, being a written testimony rather than a testimony in person. The scientific evidence, which will be the deciding factor in the case, could be tried openly which would provide the openness and transparency, allowing this evidence to be truly and openly assessed. This would increase openness, accountability and rationality in this type of decision.

Another important issue is the time it has taken the IAAF to conduct its nandrolone enquiry. The IAAF have accepted that there is a possibility that nandrolone could either be present in high levels naturally within athletes, or could be created by natural means through taking legal supplements, and have therefore commissioned an inquiry. This is to be applauded. However, the inquiry will take a year to complete[21] and, in the meantime, athletes are still to be suspended. Moorcroft has stated: 'It is disappointing that the IAAF council should go ahead with disciplinary proceedings against athletes before their own research programme is completed. What if they find a perfectly acceptable reason why nandrolone is in people's systems? You will not be able to take away the suspension they have served or the stigma attached.'[22]

This is symptomatic of the speed with which important issues are dealt within sport, as both Christie and Walker have been referred for arbitration with the Court of Arbitration for Sport, and are still, at time of writing, waiting for a date to be set three months later. This is not good enough, as an innocent result will mean little if they miss much more competition time.

---

18 Powell, D and Goodbody, J, 'IAAF rejects swift solution to dilemma' (2000) *The Times*, 14 February, p 30.

19 (2000) *Athletics Weekly*, 23 February.

20 As argued by Mike Winch in (2000) *Athletics Weekly*, 23 February.

21 *Ibid*, Powell and Goodbody.

22 *Ibid*.

CONCLUSION

Despite the criticisms levelled above, I believe I speak for athletes when I say that drug regulation is essential to the healthy future of sport. We would not like the situation to arise whereby we, as athletes, felt that we had to take drugs in order to compete on a level playing field or that those athletes who could afford the best medicine would win. However, it is also clear that doping regulations can adversely affect athletes – not least by the degree of anxiety they can generate.

Although athletes support the concepts underlying the imposition of drug regulation, things could be improved: for example, by regulation of the supplements market, a more informal approach from the agencies supposed to help athletes in this task, greater education and review of the hearing procedures. This much needed overhaul of the system would promote transparency, accountability, rationality and fairness – qualities which all athletes would welcome in an effective system of doping control.

CHAPTER 9

THE WORLD ANTI-DOPING AGENCY: PROSPECTS FOR SUCCESS

Barrie Houlihan

THE EMERGENCE OF DOPING AS A GLOBAL PROBLEM: 1950–90

Until comparatively recently, the problem of doping in sport was perceived as one that could be conveniently compartmentalised in terms of particular sports, countries or events. The rapid emergence of the problem of doping dates from the period following the end of the Second World War. Prior to the 1940s, drug use in sport was crude, relying on a variety of natural products and their derivatives, with alcohol and the opiates being the most common. The wartime period resulted in two significant developments that set the context for the modern doping problem; first, the requirements of the military boosted the scientific efforts to synthesise drugs that would maintain alertness longer or increase aggression; and secondly, the use of amphetamines and steroids within the armed forces drew attention to the potential value of these drugs outside a therapeutic context.

By the early 1960s, evidence was accumulating that steroids were being used extensively in some Olympic sports, mainly field sports and weightlifting, and that the use of amphetamines was widespread in professional road cycling. As is frequently the case, the gradual emergence of a problem prompts an equally gradual response, particularly regarding the definition of the nature of the problem to be solved and the prediction of the likely direction and pace of its development. From the 1960s to the late 1980s, the problem of doping, where it was acknowledged at all, was considered to be a feature of specific sports, countries or events. As regards forecasting the evolution of doping, the dominant perception was that the problem would remain sporadic, marginal and manageable rather than become regular, endemic and out of control. However, the overwhelming feature of the policy response to the emerging problem of doping was one of lassitude and often wilful incomprehension.

Few governments and international federations had either the determination to tackle the issue or the scientific, organisational and financial resources for a sustained policy response. The popular perception within sport was that doping was, at worst, a manageable irritation, and certainly not a central responsibility of the federations or their domestic affiliates.

Consequently, up until the mid to late 1980s, only a small number of sports bodies had taken an active interest in doping. In 1962, the International Olympic Committee (IOC) established a Medical Commission and passed a resolution condemning doping, but little action followed until later in the decade, when a re-established Medical Commission embarked on a process of policy development which led to a limited number of tests at the 1968 Olympic Games. Among the major federations, the Fédération Internationale de Football Association (FIFA) conducted a small number of tests at the 1966 World Cup, but then seemed to lose interest in the issue. Paralleling the work of the IOC, the federation for track and field, the International Amateur Athletics Federation (IAAF), formed its Medical Committee in 1972, introduced mandatory testing at its championships in 1977 and, the following year, introduced an 18 month suspension for serious doping offences. In general, however, policy development was slow and implementation was tentative, reflecting the high level of uncertainty regarding the purpose of, and responsibility for, anti-doping policy. Event organising bodies, such as the IOC and the Commonwealth Games Federation, were primarily concerned to ensure that the public perception of their events was not sullied by doping offences and, consequently, considered that in-competition testing provided a sufficient demonstration of their commitment to drug free sport and of the honesty of their own events.[1] The federations, or at least the small number that were proactive on the issue of doping, were also content to limit their involvement to the particular events for which they were responsible. In summary, most sports organisations took a very narrow view of the nature of the problem and an optimistic view of their capacity to prevent it worsening, while even the more proactive among them were constrained by uncertainty over the direction policy should take and by a growing awareness of the resource implications of a more extensive policy of testing.

There was also some policy activity by governments in this period, with Britain acknowledging doping as an issue for its newly formed Sports Council in the early 1970s and France and Belgium legislating against doping in the mid-1960s, followed by Turkey and Italy in the early 1970s. Yet, the number of governments that moved beyond routine condemnation was more than matched by the number of governments that were passive or subversive. Many of the passive governments were those which preferred to ignore the issue lest it provide a source of embarrassment for their national sports squads. Both Canada and Australia fell into this category until scandal, in the late 1980s, forced their respective governments to establish official inquiries which prompted a far more active and effective anti-doping policy to be

---

1   Voy, R, *Drugs, Sport and Politics: The Inside Story About Drug Use and its Political Cover-Up*, 1991, Champaign, Ill: Leisure.

constructed.[2] However, of greatest significance was the small group of subversive governments, which included the former East Germany, where doping was routine throughout the country's Olympic squad and was managed and funded by the government.[3] These countries ensured the rapid spread of doping not just through their own doping programmes, but also because of the effect that their actions had on other countries, such as the US and West Germany, who strongly suspected that the Olympic success of many communist States was due to doping.

By the late 1980s, anti-doping policy had reached a turning point which led, albeit very gradually, to a more concerted policy response. There were three sources of change, the first of which was governments and governmental organisations. Throughout the postwar period, the utility of international sport as a diplomatic tool had steadily grown, stimulated by the ideological confrontation between communism and capitalism that overlay the more deeply rooted nationalist rivalry. For much of the 1970s and 1980s, the imperatives of the Cold War, together with the low probability of being caught due to the lack of sophisticated testing methods and the general reticence of federations to pursue drug abusers, encouraged many governments to collude in doping or to ignore its occurrence. Up until 1984, the dependence of the IOC on State financial support for the Olympic Games provided a further disincentive to vigorous action. Furthermore, the lack of any positive drug test results at the 1980 Moscow Olympic Games was treated by the IOC as evidence of the effectiveness of existing policy rather than suspicious and grounds for an investigation of the Moscow laboratory.

However, the end of the Cold War and the improvement in the sophistication of drug testing, modest though it was, altered the balance of advantage to make government disapproval and active opposition to doping a more attractive political stance. The gradual uncovering of the East German drugs-based sports system during the series of court cases initiated in the newly unified Germany provided a basis for the condemnation of the communist system and allowed western European countries to take the moral high ground. Furthermore, the Ben Johnson case proved to be extremely embarrassing to the Canadians and acted as a warning to other countries about the risks of a passive approach to doping. Finally, as countries such as Canada and Australia changed from an apathetic to a proactive domestic policy stance on doping, they became more acutely aware of the consequences

2   Dubin, C, *Commission of Inquiry into the Use of Drugs and Banned Practices Intended to Increase Athletic Performance*, 1990, Ottawa: Canadian Government Publishing Centre; Australian Government, *Drugs in Sport: Interim Report of the Senate Standing Committee on the Environment, Recreation and the Arts*, 1989, Canberra: Australian Government Publishing Service.

3   Franke, WW and Berendonk, B, 'Hormonal doping and androgenization of athletes: a secret program of the German Democratic Republic' (1997) 43(7) Clinical Chemistry 1262.

for their Olympic and World Championship ambitions of being 'tough on doping', or at least being tougher than their sporting rivals. In swimming, for example, Canada, the US and Australia argued forcefully for sanctions against the People's Republic of China, whose government was suspected of turning a blind eye to doping among its female swimmers, if not actually colluding in the acquisition and administration of drugs. The net effect of China's success in major swimming competitions was not only to reduce the income to the swimming federations in Canada, the US and Australia, where funding was tied closely to results, but also to reduce the number of medals won and the international prestige gained, by these three traditionally strong swimming nations.

Of equal importance to the changing attitudes among individual governments was the continuing efforts of international governmental bodies such as the Council of Europe, which played a crucial role in raising the international profile of the issue of doping and encouraging European governments to treat the issue as one of public policy rather than a private matter for sports governing bodies. However, the absence within the Council; of significant resources beyond its moral authority limited its capacity to lead policy development. The second source of change was the IOC, which, during the late 1980s and early 1990s, became increasingly aware of the growing involvement of governments in drug testing and the possible consequences for the autonomy of sports organisations in general and the Olympic movement in particular. Throughout this period, doping in sport became a matter of public policy in a number of major Olympic countries, prompting governmental concern at the paucity of investment in anti-doping activities by the IOC and the apparent lack of urgency within the Olympic movement. A similar set of concerns were emerging among the major international federations, which constitute the third source of change. The international federations (IFs) were coming under increasing pressure from their domestic affiliates to improve the administration of doping control procedures, largely because the domestic federations were being put under pressure themselves by their governments.

In summary, the watershed in policy development that occurred in the late 1980s was due in part to the recognition by governments and sports organisations that doping was a much more intractable and complex problem than they had at first thought, and in part to the increasing pressure of expectations that governments were placing on sports organisations. The regularity of scandal was important in keeping the issue in the public eye and reminding policy actors of the scale of the task that faced them and their own inadequacy. Thus, at the same time that governments and sports bodies were acknowledging the greater prominence of doping on their respective agendas, they were also increasingly aware that a number of factors were combining to move an effective policy response beyond their individual capacity. The first was the realisation of the likely cost of implementing a sustained anti-doping policy. The second was the reluctant acceptance that in-competition testing was pointless when steroids were being used primarily as training drugs and therefore were highly unlikely to be present in the athlete's urine at the time of competition. Anti-doping authorities, who were comfortable with in-competition testing, which was relatively low cost and easily organised, were now faced with the prospect of having to manage a regime of out-of-competition testing with its attendant extra cost and complexity. The third factor was a consequence of the second and concerned the problems of undertaking testing among an elite group of athletes who were increasingly mobile and who were likely to be in their native country, and therefore accessible by their national doping control officers, for only part of each year. Indeed, there was a growing number of athletes who spent most of their elite career outside their home country. For example, world class Australian road cyclists spent most, if not all, of their time in Europe where the major events and teams were located. Much the same could be said for the increasing number of South American and African track and field athletes who followed the American and European calendar of competitions. Such a high level of athlete mobility required a set of anti-doping regulations that would prevent athletes exploiting the loopholes and inconsistencies found in the anti-doping regulations of various countries and domestic affiliates of international federations. The final factor concerned the increasing willingness of athletes to challenge the sanctions imposed by anti-doping authorities. Legal challenges were often based on faults in the administration of urine collection or testing rather than the positive test result. A series of high profile court cases involving such athletes as the American, Harry Reynolds, the German, Katrin Krabbe, and the Australian, Martin Vinnicombe, emphasised the need for closer co-operation between anti-doping authorities.[4] A successful legal challenge could not only call into question the reliability of the testing procedure and encourage other athletes to initiate court action, but could also prove disastrously expensive for the domestic federation.

THE EMERGENCE OF A GLOBAL RESPONSE TO DOPING: 1990–2000

Throughout much of the 1990s, policy continued to be discussed and shaped within a series of relatively discrete arenas centred around individual governments, small groupings of governments, the IOC and a limited number of IFs, despite an increasing recognition that the efforts of actors within these separate arenas were becoming progressively less effective. While policy

---

4   Houlihan, B, *Dying to Win: Doping in Sport and the Development of Anti-Doping Policy*, 1999, Strasbourg: Council of Europe. See, also, de Pencier, J, 'Law and athlete drug testing in Canada' (1994) 4(2) Marquette Sports LJ 259.

success, if measured by a reduction in the use of drugs, appeared to be diminishing, a more positive development was that a process of policy learning and innovation, largely initiated by governments, was taking place, which was to contribute to a series of important innovations in policy at the end of the decade. It was during this period that the key resource requirements of an effective infrastructure for a global anti-doping policy were being identified and, to a limited extent, established. Resources of particular importance included a supportive political context as reflected in the greater willingness to commit legislative and financial resources, organisational capacity and an international arena for policy co-ordination, technical and scientific capacity, and continued public support.

The changing political context was not just defined by the reduction in the number of subversive governments but, more importantly, by the number of governments that began to treat doping as a matter of public policy and sought to establish a domestic policy framework and began to build a network of international links. Of especial importance was the greater willingness by governments to use their legislative, organisational and financial resources to support an anti-doping strategy. Although for a number of countries, such as Canada and Australia, their enthusiasm for drug free sport was the product of international embarrassment at domestic doping scandals, there is little doubt that their new found commitment was genuine. Moreover, they shared the zeal of the convert, but found that their vastly improved policing of domestic doping was constantly being undermined by the failures of harmonisation of regulations between federations and the lack of commitment by other States.

The Council of Europe provided one arena within which activist governments could press for improved standards of doping control from other Member States as well as attempt to tackle some of the problems arising from the lack of policy harmonisation. The Council, through the formulation of the Anti-Doping Convention and the work of the Convention Monitoring Group, provided examples of good practice and also was able to use its moral authority to give a lead to its new cohort of members from among the former communist States of Eastern and Central Europe. Yet, the Council was hampered by the fact that its scope was geographically limited, for, while the Convention was open to signatories outside Europe, only two non-European States, Canada and Australia, had signed, out of a total of 41 countries, by the end of 1998. Towards the end of the decade, the slowly developing interest of the European Union (EU) in sport in general and doping in particular introduced a powerful new governmental actor into the policy arena. Following the identification of sport as a possible instrument for the development of European citizenship in the Adoninno Report[5] and the

---

5   Commission of the European Communities, *A People's Europe*, 1985, Brussels: Commission of the European Communities.

positive references to it in the Maastricht Treaty of 1991, the EU steadily increased its interest in sport, culminating in 1999 with the first meeting of EU sports ministers and the publication of a number of discussion papers, one of which concerned doping.

Perhaps of even greater significance than the new found enthusiasm of the EU for sport was the development throughout the 1990s of a series of agreements between governments. In 1996, the Nordic group of countries concluded an agreement which committed signatories to the harmonisation of penalties and doping control procedures, and also to common action to limit the availability of drugs. A second example was an agreement between the UK, Canada and Australia in 1990, which later became known as the International Anti-Doping Arrangement. By 1998, membership had increased to include New Zealand, Norway, Sweden and The Netherlands, and the group had agreed arrangements for reciprocal testing, standards for the transport of samples and an international quality control manual, which was to form the basis for ISO 9000 certification of their respective domestic anti-doping regimes. Of particular significance was that the arrangement was not limited to the harmonisation of procedures, but was also a focus for lobbying within other policy arenas to 'positively influence the sports community'.[6] In addition to the Nordic group and the International Anti-Doping Arrangement, the 1990s witnessed the conclusion of a series of other bilateral or regional agreements involving Norway, China, Cuba, Germany and the Baltic States. These governmental agreements and fora have been augmented by an admittedly more limited growth in fora among sports organisations and an even more limited number of conferences which brought together governmental and sports organisations. In many respects, the developments of the 1990s are an example of grassroots policy development filling a policy void. But, while the gradual construction of an international policy network was an important advance, it should be emphasised that it was a network that did not include those sports bodies that controlled the athletes and the major international sports events. Moreover, although the construction of the regional networks provided experience of harmonisation of policy, it also highlighted to those involved the large number of countries yet to be incorporated into the policy framework if an effective international response to doping was to be achieved.

More positively, a growing number of proactive governments were also injecting substantial resources into their own domestic anti-doping programmes. By the mid-1990s, some 40,000 doping tests were being conducted worldwide, with 90% being funded by governments, at an annual cost of $43.5 million. With the steady increase in the number of tests being conducted and in the number of countries with specialist testing agencies

---

6   UK Sports Council, Ethics and Anti-Doping Directorate, *Annual Report 1997–98*, 1998, London: UKSC.

came a parallel increase in the technical expertise in the conduct of sample collection. However, one immensely significant area where progress was less satisfactory was in relation to sustaining the level of research required to ensure that scientifically valid and reliable tests were available to cope with the steady succession of new drugs, such as erythropoietin (EPO) and human growth hormone, that were being used. Such progress as there was relied heavily on public funding, with the notable exception of the GH 2000 project, which was jointly funded by the IOC and the EU and which was intended to develop a test for growth hormone in time for the Sydney Olympic Games.

The most striking feature of policy development during the 1990s was the shift in policy initiative and leadership from sports bodies to governments and governmental organisations. Part of the explanation lay in the transition from the initial phase of policy making, where issues of principle, definition and information collection were the primary themes, to a phase where the preoccupations of decision makers were personnel, scientific research, clinical trials, and legal challenge. During the 1980s, anti-doping policy moved beyond the initial series of relatively simple and inexpensive issues to ones which were both complex and costly. Deciding the list of banned substances and practices, debating a definition of doping, undertaking limited in-competition testing and agreeing amendments to the rules and constitutions of the IFs and their domestic affiliates were comfortably within the resources capacity of the IFs and the IOC. However, once tests had been devised for the more easily detectable drugs, such as amphetamines, the escalation in research and sample analysis costs began to prove a cause of significant concern. Similarly, the increasing frequency of legal challenge to federation decisions and the urgency to introduce out-of-competition testing put great strain on the resources of domestic governing bodies, which, unlike the Olympic movement and some of the major federations, were often run on a very narrow funding base. The net effect of the shifts in the agenda for anti-doping policy was to create a vacuum, both in terms of resources and leadership, which governments were increasingly willing to fill, motivated by the twin concerns of 'protecting' the image of sport and addressing what was perceived as an increasingly urgent issue of public health. The IOC and the major federations, especially the IAAF, were acutely aware of the danger of the issue of doping being redefined as a matter of public policy rather than as an essentially private matter for sport to resolve. However, apprehension regarding the resource implications of a more proactive role and a general lack of enthusiasm among federations resulted in a pervasive lethargy that led to the gradual displacement of sports organisations to the margin of policy debate.

By the mid to late 1990s, the position regarding anti-doping policy may be summarised as follows. First, the sports organisations had lost the initiative on the issue, in part because policy implementation required resources they either did not control (for example, legislative power) or were unwilling to commit (for example, finance). Although many sports organisations were resource-poor, the same was not the case with others, especially the IOC, IAAF and FIFA, which were wealthy but were nonetheless reluctant to commit more than a token amount to anti-doping efforts. Secondly, throughout the 1990s, an increasing number of governments had strengthened their domestic policies, made links with similarly minded governments, and became more sharply aware of how little was being contributed by some international sports bodies. Doubtless, the gradual deepening of government interest in doping would have continued and would, in all probability, have led, in time, to a direct challenge to the IOC and the major IFs to make a more substantial contribution to anti-doping policy. However, it is important to recognise that, until very recently, 1998 or so, the attitude of most governments and governmental bodies was characterised by a degree of deference towards the IOC and IFs that bordered on the unctuous.

Four factors combined to alter abruptly the attitude of governments towards sports bodies in general and the IOC in particular and to encourage a far greater willingness to intervene in shaping anti-doping policy. The first factor was the simmering resentment felt by many countries at the growing arrogance and pretensions of the federations and the IOC, who exploited their power over the location of major championships such as the Olympic Games, the World Athletics Championships and the soccer World Cup, to relegate governments to junior partners in their increasingly grandiose projects. Many governments were, consequently, eager for an opportunity to deflate the collective ego of the leaders of international sport. The second factor, and the catalyst for the February 1999 Anti-Doping Conference organised by the IOC, was the near collapse of the 1998 Tour de France, one of the world's premier sports events. The scale of blood doping that was exposed was all the more dramatic because the Union Cycliste Internationale (UCI), the IF for cycling, was perceived as being one of the more active federations. However, of greater significance for the IOC and the federations was the action of the French civil authorities, which intervened directly and emphatically, and effectively ignored the UCI. The prospect of the French action being replicated in other countries caused considerable concern within the IOC. The French action reflected the widespread belief that the IOC had had its opportunity to give strong lead on doping following the 1994 Lausanne Agreement between itself and the other international sports confederations, but had failed to inject any sense of urgency into the policy process.

The third factor was the slowly unfolding story of corruption and bribery surrounding the award of the 2002 Winter Olympic Games to Salt Lake City and the 1996 summer Games to Atlanta. Although the allegations of corruption were separate from the issue of doping, they had a powerful effect in undermining the IOC's claims to moral authority based on the oft-quoted idealism incorporated in the Olympic Charter. The fact that both corruption scandals concerned America was unfortunate for the Olympic movement, as the US was not only a major Olympic power, but also the most important sponsor of the Olympic Games, both in terms of television rights and corporate sponsorship. The revelations, by the Swiss IOC member Marc Hodler, prompted a series of Congressional Committee inquiries, which kept the IOC firmly in the public eye throughout 1999. The final factor was the rapidly growing interest of the European Union in international sport. In its ruling on the *Bosman* case,[7] the EU had already made clear that it possessed the capacity to affect directly the interests of the major sports, including soccer, basketball and ice hockey. In addition, as a supranational body, the EU was less constrained in its criticism of the IOC than many individual countries, who were frequently conscious that excessive criticism might undermine their chances of hosting future Olympic Games or World Championships.

THE BACKGROUND TO THE
WORLD ANTI-DOPING CONFERENCE

The announcement by the IOC that it would convene a World Anti-Doping Conference in Lausanne in February 1999 proved to be a watershed in policy development in more ways than one. It marked a long overdue attempt by the IOC to recapture the initiative in policy making from governments, but it also forced to the surface a series of tensions that previous policy inertia had allowed to lie dormant. Reflected in the comments of politicians and public officials is a, possibly deliberate, misperception of the unity and level of co-operation between international sports organisations, especially between the IOC and the major federations. Yet, the common cause often displayed by sports organisations is at its most evident when faced by the prospect of a challenge to their autonomy from governments. In reality, the relationship between the IFs and the Olympic movement is uneasy at the best of times. For example, there is a feeling among some IFs that the Olympic Games undermines the success of their own world championships. This is most evident in soccer, where FIFA has refused to allow full strength national teams to compete in the Olympics lest it undermine the attractiveness of the quadrennial World Cup. Tensions also exist between the IOC and the federations, most notably the IAAF, over the division of income from the sale of television broadcasting rights with the Federation, arguing that it is track and field events that are the main attraction for television companies and that, consequently, the IAAF should receive a larger proportion of income. In general, the federations are keen periodically to remind the IOC that it is they who control athletes and allow them to compete in the Olympic event. However, what unites the IFs and the IOC is their collective distrust of

---

7   Case C-41 5/93 *ASBL Union Royale Belge des Sociétés de Football Association and Others v Jean Marc Bosman* [1996] 1 CMLR 645.

governments and the deeply entrenched belief that most governments treat international elite sport as a convenient political resource rather than as an important global cultural event. For their part, an increasing number of governments perceived sports organisations as unwilling, if not unable, to put their own house in order. If the February Conference was to make progress, it had to overcome some deeply entrenched hostilities.

The aim set for the Conference was to 'discuss and adopt measures allowing the fight against doping to be intensified', and groundwork had been laid for the discussion by four working parties which dealt with 'The protection of athletes' (chaired by Anita DeFrantz), 'Legal and political aspects' (Keba Mbaye), 'Prevention, ethics, education and communication' (Pal Schmitt) and 'Financial considerations' (Richard Pound). If President Samaranch expected the position statements to contain a chorus of congratulations, he was to be sadly disappointed. The position statements, most of which were from sports ministers and representatives of government anti-doping agencies, that took up much of the first day were, with only a few exceptions, fiercely critical of the IOC in general and the leadership provided by Samaranch in particular. A succession of ministers and government officials used their allotted five minutes to berate the Olympic movement for its complacency and myopia towards doping, to challenge the sincerity of its stated aims for the Conference, and to question its moral authority to oversee the proposed international agency (initially referred to as the International Anti-Doping Agency (IADA) but subsequently retitled the World Anti-Doping Agency (WADA)). The speeches given by Barry McCaffrey, Director of the US Office of National Drug Control Policy, and Tony Banks, the UK Minister for Sport, were typical. McCaffrey provided, at best, a qualified endorsement of the IOC's record and urged the Committee to ensure that the new body be truly independent, a point he was to pursue over the following six months as negotiations over the establishment of WADA progressed. However, McCaffrey did offer, on behalf of the US Government, a contribution of $1 million to the costs of running the new agency.

The intensity of criticism was lower on the second day when the reports of the four working groups were considered and the participants adopted a more pragmatic stance. Each of the four reports addressed issues central to the reinvigoration and relaunch of the anti-doping campaign, with the most pertinent issues being those raised by the working groups on financial and legal aspects. The Financial Considerations Working Group, which proposed the establishment of IADA, made suggestions about its management and remit, all of which proved highly contentious. The initial suggestion was that the agency be established:

> ... as a foundation under Swiss law ... be headquartered in Lausanne, governed by a council presided over by the IOC President, consisting of three representatives each of the IOC, the International Federations, the National Olympic Committees, athletes designated by the IOC Athletes Commission,

international governmental organisations and three persons representing sponsors, the pharmaceutical industry and the sporting goods industry.[8]

The Council would direct the work of the agency and be responsible, *inter alia*, for funding, revising the list of banned substances and practices, validating the accreditation of IOC-approved laboratories and appointing the director of the agency. As regards funding, the working group proposed the designation of an initial sum of at least $25 million to cover running costs and to commission research to develop reliable tests for the detection of natural steroids, EPO and human growth hormone (HGH).

As mentioned above, many of the politicians who spoke on the opening day supported the establishment of an international agency, but strongly argued that it should be completely independent of the IOC. Consequently, the Declaration agreed at the conclusion of the Lausanne Conference was ambiguous about the relationship between the agency and the IOC. It was agreed that an 'independent International Anti-Doping Agency shall be established so as to be fully operational in time for the XXVII Olympiad in Sydney in 2000'. The brief of the body was less clear, as this would now be determined by a new working group convened by the IOC and with membership drawn from among athletes, governments and the Olympic movement. However, the Lausanne Declaration did indicate that part of the remit of the agency would be to give consideration to 'expanding out-of-competition testing, co-ordinating research, promoting preventive and educational actions and harmonising scientific and technical standards and procedures for analyses and equipment'.[9]

If the agency was to make an effective contribution to combating doping, there were two awkward issues that the working group would need to address, namely, funding and accountability. With the steep rise in the cost of maintaining the anti-doping programme, the question of the funding of sample collection and analysis, and of research, was crucial. The $25 million offered by the IOC to support the work of IADA was a significant commitment and the offer prompted a number of countries, including the US, also to pledge financial support. However, to put the sum in perspective, it is estimated that an out-of-competition test can cost between $500 and $1,000 and that the clinical trials to confirm the effectiveness of the test for human growth hormone could be as much as $5.5 million.

Perhaps the most challenging issue to face the working group was that of the accountability of the proposed agency. The initial proposal, that IADA should be under the aegis of the IOC although drawing its membership from beyond as well as within the Olympic movement, was firmly rejected by

---

8   IOC, *Financial Considerations: Summary of Conclusions from the Meeting of the Working Group*, 5 November 1998, Lausanne: IOC, p 1.

9   IOC, Lausanne Declaration on Doping in Sport, 4 February 1999.

government representatives and politicians. The problem facing the IOC and the federations was to find a basis for the agency which did not effectively cede control over anti-doping strategy and administration to governments, many of whom, their present enthusiasm notwithstanding, have rarely demonstrated a long term commitment to Olympic ideals. A second element of the problem of accountability concerned the relationship of the federations to the agency and the willingness of the former to transfer authority. It may well be that the federations have accepted that an effective response to the problem of doping required a loss of some autonomy, but the major federations, such as FIFA, UCI and IAAF, have recently protested loudly at what they saw as attempts by the IOC to interfere in their relationship with their athletes and the organisation of their sports. When put under pressure to accept the IOC benchmark minimum penalty for steroid use of two years, FIFA and UCI simply refused. Similarly, the IAAF recently made it clear that it did not intend to recognise the Court of Arbitration for Sport in Lausanne as superior to its own arbitration panel with IAAF secretary general Istvan Gyulai expressing fundamental reservations about IOC claims to anti-doping policy leadership, arguing that 'the IOC acts like a world government, but we do not want to be dominated in this way'.[10]

Despite the intensity of criticism from politicians, the overall outcome of the February Conference was positive. When the rhetoric of the government representatives was stripped away, along with the posturing designed to satisfy domestic constituencies, there was an acknowledgment that a global body similar to that proposed by the IOC was essential if progress in the anti-doping campaign was to be made. The central issue was, therefore, not whether there should be an international anti-doping body, but who would control it. It was this issue that preoccupied the working group during the subsequent six months.

The working group met on five occasions with a membership that reflected the two key interests in doping policy, namely, government and sports organisations, plus a series of organisations with a more general interest, such as international police and drugs agencies.[11] Over the five meetings of the working group, the initial proposals formulated at the Lausanne Conference were significantly amended. However, the focus and remit of the by now retitled IADA remained largely intact and were

---

10 Quoted in (1997) 29(11) Sport Intern.

11 The organisations represented on the working group were: Arabic Confederation of Sports; Association of National Olympic Committees; Association of Summer Olympic International Federations; IOC Athletes Commission; Council of Europe; Association of International Winter Sports Federations; CAS; EU; IOC; Interpol; Supreme Council for Sport in Africa; UN International Drug Control Programme; World Health Organisation.

summarised as follows in the IOC press release, issued after the fifth meeting of the working group:[12]

> The Agency's principal task will be to co-ordinate a comprehensive anti-doping program at international level, developing common, effective, minimum standards for doping control ... Among its duties, the new Agency is expected to commission unannounced out-of-competition controls in full agreement with [the] public and private bodies concerned.
>
> The Agency is expected to work with existing authorities to promote the harmonization of anti-doping policies and procedures, identify a reference laboratory to advise the accredited testing laboratories, and co-ordinate the numerous educational efforts now underway. It also is expected to publish an annual list of prohibited substances.

It was acknowledged that the agency would not seek responsibility for the determination of doping infractions, nor for the imposition of sanctions: both these responsibilities would remain with the federations. The most significant change to the details announced at the end of the Lausanne Conference was that the agency would now be far more independent of the IOC. Following pressure from the Council of Europe, the EU and especially the US, it was suggested by the IOC that the governing board of the agency would comprise 24 members, only three of which would be nominated by the IOC itself. Other seats were to be allocated as follows: three each to the National Olympic Committees, the IFs and athletes, with the remaining 12 allocated to non-sports organisations, including governments. An equally awkward issue concerned the funding of the agency. If the agency were to be fully independent, it required the various interests represented to contribute to its operating costs. While the US offered $1 million at the February Conference, it was recognised by the IOC representatives on the working group that it would take some time for governments to agree to release funding. In addition, there was still disagreement about whether all countries involved should make a financial contribution, whether there should be a sliding scale according to wealth, or whether some, mainly poorer, countries should be excused from making a contribution. As a consequence of these unresolved questions, the IOC offered to fund the agency for the first two years, at the rate of $4 million per year, thus allowing time for governments to process their funding decisions. Half of the total of $4 million would be used to fund 5,000 out-of-competition tests, a total which represents a 12% increase on the number of out-of-competition tests currently undertaken globally: the remainder of the funding would be used to cover the other activities of the agency, including the production of educational materials, the provision of information and administration. Research would be funded separately. As

---

12 IOC press release, 9 September 1999. The title 'World Anti-Doping Agency' was preferred to the original suggestion (International Anti-Doping Agency) because of the possibility of the acronym IADA causing confusion with the International Anti-Doping Arrangement, which is a multilateral agreement between a group of States.

regards location, the IOC proposed that, initially at least, WADA should be established in Switzerland. However, the Committee did acknowledge the objections expressed by the EU and the US and agreed to invite offers from other countries to host the agency.

American suspicion of the IOC was further fuelled by the announcement on 7 November that the first President of WADA was to be IOC Vice President Richard Pound. Although Pound has been a vigorous supporter of anti-doping policy and was chair of the working group that suggested the establishment of a global anti-doping agency at the February Conference, he was considered by many, including McCaffrey, as having a conflict of interest, by virtue of the fact that he was an IOC Vice President and, more importantly, was responsible for the marketing of the Olympic Games – a product that can only be damaged by revelations of doping. However, following a meeting with Pound, McCaffrey felt sufficiently reassured that Pound would only act as interim President to lend him his support.

The changes made to the February proposals were a clear reflection of the recognition by the IOC of its increased resource dependence on governments and the greater determination of the latter to tackle doping. The IOC was especially conscious of the potential influence of the EU, which was confirmed by the newly appointed President of the European Commission, Romano Prodi, who, as President-designate, told the European Parliament that one of the issues that he intended to make a priority for the new Commission was doping, 'an issue where decisive, co-ordinated transnational action is clearly needed'. From the perspective of the IOC, the EU has a range of existing programmes that could support the work of WADA, particularly in relation to the funding of scientific research, furthering the harmonisation of laws among Member States and the funding and co-ordination of public health campaigns aimed at doping in sport. But, while the IOC was doubtless aware of the value of harnessing EU resources to the anti-doping campaign, they were probably more acutely aware of the EU's interventionist and regulatory culture and the threat that that posed to the independence of sports organisations.

THE FORMATION OF THE WORLD
ANTI-DOPING AGENCY

The period between the publication of the revised proposals from the IOC working party in early October 1999 and the establishment of WADA on 10 November was marked by an intense round of bargaining between the IOC and governmental interests, especially the US Government. Although the EU was important in negotiating the final structure and remit of WADA, it was the US that held centre stage. That the US should have become so interested in the policy towards doping in sport was due to three factors. First, a recognition that doping in sport was no longer a minor sub-category of drug use confined to a small group of elite athletes, but was developing many of the criminal features of mainstream illegal drug use such as smuggling, illegal manufacturing and sale to minors. Secondly, that the drugs used initially by athletes alone were gradually becoming widely used as social or cosmetic drugs among young Americans. McCaffrey quoted evidence of extensive use of steroids by high school girls, with one report concluding that 175,000 high school girls admitted taking anabolic steroids at least once. Wadler also pointed out that steroid use, at 3% of 9–13 year olds, was at the same level as cocaine use for the same age group[13] and that sales of the drug androstenedione, which the US baseball star Mark McGwire admitted using, had risen fivefold in one year. Thirdly, the attitude of Barry McCaffrey, who saw in WADA an opportunity to take effective action to limit growth in a new drugs market.

Perhaps because the US was considered to be one of the countries that was least enthusiastic about controlling doping, the intensity of McCaffrey's pressure took many in the IOC by surprise. Once McCaffrey emerged as a central actor in discussions concerning the new agency, he was able to exercise substantial leverage over the IOC due to support from within Congress and also due to the dependence of the IOC on US business. Congressional Committee hearings into doping in sport were held in October 1999 and were highly critical of the lack of urgency within bodies such as the IOC towards the issue. Of greater significance was the awareness within the IOC of the significance of US corporate sponsorship for the Olympic movement. Not only is the US broadcasting system the major purchaser of rights to the Olympic Games, with NBC recently paying $3.5 billion for the rights to the next five Games, but corporations pay approximately $90 million each year to the IOC in sponsorship. Indeed, nine of the eleven major corporate sponsors of the Olympic movement are US companies and 60% of all IOC income is from the US. Consequently, expressions of unease among traditional corporate sponsors, such as John Hancock Mutual Life Insurance, coupled with threats from members of the US Congress to revoke the IOC's tax-exempt status and make the Committee subject to the Foreign Corrupt Practices Act, had potentially serious implications for Olympic finances.

McCaffrey's initial response to the October proposals from the IOC working party was that it constituted a strategy designed to pre-empt democratic decision making and exclude an input from governments: 'It's unilateral, it's arbitrary, it's unacceptable.'[14] Victor Lachance, Director of the Canadian Centre for Ethics in Sport, echoed these sentiments, suggesting that

13 Wadler, G, written statement to the Senate Committee on Commerce, Science and Transportation, 20 October 1999.

14 Associate Press Worldstream, 27 October 1999, available at www.ap.org.

the IOC's haste was a strategy to 'head off General McCaffrey'.[15] McCaffrey countered the IOC proposals with a set of his own which emphasised that WADA must be 'truly independent and accountable', that there should be 'no statute of limitations for violations' and that urine samples should be preserved indefinitely so that they could be analysed when more sophisticated laboratory techniques became available.[16]

Additional pressure came from the newly appointed EU sports commissioner, Viviane Reding, who was also concerned to ensure that the IOC could not dominate WADA. However, she was also critical of the Americans who, while being aggressive at the international level had an extremely lax system of doping control in their own country. As regards WADA, Reding stated that EU support was conditional upon, first, a unified list of proscribed practices and substances; secondly, an agency with the power to carry out unannounced tests without the prior agreement of athletes (and, by implication, their IF); and, thirdly, independent accreditation of test laboratories. The EU was also keen for the permanent location of WADA to be in one of its Member States.[17]

McCaffrey argued that the IOC-proposed agency would not be independent, would not publish test results, and that it could only advise the IOC regarding its anti-doping code. Moreover, a central concern for McCaffrey was the number of potential conflicts of interest facing the IOC. Consequently, he objected to the IOC role in the accreditation of doping control laboratories. He also argued that it was not plausible to expect an organisation that makes millions of dollars from the Games to pursue drug-using athletes with the necessary vigour because of the damage that might be inflicted on the image of the Games. McCaffrey's criticisms of the IOC anti-doping efforts prompted a caustic, and not altogether unjustified, riposte from IOC Vice President Richard Pound, who pointed out that the Americans should tackle the endemic doping in their major professional sports before accusing the IOC of being dilatory. In rejecting McCaffrey's demand for a fully independent WADA, Pound reminded him that it was the IOC that was funding the new agency with $25 million. Although Pound's claim that the IOC had been at the forefront of the fight against doping was a gross overstatement, it had some justification when the IOC's involvement over the last 30 years is compared to that of many governments, including that of the US. To be fair to McCaffrey,

---

15 (1999) *Salt Lake Tribune*, 7 November.

16 White House Office of National Drug Control Policy, *Recommendations Concerning Strengthening the Anti-Drug Programs Within the Olympics and International Sport*, 1999 Position Paper, available at www.whitehousedrugpolicy.gov/newscommentary/paper/intro.html.

17 In early 2000, the most likely location was one of the following European cities: Athens; Bonn; Lille; Lisbon; Luxembourg; Madrid; or Vienna, although the Canadian Government recently announced that it would be bidding to host the agency in Montreal.

he was just as critical of the anti-doping efforts of the US Olympic Committee and was instrumental in persuading them to increase the number of tests conducted from 5,000 to between 6,000 and 8,000, which is a significant improvement, but one that looks less impressive when compared to the UK, for example, which conducted just over 4,000 tests in 1998–99 and has a population approximately one-fifth that of the US. In addition, McCaffrey reminded Pound of the US offer of funding for WADA and of the offer of the services of the US-based National Institute on Drug Abuse, which currently 'supports 85% of all worldwide research on drugs'.[18]

Agreement was reached in early November between the EU and the IOC on the draft statutes for WADA and on a series of initial policy priorities and responsibilities, which included the following: first, responsibility for the determination of an agreed list of banned substances and practices using the current IOC Medical Commission list as its starting point; secondly, the transfer of responsibility for the accreditation of testing laboratories from the IOC to the agency; thirdly, planning and co-ordinating out-of-competition testing with the IFs; fourthly, the board of directors will have equal representation of governmental and sports interests; and, fifthly, that Lausanne will only be a temporary location for the agency. The EU statement was an important item on the agenda of the Drugs in Sport Conference held in Sydney in mid-November 1999, where representatives of 25 countries agreed to establish a steering group to be jointly chaired by Canada and Australia, to liaise with WADA and to provide a constituency from which government representatives on WADA could be selected.

In mid-December, McCaffrey and Samaranch met and issued a joint statement on the operation and role of WADA. Included among the 12 points were the following: agreement to reserve four seats on WADA's board for athletes from among the seats allocated to sports organisations; permission for observer status to be granted to bodies such as the World Health Organisation; WADA meetings should normally be open to the public; WADA would encourage the adoption of ISO standards for the operation of doping control procedures; and WADA should work towards effective sanctions against those who aid and abet doping. The joint statement marked a ceasefire in the hostilities between the US Government and the IOC over doping control, rather than a settlement. While the IOC clearly felt obliged to placate the Americans, McCaffrey also diluted some of his original proposals. For example, whereas he had initially demanded that there be no statute of limitations for drug abusers, the joint statement merely required the IOC to consider the appropriate statute of limitations. More significantly, McCaffrey had to admit that the joint statement was not binding.

---

18   White House, 1999.

WORLD ANTI-DOPING AGENCY: 'MORE PUBLIC RELATIONS PLOY THAN PUBLIC POLICY SOLUTION'?[19]

Despite the friction that surrounded the establishment of WADA, there is no doubt that it marks a major development in establishing an effective policy response to doping. Twelve months ago, the voice of government in anti-doping policy was fragmented and, consequently, relatively ineffective. Since then, governmental interests have been substantially co-ordinated around three intergovernmental bodies, namely, the Council of Europe, the EU and the Canadian/Australian steering group, which includes the US Government. Given the broad consensus between these three bodies and the extensive overlap of membership, the collective influence of government on the IOC and on WADA is formidable. Moreover, the corruption scandal over the selection of host cities as well as the public scepticism towards the IOC's leadership on doping has greatly reduced, if not eliminated, the traditional deference of governments towards the Olympic movement, with the result that government officers and ministers are much more willing to challenge the actions (and inaction) of the IOC.

More significantly, WADA's commitment to add 5,000 tests to the global total and to seek to co-ordinate more tightly the distribution of the current 40,000 or so tests, so as to enhance the effectiveness of the international programme, is clearly a development to be applauded. In many respects, the establishment of WADA has the potential to complete the organisational infrastructure necessary to direct and manage an international response to a global and rapidly evolving problem. However, optimism at the progress that has been made since February 1999 needs to be tempered with an acknowledgment of the challenges that lie ahead and the tensions that have been pushed, temporarily, into the background.

Although the publication of the agreements between the EU and the IOC and the US Government and the IOC should provide the necessary reassurance that the agency will be both accountable and transparent in its operation, there is still a large measure of unease. First, while the government representatives on the board can claim to be from countries that have put in place a reasonably effective anti-doping programme at domestic level, the same cannot be said for some of the early nominees to the seats reserved for sports organisation. Particular surprise was expressed at the announcement that one of the IF seats would be taken by Hans Verbruggen, President of the UCI, which had proved so spectacularly unsuccessful in controlling doping in the 1998 Tour de France.

---

19 Barry McCaffrey, in a statement to the US Senate hearings on doping, October 1999.

A second concern is that so much of the future success of WADA assumes that the mutual suspicion between the IOC and the IFs can be subsumed by their common fear of greater government intervention. At the meeting of General Assembly of International Summer Olympic Federations in November 1998, the federations made it clear that, while they supported the IOC in its drive against doping, they were unwilling to transfer control over 'their' athletes to the Committee. The eventual compromise that was negotiated would make any athlete who wanted to participate in an Olympic Games subject to out-of-competition testing, as set out in the IOC's new Anti-Doping Code, even if their IF did not have the same anti-doping rules as the IOC. In return, the IFs, along with the National Olympic Committees, would be represented on the board of WADA. However, of far greater importance is that it is the IFs that will still decide how to respond to a positive test result and determine the application of sanctions. To an extent, the IOC is caught between the governments on the one hand and the federations on the other. While the EU and the US Government are pressing the IOC for a decisive lead, the IFs are quietly threatening the IOC that, if it seeks to enhance its role in doping policy at the expense of the federations, they will be far less co-operative over the scheduling of their own world championships and the release of athletes. FIFA, which is especially resistant to the IOC lead on doping, already has an age restriction on soccer players participating in the Olympics and has discussed openly the possibility of holding the World Cup every two years, thus bringing it into direct competition with the Olympic Games for broadcasting revenue. A key test for the credibility of WADA is whether it is able to gain the commitment of those IFs such as soccer, tennis, cycling and rugby union that have so far been, at best, lukewarm towards anti-doping efforts.

A third problem facing WADA is securing a sufficient resource base. The scale of the funding problem is easily illustrated. According to Dr Don Catlin, one of the most respected authorities on doping in sport, 'the labs' ability to respond to [doping] are restricted by funding because doping has never been a serious priority for sport'.[20] He added that, although the US Olympic Committee had paid $500,000 for a high resolution mass spectrometer, his laboratory did not have the funds to employ staff with the necessary qualifications to make the machine fully operational. John Hoberman went further and talked of a strategy of 'calculated underinvestment' by the IOC and the major federations. While the IOC has committed the modest sum of $25 million, it is as yet unclear how much new money governments will contribute to WADA or whether they will simply claim that their current domestic expenditure is their contribution.

---

20   (1999) *Salt Lake Tribune*, 20 October.

The necessity for substantial funding is underlined when account is taken of some of the scientific challenges that lie ahead as a result of the continuing experimentation by athletes with new drugs. Just as scientists are struggling to refine a method to detect EPO, a new drug, perfluorocarbon (PFC), with 'enormous oxygen-carrying capacity', is allegedly being used by some speed skaters and cross-country skiers.[21] Another new drug is IGF-1, a polypeptide that is responsible for the growth-promoting effects of HGH and is currently undetectable. There are also rumours of genetically engineered blood substitutes that will allow IGF-1 to be used without there being any adverse effects on the rest of the body.

There are also a number of fundamental, yet complex, issues still to be resolved, including providing a clear and legally robust definition of 'doping'. The newly published Olympic Movement Anti-Doping Code prohibits, *inter alia*, 'an expedient (substance or method) which is ... capable of enhancing their performance'. As Wadler notes, 'taken literally [the Code] would have the effect of banning training', as it is a method of enhancing performance. The search for a satisfactory definition of doping is crucial, yet has proved elusive for over 30 years.

At a more general level, there is a well grounded concern at the temporary appointment of Richard Pound as head of WADA. Although Pound has suggested that he will remain in office for no more than two years, they will be crucial years, during which the Chief Executive and other key personnel will be appointed and operating procedures and culture established. While Pound has a reputation for integrity, it can be argued that he is too deeply steeped in the culture of the Olympic movement to be able to establish the sort of assertive, iconoclastic and vigorous agency that WADA needs to become.

Rather than being the culmination of a process of policy making, the establishment of WADA merely marks a stage, albeit an important one, in the long term campaign to eradicate doping from sport. The challenges of keeping a very disparate and, at times, intensely suspicious, group of policy actors together and, at the same time, maintaining momentum on the central issue of harmonisation of policies and processes between sports and between countries, is a daunting task. Thus, while the establishment of WADA is no guarantee of success, the failure to establish WADA would have been a sure guarantee of failure in the anti-doping campaign.

---

21 *Op cit*, Wadler, fn 13.

CHAPTER 10

HARMONISATION: A BRIDGE TOO FAR? A COMMENTARY ON CURRENT ISSUES AND PROBLEMS[1]

Emile N Vrijman

INTRODUCTION

The central theme underlying the 1999 International Olympic Committee (IOC) World Conference on Doping in Sport was, without any doubt, the issue of harmonisation. Of all issues confronting international sports, the harmonisation of current anti-doping rules and regulations remains one of the most difficult and potentially discordant topics under current debate. This review will re-examine the key issues of the topic, analyse and comment on the depth and breadth of adherence to new protocols developed to harmonise current anti-doping procedures and regulations, and determine the progress of the harmonisation process over the past five years. It is hoped that this review will assist and augment the processes of evolution and change in current anti-doping regulations and policy.

HARMONISATION

The harmonisation of the anti-doping rules and regulations of international sports governing bodies is generally considered important for a variety of reasons. Some consider that increased harmonisation will further fairness doctrines by preventing the unequal treatment of athletes having committed similar offences, albeit in different sports. As has often been asked, 'why should a professional cyclist only receive a conditional suspension for a first time offence of anabolic steroid use, while a weightlifter could be banned for life?'. This question certainly deserves to be answered.

It has also been claimed that, by harmonising doping control procedures, a reliable and uniform system for conducting doping controls would be created, thus ensuring the similar treatment of athletes in every sport: this would enable a governing body to fully accept the results of doping controls

---

1   This chapter is based upon the results of an earlier study: Vrijman, EN, *Harmonisation: Can it Ever be Really Achieved?*, 2nd edn, 1995, Rotterdam: NeCeDo; also issued as T-DO (95) Inf 5, Strasbourg: Council of Europe.

conducted in another sport from any geographic location.[2] The need and importance of creating harmonised, universally accepted doping control procedures is illustrated by the recognition of the global character of elite sports circuits and the high level of international mobility of elite athletes.[3] According to Professor Houlihan: 'There is little point in the government and domestic governing bodies of sport in one particular country having a clear set of regulations regarding doping, if their elite athletes do not train in their home country nor participate in competition in that country.'[4] In his view, it is therefore important that there is a uniformity of regulation 'so that drug abusers are not able to exploit differences and inconsistencies between countries, domestic governing bodies and international federations'.[5] Finally, a strong motive for harmonisation is the desire of sports governing bodies to resist what has been labelled 'the increasing intrusion of the civil courts in sports', as well as the increased litigiousness of athletes. Harmonisation, from this perspective, helps to support the arguments of sports governing bodies in doping cases when it appears that precedent has already been established through the widespread adoption of standardised policies by numerous sports governing bodies around the globe.

We must not, however, simplify a complex issue. Harmonisation also has potential disadvantages. As a result of this process, it may become increasingly difficult for individual sports governing bodies to take into consideration the special demands of their sport when implementing internationally agreed harmonised anti-doping rules and/or policies.[6] Some established professional sports have thus argued that they should not be expected to adhere to the same doping rules as 'amateur sports'.[7] This has also

---

2   Harmonisation of disciplinary rules, with careful attention to the rights of athletes, will certainly also be necessary in order for sports governing bodies to be able to mutually recognise sanctions imposed for doping infractions. If these rules differed substantially between individual sports governing bodies, mutual recognition of sanctions imposed for doping infractions would become very difficult, or indeed impossible, due to the various legal obligations the courts could impose on sports governing bodies. See, eg, the decision of the Irish High Court in *Quirke v Bord Luthchleas na hEeireann* (1988) unreported, 25 March, where the IAAF failed to provide the athlete with a hearing before deciding on sanctioning.

3   Houlihan, B, *Dying to Win: Doping in Sport and the Development of Anti-Doping Policy*, 1999, Strasbourg: Council of Europe, p 154.

4   *Ibid.*

5   *Ibid.*

6   Harmonised anti-doping rules might make it difficult for a specific sport's governing body to test for certain banned substances which, while relevant for that specific sport, might not be relevant as a banned substance at all for the majority of international sports governing bodies, or vice versa.

7   Not surprisingly, athletes active in these sports regularly use the argument that, as sport provides their livelihood, they should consequently be allowed more leeway regarding the range of permissible drugs. Not surprisingly, all of the major league organisations in the US apply lists of banned substances which are vastly different from the IOC list of prohibited classes of substances and methods.

happened in relation to non-Olympic sports when discussing the application of Olympic doping rules and regulations. It has been argued that harmonisation could result in weaker rules, because all the sports governing bodies participating in this process ultimately have to agree to a lowest common denominator.[8]

Where, then, is this process currently? The last significant international meeting where harmonisation was discussed, preceding the 1999 IOC World Conference on Doping in Sport, occurred in Lausanne, Switzerland, in January 1994. At this forum, the IOC, the Associations of both Summer and Winter Olympic Federations and the International Olympic Federations, as well as various continental organisations of National Olympic Committees (NOCs) and representatives of athletes, decided to unify their respective anti-doping rules and procedures according to the principles laid down in the document, *Preventing and Fighting Against Doping in Sport*.[9] The then IOC anti-doping rules and regulations were selected as the basis for this attempt at harmonisation. In order to further the process of harmonisation, the IOC Medical Code was published in 1995, bringing together, for the very first time, within one single document, all of the IOC anti-doping rules and regulations.

The presentation of harmonisation as the central theme of the 1999 IOC World Conference on Doping in Sport, therefore, was neither altogether a surprise nor unique and, consequently, should only be viewed as the most recent attempt to revive the process of harmonising the anti-doping rules and regulations of international sports governing bodies.[10] The attention being paid at the conference to the role played by the public authorities and the necessity of harmonising (inter)national legislation concerning doping 'in

---

8 Coni, P, 'Harmonisation of international rules and regulations, restraint of trade and right to work', session 7 in IAF International Conference on Sport and Law, *Official Proceedings*, Monaco, 31 January–2 February 1991, p 160.

9 IOC, *Preventing and Fighting Against Doping in Sport*, 1994, Lausanne: IOC.

10 The so called 1989 Multilateral Agreement on Unification of Actions in the Struggle Against Doping in Sport, as well as the 1989 decision of the General Association of International Sports Federations, provide examples of such attempts. Some of these attempts at harmonisation, however, such as the Nordic Anti-Doping Convention; the International Anti-Doping Arrangement between the governments of Australia, Canada, New Zealand, Norway and the UK; the Baltic States Anti-Doping Convention; the Co-operation Agreement between the Chinese Olympic Committee and the Australian Sports Drug Agency (ASDA); the Trilateral Agreement between ASDA, the US Olympic Committee and the Canadian Centre for Ethics in Sport; and, most notably, the Council of Europe's Anti-Doping Convention, represent instruments of harmonisation developed and agreed upon by national governments and/or national sports confederations which also define and impose sanctions on athletes for doping and non-doping infractions. As has been rightly pointed out by de Pencier, legal counsel to the Canadian Centre for Drug Free Sport and current Chair of the Legal Working Party of the Council of Europe's Monitoring Group, these additional layers of anti-doping measures (while beyond the scope of this chapter) alert us to another level of harmonisation which may provide complications for the process of harmonisation, as discussed in this chapter.

consultation with the Olympic movement' did, however, provide a new and important addition to the current debate.[11] Since both the Olympic movement and the public authorities of many countries were represented at this meeting, the harmonisation process still has a potential for future development.

Given the 1999 IOC World Conference on Doping in Sport and the previous attempts at harmonisation, this review intends to examine where the harmonisation process currently stands and to determine whether the 1999 Lausanne Conference has had any impact on the current anti-doping rules and regulations of international federations (IFs).

STRUCTURE AND SCOPE OF THE STUDY

In order to examine where the harmonisation process currently stands and to determine the impact of the 1999 Lausanne Conference, the following elements of anti-doping rules and regulations of 29 international sports governing bodies have been selected for comparison with results of a similar study conducted in 1995, as well as with the current IOC anti-doping rules and regulations:[12]

- the definition of doping;
- the list of banned classes and methods of doping;
- timing of doping controls;
- the laboratories used for analysis;
- sanctions imposed;
- recognition of sanctions imposed by other sports governing bodies;
- the right to a hearing;
- the waiver of minor procedural mistakes;
- blood sampling; and
- the recognition of the Court of Arbitration for Sport (CAS).

---

11 It is fair to say that the increasing involvement of governments in international discussions regarding doping, initiated by the Council of Europe's Anti-Doping Convention and its continuing work in that area, has provided an important and much needed impetus to the ongoing harmonisation process, as it put considerable pressure upon international sports organisations to continue the fledgling harmonisation process.

12 When reference is being made in this review to the 'current' IOC anti-doping rules and regulations, the 1999 IOC MC is being addressed, as it allows for a better comparison with the anti-doping rules and regulations existing in 1995. The 2000 Olympic Movement Anti-Doping Code will be referred to explicitly, if necessary.

With the exception of the issues defining 'doping',[13] the right to a hearing[14] and the waiver of minor procedural mistakes,[15] all the elements selected mirror the guiding principles of the 1994 Lausanne decision, which should be regarded as the actual starting point of the current harmonisation process. The blood sampling issue, as well as the recognition of the CAS as a sport's governing organisation's ultimate appellate body, have been added, given their current importance concerning recent developments in the field of anti-doping science and policies.[16]

The anti-doping rules and regulations of 54 international sports governing bodies reviewed in 1995[17] were compiled and published by the Doping Control Unit of the UK's Sports Council in the 1993 *Directory of Anti-Doping Regulations of International Sports Federations*.[18] In order to be able to compare the 1995 situation with the current one, a compilation of the anti-doping rules and regulations of 37 international sports governing bodies, brought together in 1999 by the TMC Asser Instituut in The Hague, The Netherlands, has also been analysed.[19] Given the different number of anti-doping rules and regulations of the international sports governing bodies contained within both publications, only the rules and regulations of those international sports governing bodies contained within both publications have been used for comparison and subsequent analysis. In order to assess the current status of the harmonisation process, as well as its development and relative success, the current anti-doping rules and regulations of 29 international sports governing bodies were compared with their 1995 edition.[20]

---

13 This issue was added by the author in 1995 on the basis of its apparent significance.

14 This issue was added in 1995 upon the request of the Legal Issues Working Party of the Council of Europe's Monitoring Group: *Meeting Report: Working Party on Legal Issues*, T-DO (94) 22, 1994, Strasbourg: Council of Europe, p 9.

15 *Ibid*.

16 The recent announcement and subsequent testing at the 2000 Sydney Summer Olympic Games by the IOC justifies adding the blood sampling issue as an element for consideration in this review.

17 *Op cit*, Vrijman, fn 1.

18 Doping Control Unit, *Directory of Anti-Doping Regulations of International Sports Federations*, 2nd edn, 1993, London: UKSC. Although several IFs have changed their anti-doping regulations since this study was initially conducted, an update of this publication is currently still pending. Given the absence of an update, the author decided to adhere to the original results of his study.

19 Siekmann, RRC, Soek, J and Bellani, A (eds), *Doping Rules of International Sports Organizations*, 1999, The Hague: TMC Asser/Kluwer.

20 The anti-doping rules and regulations of the following international sports governing bodies were examined, both in 1995 and in 1999: AIBA, FIBA, FIBT, FIC, FIE, FIFA, FIG, FIH, FILA, FINA, FIS, FISA, FITA, FIVB, IAAF, IBA, IBF, IIHF, IJF, ISU, ITF, ITTF, ITU, IWF, UCI, UIPM, UIT, WCF, and WTF.

COMPARATIVE ANALYSIS

The definition of doping

As has been stated frequently over the past years by Mr Gay, legal counsel for the International Amateur Athletic Federation (IAAF), procedures in doping cases can, and almost certainly will, be lost if sports governing bodies employ defective constitutions with regard to doping.[21] These defective constitutions very often start with a faulty, contradictory or weak definition of doping.

Definitions viewed as problematic tend to include the following statements as key elements:

- a description of banned substances as 'substances which could have the effect of improving artificially a competitor's mental or physical performance';
- banning substances when used 'with the intention to enhance performance';
- the simple and unspecified application of the word 'use'; and
- the general use of the word 'competitor' or the phrase 'in competition'.[22]

These vague generalities and non-specific terms, or worse, a combination of them, contained within the definition of doping, almost certainly create an impossible burden of proof for sports governing bodies in a doping case. At least one IF recently found itself losing a case as the direct result of an indefensible definition of 'doping' in its anti-doping rules and regulations.[23] Other IFs have faced similar challenges concerning the definition of doping employed.[24]

In view of the consequences caused by weak and vague definitions of 'doping', Mr Gay advised sports governing bodies in 1993 to make the offence of doping an offence of strict liability, that is, an offence not dependent upon

---

21 Gay, M, 'The legal context', workshop 1 in Sports Council, *Conference Proceedings: 4th Permanent World Conference on Anti-Doping in Sport*, London, 5–8 September 1993.

22 *Ibid.*

23 *USA Shooting and Quigley v Union Internationale de Tir* CAS 94/129.

24 See, eg, *Haga v Fédération Internationale de Motocyclisme* CAS 2000/A/281. One should realise that, with the ascent of the strict liability approach in doping cases, the possibility for an athlete who is accused of having committed a doping offence raising a defence of moral innocence is significantly lessened. This will almost certainly lead to an increased scrutiny of the separate elements of the applicable definition of doping, as well other, more formal defences, such as the chain of custody and the laboratory analysis.

proof of intent.[25] Surprisingly, the 1994 Lausanne decision did not consider the 'definition of doping' an item for harmonisation. Since the IOC neglected to issue a unified and approved definition of 'doping' in 1995, it was decided for the purpose of the 1995 study to use the strict liability definition of the IAAF as basis for the analysis.[26] In order to maintain consistency, this approach has been continued in this review. The IAAF's current definition of 'doping' reads as follows:

The offence of doping takes place when either:

- a prohibited substance is found to be present within the athlete's body tissue or fluids; or

- an athlete uses or takes advantage of a prohibited technique; or

- an athlete admits having used or taken advantage of a prohibited substance or prohibited technique.

Of the 29 IFs studied in 1995, only one adopted the approach advocated. Not surprisingly, this governing body turned out to be the IAAF. The anti-doping rules and regulations of all other IFs applied definitions of 'doping' which, to some extent, should be viewed as indefensible, weak, vague or contradictory. Surprisingly, that situation hardly appears to have changed. Currently, only seven of the 29 IFs examined employ a strict liability definition.

The list of banned classes and methods of doping

Since its introduction in 1968, the IOC's list of prohibited classes of substances and prohibited methods has been regarded by most sports governing bodies as the reference source for compiling the applicable doping list for their own sport.[27] Over the last decades, the composition of the IOC's list has changed tremendously, however. Not only have new pharmacological classes of prohibited substances and methods been added, pharmacological classes of

---

25 *Op cit*, Gay, fn 21, pp 5–6.

26 IAAF, *Handbook 2000–2001*, r 55, p 81. The IOC's current Olympic Movement Anti-Doping Code, however, does apply a strict liability approach of some sort (Art 2, p 6). See, also, Soek, J and Vrijman, EN, 'De Olympic Movement Anti-Doping Code: de moed van de herder' (2000) 13 Sportzaken 76.

27 Even the list of prohibited classes of substances and prohibited methods of the Council of Europe's Anti-Doping Convention has been based on the doping list of the IOC. See *Explanatory Report on the Anti-Doping Convention*, 1990, Strasbourg: Council of Europe, p 13.

prohibited substances which originally were banned completely may now be used under certain circumstances or have even had their ban lifted altogether.[28]

Given the claim that most IFs have adopted the IOC's doping list and its selection at the Lausanne meeting as a key topic of harmonisation, the result of the 1995 analysis was surprising. Of the 29 IFs reviewed, only 21 had adopted the then current IOC list of classes of prohibited substances and methods. Five of these IFs had adopted an older version of the then current IOC doping list. Seven IFs appeared to have adopted a completely different list of prohibited classes of substances and methods from that of the IOC.

Currently, 28 of the 29 IFs studied apply the IOC's list of prohibited classes of substances and methods. One IF, however, does not do so.

The necessity for a continuing and timely update of the applicable doping list is clear. The use or adoption of an outdated IOC list of prohibited classes of substances and methods by a sport's governing body claiming to employ the current IOC doping list most certainly will cause problems as result of the apparent differences between both doping lists. For example, an athlete might test positive for a substance which is currently banned by the IOC but which is not part of (the version of) the IOC doping list applied by that IF.[29] Secondly, an athlete might test positive for a substance which is banned by the relevant IF on the basis of the IOC doping list it uses but which is not part of the *current* IOC doping list. Clearly, the decision of all sports governing bodies in Lausanne in 1994 to adopt the most current IOC doping list has finally provided sufficient impetus for harmonisation. However, it should be noted that it took these IFs almost five years to achieve an almost 100% degree of harmonisation on a limited technical issue, such as the applicable list of prohibited classes of substances and methods. Given the requirement for a continuing and timely update of the applicable doping list, the question remains of whether or not the current degree of harmonisation concerning this issue can be maintained.

---

28 The so called 'beta blockers' were originally banned by the IOC as belonging to category 1 'doping classes' but were moved to category 3, 'classes of drugs subject to certain restrictions', in 1993. The substance codeine, belonging to the banned pharmacological class of narcotic analgesics, had been banned by the IOC until 1993, when the IOC Medical Commission suddenly decided to remove this specific substance from its doping list altogether. See letter of the IOC Medical Commission, 18 March 1993.

29 As was the case with Spanish cyclist Pedro Delgado, who tested positive for probenecid, a masking agent, while wearing the yellow jersey during the 1988 Tour de France. Probenecid was explicitly mentioned on the IOC doping list as a prohibited method, but not so on the doping list of the UCI. As a result of this discrepancy, Delgado could not be suspended and subsequently went on to win the 1988 Tour de France.

Timing of doping controls

Until the positive test result of the Canadian sprinter, Ben Johnson, at the 1988 Seoul Summer Olympics, the majority of doping controls were conducted at competitions. As early as 1974 and 1975, individual members of the IOC Medical Commission warned that testing for anabolic steroids at the time of competition was a virtual waste of time in terms of providing an effective deterrent for their use during training periods.[30] The results of the official inquiry by the Canadian Government provided clear proof for this point of view.[31] Since then, doping controls during training, so called out-of-competition doping controls, have been introduced and constitute, according to experts, an essential component of the anti-doping rules and regulations of sports governing bodies. Not surprisingly, the ability of governing bodies to conduct out-of-competition doping controls was selected as an item for harmonisation.

In 1995, only 12 out of the 29 IFs studied had adopted provisions allowing them to conduct out-of-competition doping controls. On the basis of their current anti-doping rules and regulations, 19 IFs are able to conduct out-of-competition doping controls. Ten IFs are not, and are thus unable to provide what generally is being considered an effective deterrent regarding the use of anabolic agents. In addition, if the definition of 'doping' would be analysed specifically with regard to the use of the word 'competitor' or the phrase 'in competition', four of the 29 IFs mentioned employ a questionable and possibly defective definition.

Laboratories used

In order to ensure the quality and reliability of the results of the analysis of urine samples collected during doping controls, the IOC Medical Commission informed all NOCs in 1985 of its decision to establish 'recognised laboratories capable of screening for drugs which might be misused in sport'.[32] In 1988, the IOC Medical Commission produced its 'Requirements for accreditation and good laboratory practice'.[33] Even though the IOC accreditation procedure has been criticised,[34] it continues to function as a method for quality assurance

---

30 Armstrong, R, 'Anti-doping procedures and legal consequences: medical and ethical factors and conflicts of interest', session 4 in *op cit*, IAF, fn 8, p 63.

31 Dubin, C, *Commission of Inquiry into the Use of Drugs and Banned Practices Intended to Increase Athletic Performance*, 1990, Ottawa: Canadian Government Publishing Centre, pp 394–97.

32 Letter from the IOC Medical Commission to NOCs, 29 March 1985.

33 IOC, *The International Olympic Charter Against Doping in Sport*, 1990, Lausanne: IOC, Annex 1.

34 *Ibid*, Dubin, pp 402–11.

for all sports governing bodies, as well as national governments. The 1994 Lausanne decision, as well as the subsequent 1995 IOC Medical Code and the 2000 Olympic Movement Anti-Doping Code, each confirmed the exclusive use of IOC accredited laboratories for doping control purposes.[35]

Analysis of the anti-doping rules and regulations reveals that 22 of the 29 IFs studied employ IOC accredited laboratories for doping control purposes. Seven IFs apparently do not. However, experience has shown that, even when an explicit obligation to this effect has been omitted from their anti-doping rules and regulations, IFs still tend to employ IOC accredited doping control laboratories.

Some of the IFs studied provide in their anti-doping rules and regulations for alternatives when circumstances prevent the use of an IOC accredited laboratory, or appear to employ their own system of accreditation or approval. In practice, however, the use of IOC accredited laboratories for doping control purposes generally seems to be the rule. Given the development of a new and objective standard for the IOC accredited laboratories through the so called ISO 25 standard and the potential widespread introduction of blood sampling, new harmonised analysis procedures will become even more necessary.

Sanctions

In case of a doping infraction, the IOC currently recommends the following sanctions:[36]

---

35 The use of IOC accredited doping control laboratories has been made even more attractive, as they have been awarded a most peculiar status as 'indisputable expert witnesses' in doping cases by the IOC. See, also, *op cit*, Soek and Vrijman, fn 26, pp 80–81.

36 For the purposes of this review, the sanctioning guidelines of the IOC applicable at the time of the 1995 study are being applied here as well! These guidelines were contained within the following document: letter from the IOC Medical Commission to the IFs, NOCs, NOC Medical Liaison Officers, 17 March 1988. As can be deduced from the relevant provisions cited below, the original sanctioning instruction from the IOC hardly differs from the later sanctioning recommendations contained within the IOC MC and the Olympic Movement Anti-Doping Code. The IOC MC contained the following recommendation on sanctions for doping infractions:

'The penalty for a first time infraction by a competitor shall be disqualification, if the infraction occurred during a competition, plus:

(1) except in cases covered by paragraph (2) of this Article, a suspension from all competition for a period of two years from the later of the date of the positive results and the date on which any appeal from a decision thereon be finally determined; and

(2) in cases of a positive result for ephedrine, phenylpropanolamine, pseudoephedrine, caffeine, strychnine and related compounds, a maximum suspension of three months.'

See *Medical Code and Explanatory Document*, 1995, Lausanne: IOC, Art 3, p 20.

(1) anabolic steroids, amphetamine-related and other stimulants, caffeine, diuretics, beta blockers, narcotic analgesics and designer drugs:

- two years in case of a first offence;
- life ban in case of a second offence.

(2) ephedrine, phenylpropanolamine, codeine (when administered orally as a cough suppressant or painkiller in association with decongestants and/or anti-histamines):

- a maximum of three months in case of a first offence;
- two years in case of a second offence;
- life ban in case of a third offence.

---

36 [contd] 'The penalty for a second infraction by a competitor pursuant to the IOC Medical Code shall be disqualification, if the infraction occurred during a competition, plus, in cases referred to in paragraph (1) of Article 3, a lifetime suspension from all competition and accreditation, in any capacity, at Olympic Competitions and in cases referred to in paragraph (2) of Article 3, suspension for two years and, for any subsequent infraction, a life ban.'

See *Medical Code and Explanatory Document*, 1995, Lausanne: IOC, Art 4, p 21.

The Olympic Movement Anti-Doping Code contains the following provisions concerning sanctions for doping infractions:

'In case of doping, the penalties for a first time offence are as follows:

(a) If the Prohibited Substance used is ephedrine, phenylpropanolamine, pseudoephedrine, caffeine, strychnine or related substances:

   (i)   a warning;
   (ii) a ban on participation in one or several sports competitions in any capacity whatsoever;
   (iii) a fine up to US$ 100,000;
   (iv) suspension from any competition for a period of one to six months.

(b) If the Prohibited Substance used is one other than those referred to in paragraph (a) above:

   (i)   a ban on participation in one or several sports competitions in any capacity whatsoever;
   (ii) a fine up to US$100,000;
   (iii) suspension from any competition for a minimum period of two years. However, based on specific, exceptional circumstances to be evaluated in the first instance by the competent IF bodies, there may be a provision for a possible modification of the two-year sanction ...'

See *Olympic Movement Anti-Doping Code*, 28 May 2000, Lausanne: IOC, Art 3, para 1(a) and (b), p 6.

'(c) If the Prohibited Substance used is one other than those referred to in paragraph (a) above or if it is a repeat offence (a repeat offence being constituted by a further case of doping perpetrated within a period of ten years after the preceding sanction, whatever form it took and whatever the reason for it, became final):

   (i)   a life ban on participation in any sport event in any capacity whatsoever;
   (ii) a fine up to US$100,000;
   (iii) suspension (between four years and life) from all sports competitions.'

See *Olympic Movement Anti-Doping Code*, 28 May 2000, Lausanne: IOC, Art 3, para 2(b), p 7.

In the aftermath of the Ben Johnson case, many sports governing bodies decided to increase their penalties for doping infractions as a further deterrent. Instead of the suggested two year ban for a first offence involving anabolic steroids, a four year ban, and in one case a life ban, was adopted.[37] This trend, however, appears to have been reversed once again, resulting in a decrease of the applicable penalties for doping infractions and/or the application of these sanctions as maximum sanctions.

While there appears to be no statistical proof of the deterrent effect on the drug use patterns of athletes, increased penalties, however, have succeeded in stimulating athletes, suspected of having committed a doping offence, to start any variety of legal procedures, possibly allowing them to compete again. In case of a four year ban, athletes appear to suffer no illusion about their ability to return to competition after having been convicted for a doping offence.[38]

The 1994 Lausanne decision used the IOC recommended sanctions as a basis for harmonisation in this regard. A careful analysis revealed that, in 1995, only nine of the 29 IFs applied the IOC recommended sanctions, while five IFs did not seem to apply any sanctions at all in case of a doping infraction. The remaining 15 IFs incorporated altogether different sanctions within their anti-doping rules and regulations. Currently, 15 of the 29 IFs examined apply the IOC-recommended sanctions, while nine do not do so. Five IFs still do not seem to apply any sanctions in doping cases at all.[39]

It is important to note that the IOC recommended sanctions are related to the IOC's list of prohibited classes of substances and methods. In the past, comparison of the then current IOC doping list with the one then connected to the IOC recommended sanctions revealed a serious lack of uniformity within the applicable rules and regulations themselves. Such a lack of conformity could be problematic. Certain pharmacological classes of banned substances – even though part of the then current IOC doping list – were not explicitly mentioned in relation to the IOC recommended sanctions. This was, for instance, the case with the banned class of peptide hormones, as well as the so called beta blockers.

---

37 In 1991, the IAAF increased the period of ineligibility for a first offence involving anabolic steroids from two to four years. After a decision by the regional Appeal Court in Munich, Germany, declaring the three year suspension of Katrin Krabbe invalid because a suspension of 'more than two years contravenes the constitutional principle of proportionality', the IAAF decided to decrease the period of ineligibility for a first offence involving anabolic steroids from four to two years.

38 *Op cit*, Gay, fn 21, pp 1–2.

39 At least when studying the anti-doping rules and regulations of these IFs. Sanctions for doping infractions, however, might possibly be contained in their disciplinary rules and regulations.

The recognition of sanctions

Preventing athletes banned for a doping infraction in one sport from competing in another appears to be the main reason for including a provision in its anti-doping rules and regulations allowing sports governing bodies to recognise sanctions imposed by other sports governing bodies. Whether or not such a provision would in fact have the desired effect remains to be seen. The application of a sanction normally represents the final step of a sometimes very complicated disciplinary procedure. Not only is an athlete suspected of having committed a doping offence entitled to the full and correct application of the relevant procedure(s) and the exercise of his legal rights, the sports governing body involved even has the duty to ensure that the athlete's legal rights are an inherent part of its anti-doping rules and regulations and/or disciplinary rules and regulations.[40]

If, for instance, the athlete's right to present his case to, and to be heard by, the relevant tribunal within that sports governing body was neither sufficiently guaranteed within the applicable rules and regulations nor allowed to be exercised, the courts might decide to annul the decision reached and the sanction subsequently imposed. The ability of sports governing bodies to mutually recognise sanctions, therefore, does not seem to depend solely on the implementation of a clause to this effect within their respective anti-doping rules and regulations. Adequate protection of the accused athlete's rights and the quality of the disciplinary procedure also play an important part in the decision whether or not to recognise sanctions of another sports governing body for doping infractions.

In 1995, only four of the 29 IFs studied included a provision within their anti-doping rules and regulations allowing them to recognise sanctions imposed by other sports governing bodies. In 1999, the number of IFs capable of recognising a sanction imposed by another sports governing body appears to have risen to 10.

The right to a hearing

The right to a hearing has been universally recognised as a fundamental principle of procedural fairness and has been codified in international treaties, as well as in national constitutions and legislation.[41] The right to a hearing not only requires that a hearing takes place, but also that it addresses the quality

---

40 See, eg, IOC, 'Rights and responsibilities of sports organisations, athletes and their entourage', in *op cit*, IOC, Annex 6, para 1.7.

41 Universal Declaration of Human Rights 1948, Art 10; International Covenant on Civil and Political Rights 1966, Art 14; European Convention for the Protection of Human Rights and Fundamental Freedoms 1950, Art 6.

of that right, that is, that the hearing be a fair one. The absence of this particular right has been qualified as the third most common weakness in constitutions regulating anti-doping matters.[42]

Judging from the preceding discussion, the right to a hearing should be viewed as a key element of the applicable disciplinary procedures within a sports governing body when dealing with doping infractions. Even if a particular sports governing body has created the opportunity to recognise sanctions imposed by other sports governing bodies, the absence of the right to a hearing in the proceedings of that other sports governing body could prevent the sanctions from being recognised and imposed.

In 1995, only 14 of the 29 IFs studied did include the right to a hearing in their respective anti-doping rules and regulations. Currently, 21 out of the 29 IFs include the right to a hearing in their respective anti-doping rules and regulations.

Waiver of minor procedural mistakes

Athletes accused of having committed a doping infraction often attempt to base their defence on alleged defects in the doping control procedure.[43] In 1988, this kind of legal challenge was put to the test in the *Gasser* case.[44] Both the IAAF Arbitration Panel and the English High Court decided that the minor breaches or defects in the doping control procedure referred to by Mrs Gasser were not sufficient to overturn a positive finding.

The amount of compliance required of an international sports governing body with regard to its anti-doping rules and regulations has to be substantial and the criterion for judgment in this matter is the question of whether or not the defect in the procedure rendered the result of the test unreliable or unfair to the athlete. Depending on the particular facts of a case and the exact wording of the relevant anti-doping rules and regulations, the judgment in the *Gasser* case would still seem, however, to leave some room for the athlete's defence of strict compliance.

In order to avoid future litigation in this regard, the IAAF introduced the following clause within its anti-doping rules and regulations, providing that:

A departure, or departures from the guidelines set out in the 'Procedural Guidelines for Doping Control' shall not invalidate the finding of a prohibited substance unless this departure was such as to cast reasonable doubt on the reliability of such finding.[45]

---

42 *Op cit*, Gay, fn 21, p 187.
43 Gay, M, in *op cit*, IAF, fn 8, session 4, p 66.
44 *Gasser v Stinson* (1988) unreported, 15 June.
45 IAAF, *Handbook 1992–1993*, 1992, London: IAAF, rr 55, 70.

Although not considered an issue for harmonisation in the 1994 Lausanne decision, procedural mistakes do occur and most often give rise to legal challenges, causing a variety of problems for the sports governing bodies involved. It should be clear that a waiver could minimise legal challenges based upon minor or trifling breaches of the anti-doping rules and regulations concerned. Furthermore, the inclusion of such a waiver could also prevent the results of a doping control from being nullified simply because of the wording used in a governing body's anti-doping rules and regulations, which might appear to be inflexible and to leave absolutely no room to allow for a possible departure, regardless of whether or not that departure would have an effect on the reliability of that test result.[46]

In 1995, only five of the 29 IFs studied included a provision within their respective anti-doping rules and regulations, allowing them to 'ignore' minor procedural mistakes when considering the results of doping controls conducted. In 1999, 10 IFs appeared to be able to do so.

The Court of Arbitration for Sport

According to Professor Houlihan, a crucial aspect of the harmonisation process today is the management of overlapping jurisdictions of the various organisations involved in anti-doping.[47] 'Superficially, the problem of overlapping jurisdictions can easily be solved through a combination of greater courtesy by agencies informing others of their intentions and actions and the fostering of a higher level of mutual confidence,' he says.[48] He admits, however, that raising the level of mutual confidence is likely to be problematic, as it may not only require sports governing bodies to trust the anti-doping work of other organisations, but require them to hand over some of their authority concerning the doping issue as well.[49]

In order to be able to trust the test results obtained by other sports governing bodies or anti-doping agencies, the correct determination, interpretation and application of applicable anti-doping rules and regulations – including, most of all, the sanctioning decisions – a judicial body is required, empowered, to reach a final decision in these matters. Such an organisation would, first and foremost, contribute greatly to the development of relevant jurisprudence in doping matters in many different sports, thus

---

46 With regard to the waiver of minor procedural mistakes, Mr Gay has remarked that it is 'one which is not commonly found in the constitutions of governing bodies conducting doping control, but is one which I think every careful drafted constitution should contain'. See *op cit*, Gay, fn 21, p 188.

47 *Op cit*, Houlihan, fn 3, pp 181–83.

48 *Op cit*, Houlihan, fn 3, pp 181–83.

49 *Op cit*, Houlihan, fn 3, pp 181–83.

allowing general principles of law to be established with regard to the manner in which doping cases are to be conducted globally. It would also contribute greatly to a harmonised sanctioning process by applying common criteria in similar matters, albeit in different sports. The establishment of the CAS in Lausanne, Switzerland, not only as just one more arbitration body, but especially as the final appellate body for sports governing bodies in doping matters, should be regarded in this context. If such an organisation is to be successful as the final appellate body in international sports, it needs widespread support, as well as acceptance in that capacity. In 1997, however, the IAAF made it clear that it did not intend to recognise the CAS as superior to its own arbitration panel. In order to ascertain to what extent the CAS has been accepted as sport's final appellate body, particularly in doping matters, the issue was included in this review as well.

While data pertaining to this issue were not a part of the 1995 study, the 1999 anti-doping rules and regulations of the 29 IFs examined show that 11 IFs have included provisions within their anti-doping rules and regulations establishing the CAS as their final appellate body in doping matters. Eighteen IFs do not do so.

Blood sampling

As a result of the IOC's announcement on 1 August 2000 that the long awaited erythropoietin (EPO) test would finally be implemented at the Sydney 2000 Summer Olympic Games in Australia, the issue of blood sampling suddenly changed from a potential future issue for harmonisation to one that was in need of instant attention. Now that a scientifically approved method of testing blood for the banned substance EPO had been developed and approved for implementation, relevant legal issues related to the introduction of blood sampling need to be addressed urgently in order to be able to conduct such testing.

Blood sampling has been used experimentally over the past 10 years by a number of different IFs, such as the Fédération Internationale du Ski (FIS), the Union Cycliste Internationale (UCI) and the IAAF. Blood sampling was conducted for the first time in 1994 at the Lillehammer Winter Olympic Games, when the IOC had granted the FIS permission to carry out 55 of such tests. While all of the aforementioned IFs introduced such testing in order to be able to detect doping with EPO, the criteria applied to detect such doping differed surprisingly. While the UCI blood test screens for manipulation of the cyclist's blood by determining whether or not the rider's haemoglobin and haematocrit levels are significantly elevated, the FIS only screens the skier's blood for elevated levels of haemoglobin. The tests conducted by the IAAF were largely intended to gain experience with blood sampling and to identify relevant issues which would need to be addressed if blood sampling would become prevalent.

It is clear that, because blood sampling requires an invasive technique to obtain a sample – as opposed to urine sampling, a wide range of potential legal problems will present themselves for consideration.[50] The premier issue to be considered, however, is whether or not the applicable anti-doping rules and regulations of IFs would allow such tests to be conducted in the first place. In order to ensure that it would indeed be able to conduct blood sampling at the Sydney 2000 Summer Olympic Games, the IOC introduced, shortly before the commencement of these Games, a doping control protocol specifying the possibility that blood samples could be obtained from athletes participating at Sydney 2000. While the IOC sought to obtain the athletes' consent by having all those who intended to participate sign an entry form, specifying, among other issues, their agreement to be tested in accordance with the aforementioned doping control protocol, and thus create the required legal basis for conducting blood sampling at the 2000 Olympic Games, almost all of the Summer Olympic IFs did not.

Of the 29 IFs examined, only five possess the necessary provisions allowing them to conduct blood sampling in order to determine whether or not a doping offence has been committed. This means that an athlete testing positive at the Sydney 2000 Summer Olympic Games as the result of blood sampling can be disqualified from the competition on the basis of the applicable IOC Olympic Movement Anti-Doping Code, but subsequently cannot be suspended from competition if the relevant IF's rules and regulations do not consider test results obtained through the analysis of the athlete's blood samples.

CONCLUSIONS

Based on the evidence presented, the results of both Lausanne decisions have, given their potential for success, been disappointing.[51] International

---

50 Issues to be considered range from liability for injuries received or illness contracted as a result of the blood sampling conducted, to the requirements of national health legislation concerning the collection, storage and transportation of blood samples, to issues concerning medical confidentiality, ownership of the blood sample and constitutional issues. It has been precisely for this reason that the author, as representative of The Netherlands at the Council of Europe's Monitoring Group, argued that blood testing should only be introduced when it could be established more clearly that the advantages of the method outweighed the additional cost and difficulties in replacing the well established system of doping control based on urine analysis. See *op cit*, Houlihan, fn 3, pp 178–79; see, also, Vrijman, EN, *Blood Sampling and Doping Control*, 1995, Rotterdam: NeCeDo.

51 The current state of affairs has been aptly described as a period of 'quasi harmonisation'.

federations are still not consistent and fail to adapt their anti-doping rules and regulations to evolving anti-doping policies, new jurisprudence and developments concerning the availability of new substances, methods, detection methods and doping control material. While progress has indeed been made concerning harmonisation issues of a technical nature,[52] other issues have failed to show any evidence of progress being made.[53] As stated by Professor Houlihan:

> Put starkly, it may well be possible to perfect a series of effective tests for the current crop of new drugs, it may also be possible to establish publicly verifiable quality standards for the sampling and analysis process, and it may be possible to reach consensus on a scale of penalties for particular doping infractions, but these achievements will count for little if there is not a harmonisation of commitment to tackle the problem of drug abuse by athletes. In other words, alongside the technical questions is a parallel set of questions concerning the values, beliefs and attitudes, necessary to ensure the maintenance of momentum for implementation.[54]

Given the IOC's pre-eminence with regard to the issue of doping, as well as the fact that the Lausanne decision uses the IOC's anti-doping rules and regulations as the basis for harmonisation, it is suggested that a number of new initiatives be introduced to further the harmonisation process with regard to both technical, as well as policy issues. The initiatives are detailed as follows:

- the IOC organise, on a regular basis, expert meetings to discuss current developments in anti-doping and their significance for anti-doping rules and regulations of sports governing bodies. Such a mechanism would allow, within a certain time span, for an update of all the anti-doping rules and regulations of all IFs and could provide the necessary external stimulus for continued efforts at harmonisation;

- the IOC announce changes concerning its anti-doping rules and regulations, in particular those concerning the IOC doping list, on pre-established dates. Establishing a pre-determined and regular date for revisions to the anti-doping rules and regulations would allow IFs time to

---

52 Such issues include the acceptance of the IOC's list of prohibited substances and methods; the sampling procedures; the use of IOC accredited doping control laboratories; the use of the IOC requirements for good laboratory practice; and the development of an ISO benchmark (ISO 25) for the verification of quality standards in doping control.

53 This would include such issues as the role of CAS, sanctions, recognition and other, more policy-oriented issues.

54 *Op cit*, Houlihan, fn 3, p 172.

plan and prepare for the impact that changes might have on their respective rules and regulations;[55]

• introduce a periodical evaluation of the harmonisation process similar to that developed in this chapter.

By evaluating any progress or structural changes in the ways and means of harmonisation, the process will be viewed less as crisis management and more as part of a necessary consequence of changes in science, technology, policy and jurisprudence. In addition, the periodic evaluation of current efforts will allow for the ongoing and continued exchange of ideas and methods.

In closing, the harmonisation of anti-doping rules and regulations of sports governing bodies is an important element in the public perception of the existing system of doping controls. The public acceptance of such a system relies, to a large extent, on the belief that it is effective and just. If, however, due to a lack of harmonisation, athletes in different sports are being treated differently and the applicable anti-doping rules and regulations appear unclear, outdated, biased, confusing and contradictory, faith in the ability of the governing bodies honestly, fairly and efficiently to deal with the doping problem will be lost. Given the dynamic relationship between athletes, fans and sport, it is critical that sports governing bodies adhere to the principles of just and fair governance and that such governance be seen as timely, clear and equitable.

---

55 To allow for a certain flexibility in this regard, an emergency procedure, as employed by the Council of Europe's Monitoring Group, for adjusting the Anti-Doping Convention's list of prohibited classes of substances and methods should be implemented by the IOC as well.

CHAPTER 11

THE INTERNATIONAL OLYMPIC COMMITTEE, TRANSNATIONAL DOPING POLICY AND GLOBALISATION

Simon Boyes

The regulation and control of drugs and doping practices is the most high profile and highly sensitive issue facing international sport at the present time. Recent developments include disputes regarding a spate of nandrolone-related 'offences' committed by athletes as well as controversy surrounding the introduction of blood and urine testing for the substance known as EPO (erythropoietin), which commenced at the Sydney Summer Olympic Games in 2000.

The view which is very often adopted by those bodies that have assumed responsibility for the governance and regulation of doping practices is that doping, however defined, is intrinsically 'bad' and should be eradicated by whatever means possible. The purpose of this article is to step back from the moral and ethical arguments that often rage around the regulation of doping and to consider the issue in a broader, global canvas. It is hoped that this will allow consideration of the more practical implications and limitations of attempting to regulate doping practices at an international level. The application of abstract models of globalisation and governance will demonstrate some of the fundamental problems surrounding global doping regulation. In order that these models can be properly applied, it is first necessary that the context and structure of the international regulation of doping in sport is established.

THE DEVELOPMENT OF INTERNATIONAL DOPING POLICY

There is little doubt that the world's dominant sporting organisation is the International Olympic Committee (IOC). As the driving force of the Olympic movement, and having effective control over the Olympic Games, the IOC is in an extremely strong position to dominate and control the regulation of sport in any number of regards. Indeed, the IOC has, in some quarters, come to be considered as being on a par with a specialised body of the United Nations.[1] Though the IOC is active across a broad spectrum of sporting activity, it is most noticeably in the field of anti-doping that the IOC has been the vanguard of regulation and control.

---

1   Nafziger, JAR, *International Sports Law*, 1988, New York: Transnational, p 3.

The development of an anti-doping policy is a relatively recent occurrence; significant developments first began in the 1960s and have since snowballed in terms of both scope and complexity. The IOC's Medical Commission was created at the Committee's session in Athens in 1961, initially as a result of growing concerns over the use of amphetamines in sport. It was not until the IOC's 1967 session in Tehran that the list of banned substances and practices was set out and applied for the first time at both the Winter and Summer Olympic Games of 1968, in Grenoble and Mexico City respectively.

At the session of 1967, the basic principles underlying the IOC's Medical Code was set out by the newly appointed Chairman of the Medical Commission, Prince Alexandre de Merode of Belgium:

- the protection of athletes' health;
- the defence of sports ethics; and
- equality for all participants at the moment of competition.

Despite being the subject of much criticism,[2] these principles have been maintained as those underlying the now much expanded controls that are placed upon athletes as regards the substances that they may ingest or practices in which they may indulge. It is not intended that these underlying principles be dissected and their moral and ethical correctness or otherwise be assessed. Instead, it is these principles that will be considered against the background of increasing globalisation.

GLOBALISATION AND WORLDWIDE ANTI-DOPING POLICY

Any stance adopted by the IOC would be inconsequential and unworthy of examination and comment if it did not have an impact across both a broad range of different sports and across those Nation States wishing to involve themselves to any great extent in international sporting competition. As the body that regulates the Olympic Games, the IOC is in a position of considerable power. Involvement in Olympic competition has the potential to raise the profile of any particular sport. Any such elevation is often associated with a growth in popularity, both in terms of participation and spectator interest. This, in turn, expands commercial and economic possibilities for those sports. Inclusion in the Olympic Games appears to confer a kind of

---

2   See, amongst many others, Frost, NC, 'Ethical and social issues in anti-doping strategies in sport', and Schneider, AJ and Butcher, RB, 'The mesalliance of the Olympic ideal and doping: why they married, and why they should divorce', both in Landry, F, Landry, N and Yerles, M (eds), *Sports ... The Third Millennium,* 1990, Sainte-Foy: Université Laval.

kudos and legitimacy upon a given sport. This has a number of implications. First, federations governing individual sports are particularly keen to have their events included in the Games. This clamour to be involved gives the IOC, as the ultimate authority on sports' inclusion in the Games, a great deal of power and influence over individual sports federations and, to some extent, an indirect control of the manner of sports regulation. Inevitably, this control extends to the regulation of anti-doping policy, though the IOC would argue otherwise:

> Other than matters for which it has a clear constitutional responsibility, the IOC has no power to impose its will on any of the autonomous organisations within the Olympic Movement. There is a widespread misconception that the IOC is in a position to control organisations such as [International Federations] and [National Olympic Committees]. It is not in such a position. The IOC depends on developing a consensus amongst them and using its moral suasion to bring about courses of conduct which it considers beneficial to the Olympic Movement and the development of sport.[3]

It is suggested that the development of a 'consensus' may be a relatively simple target for the IOC to achieve, when the sanction for failing to adhere to it could be the exclusion of a particular sport from the Olympic Games, accompanied by a reduction in participation and public interest and the resultant economic disadvantages. Rugby Union provides a recent example of this, where the economic and development benefits for the sport have been cited by the International Rugby Board as a key reason to seek acceptance as an Olympic sport. It appears that only two International Federations (IFs) are in a powerful enough position to be able to operate with a certain degree of autonomy. The Fédération Internationale de Football Association (FIFA)[4] and the International Amateur Athletics Federation (IAAF) appear to be able to act, at least to a certain extent, independently of the will of the IOC. However, other federations are largely subservient to the will of the IOC, despite any protestations to the contrary. This is specifically endorsed with particular reference to the regulation of doping by Art 5 of the IOC's Medical Code:

> It is a condition for recognition of any international federation and any national Olympic committee that its statutes incorporate the IOC Medical Code by express reference and that its provisions apply, *mutatis mutandis*, to all persons and competitions under their jurisdiction.

Clearly, the IOC are seeking, and succeeding in, the exertion of an influence, even control, over IFs and National Olympic Committees (NOCs) that extends beyond their involvement in the Olympic Games, as the application of the

---

3   IOC Policy Commitment, submission to the International Summit on Drugs in Sport, Sydney, Australia, 14–17 November 1999; available at www.nodoping.org/drug_summit/drug_summit_policy_commit.pdf.

4   'FIFA red card for Olympic move on drugs' (1999) *The Daily Telegraph*, 5 February.

Medical Code is purportedly required to be applied in *all* competitions under the jurisdiction of those organisations. The message is clear: abide by the arbitrarily imposed anti-doping rules of the IOC or be excluded from Olympic competition suffering the attendant consequences of reduced exposure and the associated participatory and economic consequences. In effect, the anti-doping rules presented by the IOC are adhesionary to all federations and athletes. Nor is this influence limited to international sports federations or NOCs: the IOC also has considerable influence over national governments. This arises because of the immense significance of sporting competition for individuals and for societies as a whole. Participation and success in international sporting events has come to be perceived as being of immense importance for the stature and standing of Nation States. Readers need only cast their minds back to the considerable effort poured into sports by a number of Eastern European States during the Soviet era. Elsewhere, this importance is most vividly illustrated by the Australian hosts of the 2000 Summer Games, who poured considerable resources into the development of sporting academies with the goal of raising their national profile.

Readers might quite properly question the author as to what exactly is problematic about this situation. In order for sport to have any kind of meaning, it must exist in some kind of stable contextual framework. The rules of the 'game' must be known and applied, otherwise the 'game' is not being played. Organised sport as it is understood today would be impossible without rules and regulations. In addition, the principles underlying the regulation of doping appear *prima facie* admirable and consistent with more mainstream societal norms. Indeed, it might appear strange that the author is questioning these values at all, being a white, middle class academic, sitting in a university in the south east of England. These underlying values of the protection of athlete's health, defence of sports ethics and equality for all participants might very well be perceived as those that ought to be representative of such an individual. Such a perception might well be correct, and therein lies the problem – the history of the development of the Olympic Games and the background to the evolution of the Olympic ideal.

Pierre de Coubertin, the founder of the modern Olympic Games, was influenced to a large extent by the movement towards codification of rules and regulations which had taken place in Britain during the Industrial Revolution.[5] During that period, England had become a society which held values such as discipline, precision and control in high regard. These broader

---

5   Tomlinson, A, 'de Coubertin and the modern Olympics', in Tomlinson, A and Garry, W (eds), *Five Ring Circus: Money Power and Politics at the Olympic Games*, 1984, London and Sydney: Pluto; Guttmann, A, 'The diffusion of sports and the problem of cultural imperialism', in Dunning, EG, Maguire, JA and Pearton, RE (eds), *The Sports Process: A Comparative and Developmental Approach*, 1993, Champaign, Ill: Human Kinetics, p 131; Hill, CR, *Olympic Politics*, 2nd edn, 1996, Manchester: Manchester UP, pp 5–33.

societal values were largely reflected in the codification of the football sports, with the application of strict rules and precise delimitation of games.[6] Codification was also supported by the Church, which saw properly regulated sports as fostering and promoting ideals such as unselfishness, justice and health, which they were keen to encourage.[7]

This period was characterised as one of 'sportisation', linking the codification of sport with a broader societal shift towards the introduction of rules and norms to govern behaviour:

> [R]egulative and reform impulses initially dominated the making of self-consciously modern forms of sporting practice ... the creation of a new, higher, seemingly more civilised form of sporting practice than that of traditional folk games and sports required the rational organisation of spectacle, human physical contests and masculine physicality. But this could only win legitimacy as a cultural project if it could be harmonised with new class needs for labour discipline, education, and the control of public order.[8]

Thus, there was a requirement for institutional foundations to be laid in order to implement these values. These were in the form of rationalised sporting structures and the creation of codified and documented technical and moral regulations and of organisational bureaucracies. This rationalisation, of course, took place in the context of the increasing 'civilisation' taking place in British society as a whole. It was in the mould of these structures that de Coubertin's International Olympic Committee was cast, as indeed were many other international sports federations. It is notable that de Coubertin was a Frenchman and his committee almost exclusively European. The Eurocentric roots of the Games were emphasised in its constituent sports:

> Consciously hellenising, the IOC revived the discus throw and invented the marathon race. Coubertin was not an antiquarian and the Games included numerous events unknown to the ancients – weight lifting, fencing, rowing, and cycling – but the modern additions to the classic contests were clearly European in form.[9]

Though the Olympic Games are widely perceived as being international in their nature, the Games' European roots are not without significance. The motivation behind the hosting of the Games on an international basis was the spread of the Olympic ideal itself.[10] This has been emphasised in the modern era by a continuing desire that the Games be hosted in Asia and amongst developing countries, so the Europeanised ideals of the Games might be proliferated. The IOC has continued to conduct the Games in such a way that,

---

6   Eg, defined playing areas and the delimitation of the length and structure of games.
7   Cashmore, E, *Making Sense of Sport*, 2nd edn, 1996, London: Routledge, p 76.
8   Gruneau, R, 'The critique of sport in modernity: theorising power, culture, and the politics of the body', in *op cit*, Dunning *et al*, fn 5, p 88.
9   *Op cit*, Guttmann, fn 5, p 131.
10 *Op cit*, Guttmann, fn 5, pp 131–32.

even where the sports involved are 'cultural universals', occurring throughout the globe as a constituent part of man's development, it is the Western version of the sport that is represented in the Games.[11] Examples of 'cultural universals' include running, swimming and combat sports. It is significant, then, that the only Olympic sport with exclusively non-Western origins is Judo – even that sport has, to a large extent, been Westernised. Additionally, it should be noted that members of the IOC act in their capacity as a representative of the IOC in their home State, not as a representative of their State to the IOC. Similarly, members are appointed by the IOC itself and *not* the State to which the member is affiliated.

There is nothing inherently problematic in the European roots of the IOC; the majority of competitors in the early Games were drawn from societies that share a Judaeo-Christian cultural heritage and Western liberal notions of fair play and 'sportsmanship'. Indeed, it is inherent, in any paradigm which describes globalisation, that interaction will occur first between actors at a local or regional level before moving to a global plane. The problem arose when the IOC ceased to be the organising committee for a contest involving representatives of a small group of nations sharing similar values. The model that we are now presented with is one where the IOC is *the* regulator of international sport; wielding considerable power over all those involved in Olympic sports.

The danger of this position is that the IOC may be perceived as indulging in a form of cultural imperialism by imposing a Eurocentric version of sport upon the whole World. Guttman suggests that:

> This is not the result of a conspiracy on the part of the IOC. The entire structure of international athletic competition is Western. The federations that control international competition were created in Europe and have simply assumed the norms shared by Europeans and Americans.[12]

It should not be inferred from this that the IOC is solely responsible for this cultural colonisation. Indeed, the roots of this are much deeper:

> The sport of Western industrial societies is frequently initiated in those countries that have adopted the Western model of social and political development and industrialisation ... On the one hand it is regarded as being modern and, on the other, since it was originally practised by the colonial masters, as exclusive ... The import of European sport often entails the destruction of a traditional games culture.[13]

The adoption of Western forms of particular sports is largely unimportant – as noted previously, the need for a commonality of understanding as to the rules and conduct of a particular sport are unquestionable if the sport is to have any

---

11 *Op cit*, Guttmann, fn 5, p 133.
12 *Op cit*, Guttmann, fn 5.
13 *Op cit*, Guttmann, fn 5, p 144.

competitive meaning. This imposition of European norms upon disparate cultures becomes problematic when they impinge upon important indigenous standards. The regulation of doping practices is an instance of where this has occurred. This has arisen most recently in the run up to the Sydney Games in relation to the IOC's decision to adopt a new test to detect the use of EPO by athletes participating in the Olympics. The test for EPO involves athletes supplying both urine and blood samples for analysis. The giving of blood for these purposes has been met with vociferous objection by Muslim nations and religious groups. Nevertheless, the head of the IOC's Medical Commission, Prince Alexandre de Merode, has been reported as saying that refusal to provide samples on the basis of religion would lead to an athlete's expulsion from the Games:

> No one is forced to compete ... We have our rules and it is also in the constitution that they must take the test. If they don't they are out.[14]

This points to a clear seizure of sport and the imposition of the Western version upon all those who wish to compete. As noted elsewhere, this is not necessarily desirable:

> It is impossible to organise sport according to its inherent principles. On the contrary, sport must correspond to the social conditions and functions of the specific spheres of existence to which it is affiliated.[15]

Viewed in this way, the manner in which the regulation of doping in sport has developed has a certain synergy with particular views of the globalisation process more generally. The Neo-Marxist account of globalisation conceives of every actor in the global system as acting in order to maintain the global capitalist order, that the system is a reflection of the dominant class interests being supported, each actor in the system is capable of acting independently, but is highly constrained by the need to ensure the long term welfare of the international capitalist system.[16] Parallels might well be drawn with the manner in which doping is regulated under the guardianship of the IOC, the message to domestic regulators and international federations being: deal with doping in any way you will, as long as it conforms to, and supports, the IOC Eurocentric approach to the issue.

It has been argued that this has the practical effect of reducing the role of domestic regulators to the role of 'local government', with the role of providing an infrastructure and services to facilitate the operation of the global process.[17] The need for involvement in international sporting competition has the result that domestic regulation is, more often than not,

---

14 'Olympic blood tests given go-ahead' (2000) *The Guardian*, 29 August.

15 Heinemann, K, 'Sport in developing countries', in *op cit*, Dunning *et al*, fn 5, p 144.

16 McGrew, A, 'Conceptualizing global politics', in McGrew, A and Lewis, P (eds), *Global Politics*, 1992, Cambridge: Polity, p 21.

17 Hirst, P and Thompson, G, *Globalization in Question: The International Economy and the Possibilities of Governance*, 1996, Oxford: Blackwell, p 176.

brought into line with the global example, rather than face the possibility of exclusion.

In the same way that the processes by which sport is governed, including doping regulation, and have become denationalised, national actors no longer possess absolute power over their own jurisdiction. Decisions taken at an international or supranational level are internalised or take effect at the domestic level without the willing participation of the domestic regulator and decisions taken at a supranational or international level take effect irrespective of the boundaries of national jurisdictions and their core values. This disempowerment of domestic actors inevitably impacts on the individuals existing within a particular jurisdiction. Domestic regulators do not only act in a manner calculated to regulate the activities of their athletes; they also guarantee particular rights and liberties granted to those athletes. Key elements such as accountability, participation, mechanisms of redress and the exercise of other controls based on constitutional or other norms are protected by the State:

> The language of globalisation ... has failed to recognise the manner in which the internationalisation of governance can also exacerbate the 'democratic deficit'. States are not only problem solvers, their policy élite are also strategic actors with interests of, and for, themselves. Collective action problem solving in international relations is couched in terms of effective governance. It is rarely posed as a question of responsible or accountable government, let alone justice.[18]

It is difficult to see exactly how the IOC can maintain its position as the leading authority in *global* sports regulation when it maintains a dogmatically Eurocentric approach to the issue of anti-doping policies as protective of sports ethics.

This problem also manifests itself inversely, in that the IOC's attempts to maintain a global anti-doping strategy are often undermined by the very cultural disparities over which it rides roughshod. Globalisation does not represent all-conquering homogeneity, but also describes the impact of diversity in global systems. Thus, the stated aim of equality for all participants at the moment of competition is likely to be rendered problematic by the impact of disparities arising at a local or regional level. Though the IOC does wield considerable power, where the cultural norms that its regulation infringes are of sufficient import, that attempt at regulation will often be rejected at a local level:

> Much attention has been given to internationalisation's impact on domestic policy and institutions, but the discourses on 'two levelness' point to the reverse process: domestic forces and processes are increasingly penetrating

---

18 Devetak, R and Higgott, R, *Justice Unbound? Globalisation, States and the Transformation of the Social Bond*, Working Paper No 29/99, Centre for the Study of Globalisation and Regionalisation, p 10; available at www.csgr.org.

international politics. A process of *mutual interpenetration* between the domestic and the international is underway. The dual nature of this phenomenon is important. If you focus solely on the first side, you get a picture of domestic forces being subjected to a powerful, actorless process on internationalisation. If you focus on the other side, an element of *empowerment* appears: individuals, political parties, interest groups, etc, can influence events in the outside world, including the politics of institutionalisation.[19]

This is demonstrated to a certain extent by the objection of Muslim nations and organisations to the introduction of mandatory blood testing for EPO. This may only result in the exclusion of those with the objection; alternatively, where the objector possesses sufficient weight, it is often the case that regulations will be amended accordingly. Examples of this can be seen in the field of doping, where the length of bans imposed for infractions of doping regulations have been successfully challenged in law in a number of European countries. This has prompted the length of bans imposed for doping offences to be reduced on a global scale. This serves to emphasise the important role that law plays in influencing global regulation as the manifestation of the cultural and other societal values that exist in a given jurisdiction. As noted elsewhere, regulatory variation across different sports and jurisdictions in relation to anti-doping strategy can often lead to the adoption of a penalty reflecting the lowest common denominator.[20]

It is interesting that the IOC has recognised the need to incorporate flexibility into their doping regulations in order that they can be applied sensibly to individual sports.[21] It appears strange, therefore, that there has been a failure to recognise a need to articulate tolerance towards cultures and societies different from those presently informing the regulation of doping in sport. This may appear questionable when one considers that international agreements aimed at the protection of elements as significant as fundamental human rights habitually include clauses allowing local factors to be considered when defining what is and is not a breach of those rights. The European Convention on Human Rights and Fundamental Freedoms 1950, for example, contains what are known as 'claw back clauses', which allow the local context of a case to be considered. This contrasts with the application of blanket rules under doping regulations that apply irrespective of the context of a given situation.

---

19 Ougaard, M, *Approaching the Global Polity*, Working Paper No 42/99, Centre for the Study of Globalisation and Regionalisation, p 14; emphasis in original. Available at www.csgr.org.

20 Vrijman, E, 'Towards harmonization: a commentary on current issues and problems' (2000) 3(2) Sports Law Bulletin 13.

21 *Report of the Working Group on the Legal and Political Aspects of Doping*, World Conference on Doping in Sport, Lausanne, 2–4 February 1999.

It appears that, in any case, powerful actors in the system of doping regulation will, usually covertly, fail to adopt or will intentionally flout the supposedly global regime of anti-doping regulation. An example of this can be seen in the run up to the Sydney Games with the withdrawal of 40 athletes and officials, due to represent the People's Republic of China, seemingly on the basis of the likelihood of failed drug tests.[22]

Thus it may be that the IOC has failed adequately to recognise, in their anti-doping policy, the importance of the different values and cultural norms across which sporting activity extends. This has two particular results. First, it can result in the exclusion of particular nations or groups, as demonstrated by the issues surrounding the introduction of a blood test for EPO. Secondly, because of the different jurisdictions across which the regulations apply, different legal positions can result in the policy not being evenly applied at a global level. A current example of this is the dispute between the IAAF and UK Athletics, regarding the banning of four British athletes for alleged use of nandrolone, a banned substance under the IOC's Medical Code. Here, it seems that the UK body, mindful of the disastrous economic impact of the *Modahl* case[23] on the previous regulator – the British Athletics Federation – are eager not to find themselves involved in potentially crippling litigation. By way of contrast, the IAAF are keen to enforce the homogeneity at a global level. It is notable that these differences arise even where the clash occurs between two bodies sharing similar cultural and historical backgrounds.

The result of this is clear: the principle of equality for all athletes at the point of competition is negated. Despite attempts at uniformity of regulation, legal and cultural differences and the variable zeal with which the rules are upheld render the 'level playing field' justification for anti-doping regulation impractical. These difficulties only arise because of a desire to impose uniform values upon regions where they are not necessarily shared, nor welcomed. The source of those values is unimportant, but the inability to achieve the desired homogeneity is inimical to equality amongst the athletes.

The same inability renders the protection of athletes' health an unsatisfactory basis upon which to ground 'doping' regulation. If the rules lead to the exclusion of particular groups, and in any case universal application is unimportant, then the protection of health as an underlying principle can surely not be justified. Numerous other arguments exist to challenge this rationale, but, on the basis of an examination of the global impact of the anti-doping rules, such a flaw appears fundamental.

---

22 'Olympic Games: China withdraw 27 athletes from Games after drug tests' (2000) *The Daily Telegraph*, 7 September.

23 *Modahl v BAF* (1999) *The Times*, 23 July (HL).

Similar problems of localisation occur not only in relation to cultural, societal and legal disparities but also in relation to economic and physiological differences. Black and Pape note that:

Athletes turn to every possible device to improve their performance, including coaching, high altitude training, videos, amino acids, special diets, vitamins and drugs. Records continue to fall as standards improve through competition. The end result is that all athletes have been artificially produced, through coaching, dieting, training, and other factors. These devices are no different from performance enhancing drugs.[24]

The IOC does not regulate differential access to each of these elements, so it would appear inconsistent to regulate doping on that basis. Again, the globalisation/localisation paradigm comes into effect, as each of the elements highlighted by Black and Pape are undoubtedly conditional upon the geographic location of athletes. It is unlikely that a young athlete from a third world country is likely to have the same access to the quality of coaching, technology and training facilities as, for example, a contemporary from the industrialised west. Location, with its associated economic and social characteristics, undoubtedly impacts upon the standard of facilities available to athletes to aid them in their preparation. This is not limited to saying that athletes from the industrialised west are necessarily advantaged by this state of affairs. Underlying social and cultural practices have undoubtedly contributed to the dominance of African athletes in middle and long distance track events. Indeed, more controversially, it has been suggested that genetic differences between racial groups make certain individuals predisposed to be successful at different events:

[T]here is no doubt that the patterns of distribution of athletic success among different ethnic groups are strikingly pronounced. Of the 32 finalists in the 100 metres in the last four Olympics, there was not one single competitor who was not of West African origin. Over the same distance, the fastest 200 times ever recorded are shared among athletes of West African descent. More than 50% of the 100 fastest times in middle and long distance running have been recorded by East Africans (around 70% for the 5,000 and 10,000 metres) ... The finals of Sydney's Olympic swimming competitions will almost certainly look like a negative of the track sprints. Only one black swimmer has ever won an Olympic medal.[25]

The outlawing of doping practice may in fact exacerbate these regional inequalities, as only those athletes with access to technology and wealth have the capacity to stay 'ahead of the game', allowing them to make use of the most up to date doping practices which are as yet undetectable. By contrast,

---

24 Black, T and Pape, A, 'The ban on drugs in sports: the solution or the problem?' [1997] 21(1) J Sport and Social Issues 83.

25 'White men can't run' (2000) *The Observer Sports Monthly*, 4 June. See, also, Entine, J, *Taboo: Why Black Athletes Dominate Sports and Why We are Afraid to Talk About It*, 2000 New York: Public Affairs.

those without access to such technologies are unable to indulge in any kind of doping activity and are thus disadvantaged. These factors are clearly less obviously linked with *present* location in a globalised age where societies across the globe have become, and are becoming increasingly multi-racial. However, the sort of statistics highlighted above hint very strongly that the geographical roots of any particular race are significant, in that they have served to shape and determine particular physiological characteristics that impact upon the way in which athletes are able to perform in particular sporting activities.

CONCLUSIONS

The emergent pattern seems to be that the IOC is losing a battle with the very agent that it would seek to utilise in relation to the regulation of doping in sport. In effect, what the IOC seeks is the 'globalisation' of its anti-doping policies and strategies, to penetrate and pervade both a broad spectrum of different sports and the different jurisdictions within which sporting activity takes place. However, the IOC has failed to recognise the process of globalisation as being 'two way'. Though there has been a little acknowledgment of the mutual interpenetration between the local and the global by the IOC, for the most part it has sought, and continues to seek, to impose its particular (localised) views at the global level. The resultant exclusions of, and intrusions upon, individual cultures and societies must be regarded as unsatisfactory for an organisation that would purport to support access to sport for everyone as being a basic human right. However, when the ethics being protected are those of a small, localised group and not inclusive of global society as a whole, this clearly undermines the principle of protection of sports ethics as a basis upon which to regulate doping practices.

This ideological failure is compounded by the impracticality attending the imposition of such a scheme. Where resistance to the global regime has arisen at a local level, whether as a result of cultural, social or legal disparities, this has had the effect of creating a situation of imbalance, where athletes are either subject to much stricter controls or effectively allowed to act irrespective of the rules 'imposed' by the global regulator. This clearly debilitates an anti-doping policy predicated upon the principle of the 'level playing field', and also damages the attempted justification involving the protection of health.

When considered and combined with the abovementioned divergent economic, social and even physiological attributes which may facilitate an 'unfair advantage', the IOC's error becomes clear.

The exact solutions to this error are, however, less clear and will only emerge over time. The IOC must revise its attempt to enforce its anti-doping policy on a uniform and worldwide basis. The revisions must involve a holistic appreciation of the global context of sporting competition. Such an appreciation will involve considerable effort on the part of the IOC, but will at least mark the end of a period in which its failure to take differentiating factors into account has exposed its supposedly global action to damaging charges of inconsistency and tokenism.

CHAPTER 12

THE DISCOURSES OF DOPING: LAW AND REGULATION IN THE WAR AGAINST DRUGS

Ken Foster

INTRODUCTION

If you listen to the sporting federations talk of doping, you will hear the language of war. The talk is of 'fights', 'combat', 'battle' and the 'war against drugs'. The new Anti-Doping Code of the Olympic Movement begins its preamble by talking of 'the fight against doping'.[1] The European Union's latest initiative is entitled *Plan to Combat Doping in Sport*.[2] The courts also echo this language. In *Modahl v BAF*,[3] Lord Woolf MR, at the very beginning of his judgment, quotes the IAAF regulations that talk of doping as a 'deadly threat to sport'. Later in the same judgment, he cautions against courts interfering, 'as otherwise the whole war against drugs in sport could be undermined'. Likewise, Scott J, in *Gasser v Stinson*,[4] spoke of the innocent being hurt along with the guilty, as if these were regrettable but justified casualties in war. He said 'the moral innocent may have to suffer in order to ensure that the guilty do not escape'. This language allows a perception that normal legal safeguards to protect the victims of this war, the innocent athletes who suffer injustice and the destruction of their careers, can be ignored or compromised. All's fair in love and war. There are, however, always other ways of seeing the problem and talking about it. David Moorcroft, Chief Executive of UK Athletics, when the International Amateur Athletics Federation (IAAF) confirmed bans on British athletes who had tested positive for nandrolone, said: '... the IAAF have given the benefit of the doubt to the system, not the athletes.'[5] He, by contrast, talks the language of the criminal law. This implies that athletes are accused criminals who are entitled to the benefit of any reasonable doubt and who should be treated as innocent until proven guilty. Different ways of talking not only pose the problem of doping differently; they help to shape the solutions to the problem. There are many different ways of

---

1   IOC, Olympic Movement Anti-Doping Code, Lausanne, 1999, hereafter referred to as the 'Olympic Code'.
2   European Commission, *Community Support Plan to Combat Doping in Sport*, available at www.europa.eu.int/scadplus/leg/en/lvb/135003.htm.
3   (1997) unreported, 28 July (CA).
4   (1988) unreported, 15 June.
5   (2000) *The Guardian*, 22 August, p 32.

talking about the regulation of drugs. These ways of talking will be termed 'discourses'. This chapter explores these discourses and tries to assess the role that law has played in shaping them.

Sporting federations, in drafting regulations about doping and in developing reliable methods of detecting drug use, have used different discourses. These discourses have frequently conflicted with each other. The introduction of testing for erythropoietin (EPO) at the Sydney Olympics is an example. On one hand, there was a scientific discourse that established the efficiency of the tests in scientific terms. This 'followed an internationally accepted protocol for approving scientific research results'.[6] On the other hand, there was a justice discourse that worried about the legal implications of introducing blood tests as the only effective way of testing for EPO. The IOC's Juridical Committee had to 'determine whether the testing method protects the athlete's legal rights so it can endure potential legal challenges'.[7]

New patterns of global policing of doping are emerging. The IOC has taken the lead. They convened a World Conference on Doping in 1999 at Lausanne, primarily as a result of the scandal surrounding the Tour de France in 1998. This produced the Lausanne Declaration,[8] which recommended, among other things, the establishment of a new independent and international World Anti-Doping Agency (WADA). This body is now established and was fully operational for the first time at the Sydney Olympics. The Olympic movement has also introduced a much revised set of rules and regulations, its Olympic Code, which also came into force for the Sydney Games. Governments have also begun to act. Canada has brought into force, as from 1 January 2000, a new national Policy on Doping in Sport. This represents 'the common interest and consensus of athletes, coaches, sport governing bodies and governments in Canada' and aims to 'provide a consistent and effective response' to the doping problem.[9] The European Union is also active. It has supported sporting federations. They agreed the draft constitution of WADA with the IOC, and have offered financial support for research into doping.[10]

The institutions that regulate the 'problem' of drugs in sport talk in different ways and, therefore, help to constitute the 'problem' in different ways. The political strengths and influences of the regulatory institutions will determine which discourses predominate in trying to 'control doping in sport'.

There are three main institutional fields of regulation of doping in sport:

---

6   IOC press release, August 2000, available at www.olympic.org/ioc/e/org/epo-meet0007.
7   *Ibid*.
8   Lausanne Declaration on Doping in Sport, available at www.nodoping.org/declaration.
9   Canadian Centre for Ethics in Sport, *Canadian Policy on Doping in Sport*, 2000, Ottawa: CCES, Arts 1 and 2.
10   See COM (99) 643.

(a) There is self-regulation by the sporting federations themselves. This occurs at different levels. Individual sports can have their distinctive rules and procedures. Football is a good example. It has not followed the IOC's lead, and retains its own regulations. This is because it believes the level of sporting penalties is too severe for professional footballers. Other sports follow the IOC model and adopt their rules and procedures. There are also different regional levels. National federations may have different rules and different procedures from their international federations. There has been a general tendency for regulations to be harmonised, by agreeing the same definitions of prohibited substances in each sport, and universalised, by trying to ensure that national and international federations have the same procedures. Differences have been reduced, and the IOC appears to see its role as encouraging a single set of rules and a single institutional framework for all sports.

(b) National governments have become involved in the problem of drugs in sport. Again, there are different levels of regulation. The criminal laws of States may supplement the sporting 'crimes'. Intergovernmental co-operation has helped to harmonise regulation. Transnational institutions, such as the European Union or the United Nations, have also played a role.

(c) Courts may regulate by intervening when athletes bring private law actions against sporting federations.

Within these regulatory fields, there are many different discourses about doping. They can be broadly classified into two groups: the non-legal discourses and the legal discourses. However, it is not the case that these groups of discourses neatly correspond with the main regulatory fields outlined above. So, for example, the self-regulating sporting federations do not talk solely in non-legal discourses, nor do the courts talk solely in legal discourses. The total picture is much more complex and reflexive than this simple dichotomy. Sporting federations have claimed sovereignty over the non-legal discourses in order to resist the intervention of national governments. They also have tried to claim sovereignty over the legal discourses when challenged by national courts. Before looking at the regulatory picture, the different discourses will be discussed.

DIFFERENT DISCOURSES

The main legal discourses at work, and the languages that they use, are these:

- The *constitutional* discourse. Sporting organisations are independent bodies which have sovereign powers to govern themselves. This is central to self-regulation. This allows them to be independent from State interference and legal intervention. 'Courts create a lot of problems for our anti-doping work, but we say we don't care in the least what they say. We have our rules, and they are supreme.'[11] Sport has its own regulatory authorities and its own governing institutions. This gives sporting federations administrative freedom to control their affairs without the need to account for their activities to public regulatory bodies. This constitutional discourse emphasises two features: one, that sporting institutions can formulate their rules and administer their procedures without external supervision or legal accountability; two, that international sporting federations are not under the jurisdiction of national courts and are constitutionally separate. It follows that global harmonisation of anti-doping procedures is primarily a question of internal rationalisation within the sporting community by international sporting federations. The discourse is essentially a claim not to be subordinate to any other legal or regulatory regime. Sport is constitutionally independent and has its own inviolate systems of legislation and adjudication.

- The *contractual* discourse. This constitutes sporting federations as private clubs. The club has rules, and when athletes join they accept the rules of the club. The athletes agree to two main types of rules. One is the doping rules themselves. They also agree to the disciplinary processes under these rules. These rules also rest on the idea that, as a club, the sporting federation has exclusive jurisdiction over the athletes whilst they are competing or training for competitions.

- The *criminal* discourse. Doping regulations and procedures within sport read as 'criminal'. There are offences laid down in a penal code. Athletes are accused. Sentences are passed and punishments are received. The 'fight' against drugs, it is said, requires these draconian powers.

- The *justice* discourse. This talks of protecting the athletes' right to be treated fairly. It stresses procedural fairness rather than substantive justice. In other words, the accused must have a fair trial, but not question the underlying fairness of the rules. It insists on due process and natural justice in disciplinary proceedings. The more extreme forms of this discourse shade into talk of human rights, for example, the right to refuse to take blood tests on religious grounds.

- The *workers' rights* discourse. The increasing professionalism of many sports has produced a discourse that treats sport as work, not play. Elite athletes in most sports are now full time professionals. This leads to a conflict of interests when amateur administrators, the 'old farts' as Will Carling described them, take decisions that cause economic loss to athletes. In the doping context, this implies that the length of bans,

---

11 The IAAF explaining why they refused to recognise the US courts in *Reynolds v IAAF* 841 F Supp 1444 (SD Ohio 1992), p 1452.

suspensions while investigations take place, and reinstatement are all key economic issues when viewed from this discourse.

The main non-legal discourses in regulating doping are these:

- The *moral*, or *ethical*, discourse. This discourse defines what is right and what is wrong in sport. It is also the ethos of fair play. The principal sporting value is that all competitors should start on an equal footing. No one should have an unfair advantage. Drugs are precisely such an unfair advantage. A linked moral value is that of obeying the rules. Sport is constituted by rules. As an activity, it is made by the players knowing that there are rules and following those rules. Not playing by the rules on drugs is unsportsmanlike. It is can also be reformulated as an 'integrity of the sport' discourse. Winners and records are suspect in a drugs environment.

- The *medical* discourse. This talks of the health of the athletes as paramount and says that sporting federations need to protect their athletes. It also uses the imagery of cleanliness and purity. Sport is a wholesome physical activity. It needs a pure unadulterated drug free body. This discourse stigmatises drugs as unnatural, artificial stimulants.

- The *scientific* discourse. The listing and testing of drugs in sport are heavily dependent on the available scientific evidence. This science is treated as sacrosanct and cannot be challenged.

- The *penal* discourse. This discourse asks what is the appropriate penalty and what is the philosophy behind sporting punishments. The answer is both a punitive one and an educational one. The punitive one talks of exemplary punishments as a deterrent to drug abuse. The educational one says that the drug problem can be cured by educating athletes so that they police themselves. In policy terms, the penal discourse would distinguish between young and experienced athletes, between first offences and others, and between recreational and performance enhancing substances. It also encourages rehabilitation programmes to try and cure athletes of drug abuse. This is reflected in the recent moves to have discretionary reinstatement provisions in doping regulations.[12] This allows the carrot of a return to the sport after successful treatment for drug abuse to be used as an incentive.

---

12 The Olympic Code, Chapter 2, Art 3, allows the two year ban from competition to be modified if there are 'specific, exceptional circumstances'.

WHO REGULATES?

These different discourses work within each of the regulatory fields, but they are reflections of the relative power of the regulatory institutions themselves. The battle by the sporting federations to preserve their autonomy has forced them to use different discourses for different purposes.

Self-regulation

Sport has traditionally regulated itself with minimum legal interference. This self-regulation has allowed sporting federations to make whatever rules that they feel are best in fighting the war against drugs. They have their own procedures for testing and detecting the use of banned drugs in competitions. They impose sanctions that are mainly sporting sanctions, typically banning the athlete from competitions, rather than more conventional penalties such as fines. The sporting penalty is seen as the more effective punishment. They have their own system of justice with hearings and appeals. The general ideology is one of autonomy and self-regulation. This traditional autonomy has been questioned by the other two regulatory fields.

Courts have sometimes believed that the justice discourse has been ignored by the sporting federations. They have allowed athletes to challenge disciplinary procedures as not conforming to standards of natural justice and they have insisted that sporting federations have a duty to act fairly. They have also ruled illegal certain types of penalty, in particular long bans, as not giving sufficient attention to the workers' rights discourse by ruling that they are in restraint of trade.

National governments have also queried the policy of self-regulation. They perceive a failure of governance within sporting federations over the doping issue. The integrity of these sporting bodies, at both the international and national levels, is in question. They wish to make sport appear clean without necessarily devoting the resources to funding adequate detection. There are considerable sporting and commercial pressures to suggest that the image, if not the reality, of a drug free sport is a valuable commodity. There is a fear that commercial sponsorship will be lost. A link with drugs is not the image that a business partner wants. Broadcasting revenues can be threatened if a sport appears rigged or suspect.

There may, however, be sporting reasons for turning a blind eye. Tacit condoning of drug-improved performances by organising committees such as the IOC can be explained because they produce new records, better performances and a better spectacle. National governing bodies may have reasons to favour their own athletes and thus not be as assiduous in monitoring their star performers. The institutionalised doping in State regimes such as China and the former German Democratic Republic were motivated by political ideology. Yet, there are also strong incentives in other countries. A national federation will often claim credit for the performance and progress of their athletes, but will individualise a doping scandal as a rogue exception. Such a scandal will not be associated with the national federation's failure of governance, in which their control over the detection of doping has broken down. The credit for sporting success is shifted from the individual to the institution, but the responsibility for the wrongdoing is shifted from the institutions to the individual.

Sporting federations have reacted to this dual threat to their sovereignty over doping in two main ways. First, there has been a process of internal reform. Sporting federations have been forced to address their failure of governance. They have reformed their own disciplinary procedures under the threat of litigation by introducing a better 'sporting rule of law'; in other words, by trying to participate in, and respond to, the justice discourse. The institutional response to this has been the creation of an international arbitration tribunal, the Court of Arbitration for Sport (CAS).[13] This uses the contractual discourse to claim that its decisions are final and binding, and it uses the constitutional discourse to maintain that its decisions are not reviewable by national courts because they are independent arbitration awards.

Secondly, the international sporting federations have begun to take a role in furthering and promoting a policy of harmonisation of rules and procedures about doping. The IOC has a policy of trying to achieve consistency about doping. It aims at a position in which all sports have the same banned substances and methods, where the standards of liability are the same, and where the penalties imposed for offences are the same. The IOC fears that the role of harmonisation may be undertaken by national governments and they would lose their moral leadership over doping questions. The IOC insists that this process of harmonisation of anti-doping procedures is primarily a question of internal rationalisation within the sporting community:

> The only event that the IOC actually controls is the Olympic Games. All other sports events are organized under the auspices and control of [other sports federations] ... The IOC has no power to impose its own views or rules on any

---

13 For descriptions of the work of the CAS see Beloff, M, Kerr, T and Demetriou, M, *Sports Law*, 1999, Oxford: Hart, especially pp 217–20 and 256–63; Panagiotopoulos, D, 'Court of arbitration for sports' (1999) 6 Villanova Sports and Entertainment LJ 49; Raber, N, 'Dispute resolution in Olympic sport: the Court of Arbitration for Sport' (1998) 8 Seton Hall J Sport Law 75; Kaufman, SA, 'Issues in international sports arbitration' (1995) 13 Boston U International LJ 527; Paulsson, J, 'Arbitration of international sports disputes' (1994) 11 Entertainment and Sports Lawyer 12; Polvino, AT, 'Arbitration as preventive medicine for Olympic ailments: the International Olympic Committee's Court of Arbitration for Sport and the future for the settlement of international sporting disputes' (1994) 8 Emory International L Rev 347.

such events. Despite its limited jurisdiction, what the IOC has tried to do, in addition to testing for prohibited substances and prohibited methods at its own event, is to persuade the other elements in the Olympic movement to adopt its rules in respect thereof, or, at the very least analogous rules. The politics of organizational autonomy, however, make simple adoption of an IOC rule unattractive to such organizations.[14]

The dominant perception of the doping problem by the IOC is that the level of regulation needs to be moved upwards within the international sporting world. The IOC has tried to act as the global sports legislator and take the lead in this process of harmonisation and standardisation.

National governments

There are many reasons why national governments become involved in doping issues. There may be a feeling that the sporting authorities cannot or will not solve their own doping problem. Individual sports federations cannot necessarily be trusted to administer their own procedures because they have self-interested reasons for not being as vigilant as possible. Cycling, especially in long distance events such as the Tour de France, has had a long standing problem with drugs. Evidence of abuse has been available for a long time. It is significant that the scandal that surrounded the 1998 Tour was precipitated by the activities of the State authorities in Belgium and France, and not by the governing body of cycling. Drugs were seized by customs officials when trainers were entering the country and criminal investigations were undertaken by magistrates. If regulation at the level of the individual sport is inadequate, it also possible that regulation at the level of the national sporting federation may be equally inadequate. The well documented evidence of systematic State sponsored doping of athletes by the former German Democratic Republic implies that to make the national federation the main agency for drug testing is also doomed to failure. Governments prefer independent testing institutions.

National laws can supplement or replace the efforts of the governing bodies of sport. It may be that criminal sanctions, such as imprisonment, are a greater deterrent than sporting sanctions. The process of testing and detection of offences can be better financed and undertaken by State authorities. National laws can criminalise trafficking in, or supplying, drugs. There is also the further sanction of government funding being withdrawn from the sport. Many sports, and individual athletes, are dependent on such State funding.

---

14 IOC, *Policy Commitment of the IOC*, paper submitted to the International Summit on Drugs in Sport, Sydney, Australia, 14–17 November 1999, p 8; available at www.nodoping.org/pos_drugsinsports_e.html.

There has also been intergovernmental action. An early effort in this direction was the Council of Europe's Anti-Doping Convention, agreed in 1989.[15] This defined the role of the State in anti-doping policies. It was agreed that legislation to restrict the availability of banned drugs was needed. Public subsidies to sports organisations should only be available if they have effective anti-doping regulations. International co-operation was emphasised by encouraging the exchange of information on drugs and by encouraging mutual recognition of sporting sanctions imposed in other countries.

Houlihan has recently stressed the importance of these initiatives by the Council of Europe. He argues that the IOC were relatively unprepared 'to address the issues of harmonisation when its own policy was only weakly formulated'.[16] They acted to avoid losing their control over policy and reluctantly 'accepted a broader role ... out of a concern that it will forfeit policy leadership to other sports organisations, or more serious still, to governments'.[17] There was no real commitment to transnational non-governmental action by the IOC until this initiative.

The political discourse at work here is increasingly one of partnership between national governments and sporting federations. The sovereignty and autonomy of sporting federations can only be retained if there is partnership and co-operation. This is a shared autonomy in which the Nation States are increasingly involved because they see a failure of internal order and governance within the sporting world.

Legal regulation

Athletes accused of doping offences have also been prepared to mount legal challenges. This has been an international phenomenon. One of the most famous examples was the litigation begun in the US by Butch Reynolds.[18] In the UK there have been several cases in the past two decades.[19] Katrin Krabbe was able to get her ban reduced by appealing to the German courts. These legal challenges have had their effect. They have contributed to internal

---

15 ETS No 135, agreed at Strasbourg, 16 November 1989.
16 Houlihan, B, 'Anti-doping policy in sport: the politics of international policy co-ordination' (1999) 77 Public Administration 311, p 328.
17 *Ibid*, p 327.
18 *Reynolds v IAAF* 841 F Supp 1444 (SD Ohio 1992); 23 F 3d 1110 (6th Cir 1994); 115 S Ct 423 (1994).
19 *Reel v Holder* [1981] 3 All ER 321 (CA); *Angus v British Judo Association* (1984) *The Times*, 15 June; *Gasser v Stinson* (1988) unreported, 15 June; *R v Disciplinary Committee of the Jockey Club ex p Aga Khan* [1993] 2 All ER 853 (CA); *Edwards v BAF* [1997] Eu LR 721; *Modahl v BAF* (1996) unreported, 28 June (QBD); (1997) unreported, 28 July (CA); (1999) *The Times*, 23 July (HL). *Wilander v Tobin (No 2)* [1997] 1 Lloyd's Rep 195 (Ch D); [1997] 2 Lloyd's Rep 293 (CA). *Korda v ITF* (1999) *The Times*, 4 February 1999 (Ch D); (1999) unreported, 25 March (CA).

reform by sporting federations of their rules and procedures. They have made rules more precise and consistent. They have reformed disciplinary procedures by allowing athletes to be heard and to be legally represented. The result has been revised penalties, shorter bans and legal questions about mandatory sentences. The justice discourse has been inserted by the courts into the institutions of self-regulation.

Courts have also questioned the independence of committees that have made decisions on doping matters. In other words, they have queried the constitutional discourse. This has led to individual sports or national associations having more independent bodies to decide doping cases. Sporting federations have taken care to separate the investigatory and adjudication functions from each other and not to act as both judge and jury. Disciplinary committees of sports federations more frequently have legal chairs. The findings of these committees can usually be appealed. Many rule books also now allow a final appeal by way of binding arbitration to the IOC's CAS.[20] All these measures are designed to provide procedural justice for the accused athlete but at the same time attempt to retain institutional autonomy for the sporting federations.

LEGAL QUESTIONS

Despite these previous legal interventions by courts, there still remain a number of unanswered legal questions.

Definition of 'doping'

The dominant discourse in dealing with the internal rules of sporting federations has been the criminal discourse. Doping rules and the procedures under them are treated as if they were legal rules. They speak like the criminal law. They create offences, they have a process of investigation and trial and they result in penalties. The discourse is 'criminal', and it demands to be analysed as if it were law. The move to international harmonisation of rules within different sports has meant that the rules of the IOC have acquired a particular significance. The introduction of a new Code by the Olympic movement is an important event. The Code was introduced in 1999 as a result of the Lausanne Conference on Doping earlier in that year. It was fully operative for the first time at the Sydney Olympics in 2000.

The Code has mixed aims and its preamble discloses various discourses at work. It begins by stressing the constitutional dominance and autonomy of

---

20 The Olympic Code, Chapter 3, Art 1, states that any participant affected by a decision may appeal to the CAS.

the IOC. It then stresses the ethical discourse of sport by talking of the 'spirit of fair play'. But the main discourse is medical. It claims to protect the athletes' health. The justice discourse comes later in the Preamble, by stating that the athlete's rights to justice must be safeguarded, almost as an afterthought.

The central crime in the Code is that of 'doping'. This is defined in Art 2 of the Code as:

1   the use of an expedient (substance or method) which is potentially harmful to athletes' health and/or capable of enhancing their performance, or

2   the presence in the athlete's body of a Prohibited Substance or evidence of the use thereof or evidence of the use of a Prohibited Method.

This is an extremely wide definition, for several reasons. The list of prohibited substances referred to in the second part of the definition is a long one. There are over 100 listed substances. There are two classes. The main class lists those that are banned in all Olympic sports, and so will be applicable to most sports.[21] A secondary class lists those that may be prohibited 'where the rules of a responsible authority so provide',[22] or allows other groups of substances, mainly painkillers, to be used if notified to the relevant authorities. The main list tries to classify by using generic classes as well as naming specific substances. Each class of prohibited substances is presented as an open ended list. Uncertainty is introduced by two phrases in this part of the definition. The list is said only to be 'examples'; and the list adds the phrase 'and related substances'. In listing examples of prohibited substances, the Code warns: '... this is not an exhaustive list ... Many substances that do not appear on this list are prohibited under the term "and related substances".'[23] This produces a considerable 'penumbra of uncertainty'.[24] It also tries to overturn the ruling of the CAS at the Atlanta Games in 1996, where Russian athletes who had used bromantan were exonerated, as it was not on the prohibited list even though it was, chemically, a 'related substance'.[25]

The master definition also tries to be comprehensive by including the 'use of an expedient ... which is potentially harmful to athletes' health and/or capable of enhancing their performance'. In a criminal discourse, the use of 'and/or' is unfortunate, but it appears to produce the result that anything that improves performance can be considered to be doping and anything that harms the health of the athlete is also doping. This seems to cover practically anything unless 'expedient' (which has a pejorative undertone in English)

---

21   Olympic Code, Appendix 1.

22   Olympic Code, Appendix 2.

23   Olympic Code, Appendix A, Pt IV.

24   The phrase is that of HLA Hart, in *The Concept of Law*, 2nd edn, 1997, Oxford: Clarendon.

25   A similar argument was used by Katrin Krabbe, who tested positive for clenbuterol in 1993, which was not then on the prohibited list. She was, however, banned by the German Federation for 'unsportsmanlike conduct'. The ban was upheld by the IAAF, who treated it is as 'conduct likely to bring the sport into disrepute'.

implies intentional cheating. Overall, the definition has the makings of a legal minefield if it used by sporting associations outside the substances that are actually listed. The definition shows a conflict between different discourses. The criminal discourse strives for certainty in definition. The medical discourse attempts to anticipate pharmaceutical advances by using the phrase 'related substances' and wants its autonomy to prevail. The ethical discourse is not uneasy with a comprehensive definition, as trying to circumvent the precise banned method is, in itself, considered to be cheating because it is against the spirit of the rules, if not the letter. The constitutional discourse favours a wider definition so that discretion to take proceedings lies with the sporting institutions. The justice discourse insists that crimes should be specified, and not subsumed under such vague headings as 'related substances'.

Strict liability

The new Olympic Code appears to create a strict liability offence, in which the mere presence of a prohibited substance suffices for the offence to be committed. There is no defence available for the athlete. The defence of 'innocent ingress' is apparently not allowed and the possibility of accidental consumption is discounted. This reproduces in substance the rule of the IAAF.[26] It is interesting to note that its Panel has rejected defences that include being given the substance by others; having drinks spiked; eating natural foods such as beef that contain steroids; taking food supplements that contain prohibited substances; and being prescribed medicine by a doctor. Beloff claims that the IAAF's Arbitration Panel appears to have accepted that their rule creates an offence of strict liability.[27] However, the interpretation of the Chairman of the Panel at the time of most of these decisions is different.[28] He argues that the general principle of *nulla poena sine culpa* (no penalty without fault) applies and that the wording implies that the athlete must show an absence of intent or negligence. In other words, the issue is one of shifting the presumption of guilt that the rules impose once the presence of the substance in the athlete's body has been factually established. In the *Bevilacqua* case (1996), the Panel rejected an argument that the athlete had taken health pills containing the drug without it being listed on the label. Given the IAAF's rule[29] placing responsibility on the athlete for whatever is in their body, the Panel concluded that she had not done enough to displace the presumption of

26 IAAF Rules and Regulations, r 55 defines doping as occurring where 'a prohibited substance is found to be present in an athlete's body tissue or fluids; or an athlete uses or takes advantage of a prohibited technique'.

27 *Op cit*, Beloff *et al*, fn 13, p 186.

28 Tarasti, L, 'When can an athlete be punished for doping offence?', paper presented to the IOC Conference on Doping in Sport, Lausanne, February 1999.

29 IAAF Rules and Regulations, r 55.4: 'It is the athlete's duty to ensure that no substance enters his body.'

guilt. The Panel remarked that 'those health pills were not everyday food that one consumes'.[30] This implies that it is at least negligent for the athlete to take supplements without establishing that they are drug free. In a subsequent award in the *Capobianco* case (1997), the Panel again listened to an argument of innocent ingress. The athlete claimed that the drug in his body was the result of eating beef from cattle that had been given steroids. This argument was rejected, on the basis of scientific evidence that this was an extremely unlikely occurrence. These awards seem clearly to indicate that the apparent 'strict liability' rule was being interpreted as a question of the burden of proof. Beloff disagrees with this interpretation. He says that 'presence is a question of pure fact'.[31]

This is an important argument because national courts may not be prepared to accept as valid rules of sporting federations that create strict liability, at least where there is clear evidence of innocent ingress. Some commentators think 'strict liability' rules are *per se* illegal.[32] The justice discourse says that strict liability is unacceptable because it increases the chance that miscarriages of justice will occur. The English courts, however, appear ready to accept such rules. In *Gasser v Stinson*,[33] it was said that the innocent must suffer with the guilty. Scott J was not prepared to rule that the IAAF's regulations were an unreasonable restraint of trade. He said, 'I am not persuaded that the IAAF's absolute offence and mandatory sentence applicable to an athlete who is found to have dope in his or her urine is unreasonable. On the contrary, I think that in the circumstances, the restraints are reasonable'.

This aspect of the court's reasoning was followed in *Wilander v Tobin (No 1)*.[34] Here, too, the High Court refused to declare void as a restraint of trade the anti-doping regulations of the International Tennis Federation (ITF). This was despite the interpretation of these regulations as creating a strict liability rule, having mandatory sentences, and placing the onus of proof on the athlete to rebut the scientific evidence. As most sports have similar regulations to those of the ITF, it appears on this precedent that most would survive a legal challenge that the rules themselves are void.[35] This judgment downplays the criminal and the workers' rights discourse.

---

30 *Op cit*, Tarasti, fn 28.

31 *Op cit*, Beloff *et al*, fn 13, p 187 and the helpful references in fn 37.

32 See Wise, A and Meyer, BS, *International Sports Law and Business*, 1998, The Hague: Kluwer, Vol 3, p 1469; Wise, A, 'Strict liability drug rules of sports governing bodies' (1996) 146 NLJ 1161.

33 (1988) unreported, 15 June.

34 (1996) unreported, 19 March. Elements of the reasoning can be found in the reports of the subsequent litigation: *Wilander v Tobin (No 2)* [1997] 1 Lloyd's Rep 195 (Ch D); [1997] 2 Lloyd's Rep 293 (CA).

35 See *ibid*, Wise.

If the legal conclusion is that such rules only move the onus of proof and place the burden of displacing the presumption of guilt on the athlete, then the question as to the standard required to displace it also arises. In *Wilander v Tobin (No 1)*, in the Court of Appeal,[36] Neill LJ said that the ITF's regulations effectively reversed the burden of proof. He found this presumption of guilt troublesome, but not unreasonable, as long as the regulations were interpreted as meaning that this presumption could be rebutted on the balance of probabilities. He said: 'I do not understand the words ... used in the relevant paragraph of r 53 to be more than on a balance of probabilities.' The burden of proof is, in English lawyers' eyes, the civil burden of proof.

Penalties

The new Olympic Code tries to address the problem of innocent ingress as not a matter of liability, but as a question of sentencing. In other words, it uses the penal discourses over which it claims sovereignty. This is part of a wider move away from single fixed penalties for doping offences. The Code has different levels of penalty. For minor stimulants, such as caffeine, the ban can vary from one to six months, or may be just a warning. For all other substances, the ban is for a minimum of two years unless there are exceptional circumstances.[37] These apply to non-intentional doping. If intentional doping, or activities such as using a masking agent or refusing to take a test are established, then the penalties are more severe. The ban is then two to eight years for minor substances and four years minimum to life for all other substances. 'Intentional doping' is defined as acting 'knowingly or in circumstances amounting to gross negligence'.[38] The reasons for moving away from fixed penalties despite the pressures of harmonisation have been explained by de Merode, the chairman of the IOC Medical Commission:[39]

> We think ... that as sport has become an important aspect of life in society, it should gradually adapt to the life of society. It should therefore abandon the system of private club sanctions in favour of the system that applies to all forms of activity governed by the criminal law. We therefore need a sliding scale of sanctions that have minimum and maximum values, with a degree of discretion on the part of the bodies responsible for deterring guilt and passing sentence as to how they apply them.

The length of the ban is another tricky legal problem. Long bans run the risk of being declared illegal by national courts when applied, in accordance with the rules of the international sporting federation, by a national federation.

---

36 (1996) unreported, 26 March.

37 Olympic Code, Chapter 2, Art 3.1.

38 *Ibid*, Chapter 1, Art 1.

39 Introduction to IOC's *Handbook 1999*, Lucerne: IOC.

Here, the workers' rights discourse predominates. As athletes become more professional, then restraint of trade laws that depend on the right of the athlete to earn a living come into play. It was a fear that four year bans would be declared illegal that led the IAAF to change their maximum ban from four to two years. A four year ban can be a 'functional death penalty' for an athlete. Most top athletes have a short career. In minor sports, the peak that is aimed at is the Olympics and a four year ban at one Olympic Games will mean an effective ban of eight years.

Economic loss

The question of whether the athlete is entitled to any financial compensation when they are wrongly convicted by the sporting federation was the real issue behind the *Modahl* litigation.[40] Diane Modahl tested positive for drugs just before the Commonwealth Games in 1994. She was eventually cleared by an independent appeal panel of the British Athletic Federation (BAF), which accepted that the testing procedure was faulty. She also alleged that the original disciplinary committee, which upheld the original finding, was biased and so had breached the rules of natural justice. Her argument was that the BAF had broken the implied term in their contract that she would receive a fair and impartial hearing. The BAF argued that, as her internal appeal had been successful, the overall proceedings were not flawed; therefore, there was no breach of contract, and so she was not entitled to any damages. This meant that the economic loss that had resulted from her suspension was not recoverable. The Court of Appeal[41] did not clearly resolve the issue, for the proceedings were interim and the question was whether there was an arguable case. Morritt LJ accepted that the athlete may have a case. The Federation's case, he said, was not so compelling as to conclude that she did not have a reasonable case, especially as the suspension was mandatory and could not be lifted while the case was heard. This seems to respect the workers' rights discourses. Pill LJ agreed. He also emphasised the automatic duty on the BAF to suspend the athlete. The consequences were 'very serious for the athlete' and it was arguable that 'the athlete is entitled to fairness at each stage of the procedure'; and, as this is a contractual term, merely getting a final satisfactory result 'was an inadequate remedy' for the athlete. Lord Woolf MR argued differently. He saw no reason to treat public law and private law principles differently. The standard of fairness required of a sporting

---

40 *Modahl v BAF* (1996) unreported, 28 June (QBD); (1997) unreported, 28 July (CA); (1999) *The Times*, 23 July (HL).

41 Although the case went to the House of Lords, this was on a technical question. The testing laboratory had ceased to be officially accredited because it had moved premises without informing the IOC or the IAAF. The House of Lords agreed that there was not an arguable case that this constituted a breach of contract between the BAF and the athlete.

disciplinary body was the same as that of a public body. Damages cannot be awarded against a public body without bad faith or malice. Therefore, he argued that there could be no damages awarded for the breach of contract. This gives the sporting federation the best of both worlds. They cannot normally be subject to judicial review because they are not a public body.[42] The reasoning behind this conclusion is that there is an alternative contractual remedy. It then seems perverse to argue that the contract does not allow damages because none would be available if they were a public body. Lord Woolf also warned that, by requiring each part of the disciplinary procedure to be fair, 'the courts will have to take care not readily to interfere by injunction, as otherwise the whole war against drugs in sport could be lost'. Lord Woolf felt that was a danger of challenges at every stage of the procedure. The obvious answer to this point is to refer to the well established rule that internal appeals must be exhausted before an aggrieved party can appeal to the courts.

The rules of some sporting federations provide for automatic suspension of the athlete as soon as there is a positive test. This mandatory suspension clearly caused Court of Appeal some unease in the *Modahl* case. It appears to have been shared by the judge in Dougie Walker's case in July 2000. Walker tested positive for nandrolone and was suspended according to the IAAF regulations. He was granted an injunction by Hallet J, allowing him to compete pending the outcome of the IAAF's Arbitration Panel's hearing.[43] This ruling seems to reinforce the workers' rights discourse and, moreover, the criminal discourse standard of 'innocent until proven guilty'.

Vicarious liability

There is a wide range of people, other than the athlete him or herself, who may be considered guilty of a doping offence. The new Olympic Code applies to any participant. These are defined as including 'coach, trainer, official, medical or paramedical personnel working with or treating athletes participating in or preparing for sports competitions'.[44]

This wide definition of vicarious liability does not extend to the national federations. If they have jurisdiction over athletes, why are they not also liable? On the one hand, it could be argued that vicarious liability is only justified where the superior body can control the activities of those for whom it is made responsible. On the other hand, such a policy would ensure that institutionalised doping is not encouraged or condoned by the national governing body. FINA, the international sports federation of swimming, has

---

42 *R v Disciplinary Committee of the Jockey Club ex p Aga Khan* [1993] 2 All ER 853 (CA).

43 (2000) *The Guardian*, 27 July, p 26.

44 Olympic Code, Chapter 1, Art 1.

introduced the 'four strikes rule'.[45] This states that, if four swimmers under the jurisdiction of any national governing body test positive for drugs in a 12 month period, then the national federation is suspended from international competitions for two years.

Can sporting federations prevent athletes from going to court?

The exclusive claim to adjudicate its disputes is made by the IOC. It wants non-interference by national courts, especially in doping cases. If its justice discourse enjoys its own integrity and independence, then the final court of appeal is the CAS and its awards are legally binding. The awards of the CAS are intended to have international effect, but this needs a procedure whereby such awards are recognised by national courts as binding and enforceable. There are various reasons why national courts may declare doping rules, and especially the sanctions imposed under them, unenforceable.

English courts have traditionally maintained that the decisions of private, or domestic as they are sometimes termed, tribunals exercising disciplinary power can be challenged, at least where there is an economic power. This rule has its origins in trade union cases, where it was clearly motivated by a workers' rights discourse to protect workers against trade unions who ran closed shops. This was stated clearly in *Lee v Showmen's Guild*,[46] a trade union case. It was confirmed as applicable to sporting authorities in *Baker v Jones*,[47] a case concerning the British Amateur Weightlifters' Association. The Scottish courts take the same view. In *St Johnstone FC v Scottish FA*,[48] Lord Kilbrandon interpreted the rules of the Scottish Football Association (FA). One rule described the Council as 'the sole judges', and another rule prohibited members taking legal proceedings on any matter without the consent of the FA. These rules, he said, could produce 'some remarkable consequences because it seems to import an agreement between the members and the association that members will renounce the jurisdiction of the courts'.[49] If this was the correct interpretation, Lord Kilbrandon said, 'the rule is to be construed as depriving the members of the association of the right to appeal to the courts of the land ... then such a construction would be contrary to public policy, and ought not to be countenanced by these courts'.[50]

---

45 See Galluzzi, D, 'The doping crisis in international athletic competition: lessons from the Chinese doping scandal in women's swimming' (2000) 10 Seton Hall J Sport Law 65.

46 [1952] 2 QB 329.

47 [1954] 2 All ER 553.

48 1965 SLT 171.

49 *Ibid*, p 175.

50 *Ibid*.

The conceptual reasoning behind these and similar decisions is important in answering the question of whether an express agreement to exclude the courts is valid. Using the contractual discourse, it may be possible. Anti-doping rules are contractual rules to which the athlete expressly or implicitly agrees when they join a sporting association or when they enter a competition. In a contract, they can agree to final and binding arbitration of their cases. Under the new Olympic Code, athletes are presumed to accept this 'by the very fact of participation' in the Games. But, such an agreement would not, arguably, extend to the wrong legal interpretation of the rules by a sporting tribunal, or to the sporting association's duty to act fairly. On this view, the rules and regulations are quasi-legislative in character and they operate independently of contract. The classic statement of this position was made by Lord Denning in *Breen v AEU*.[51] He said that the 'rules are in reality more than a contract. They are a legislative code ... This code should be subject to control by the courts'.[52] The implication of this analysis is that the duty to act fairly, or the rules of natural justice, cannot be excluded, even by agreement. This implication was spelt out in *Wilander v Tobin (No 2)*.[53] The key question in this case was whether the athletes had had a proper appeal under the ITF's rules. But Lord Woolf said, in the Court of Appeal of the Appeals Committee of the ITF, that:

> ... because it is not a public body, this does not mean that it escapes the supervision of the High Court. The proceedings out of which this appeal arises are part of that supervision ... If the Appeals Committee does not act fairly or if it misdirects itself in law and fails to take into account relevant considerations or takes into account irrelevant considerations, the High Court can intervene. It can also intervene if there is no evidential basis for its decision.[54]

In *Korda v ITF*,[55] the Court of Appeal was faced with a doping case in which the governing body had tried to prevent disputes over its rules from ever reaching the courts. Korda had tested positive for drugs. The ITF's rules provided for a mandatory sentence of one year's suspension. Its regulations provide for a hearing before an Appeals Committee and its decision was described by the rules as being 'the full, final and complete disposition of the appeal and will be binding on all parties'. The Appeals Committee accepted Korda's defence that he did not know that he had taken the drug. The Committee then decided to lift his suspension, relying on their power to

51 [1971] 2 QB 175. It should be noted that this was a trade union case and Lord Denning's was a dissenting judgment.
52 [1971] 2 QB 175, p 190.
53 [1997] 1 Lloyd's Rep 195 (Ch D); [1997] 2 Lloyd's Rep 293 (CA).
54 *Ibid* (CA), p 300.
55 (1999) unreported, 25 March.

reduce the sentence if 'exceptional circumstances' are established.[56] The ITF contended that the Appeals Committee had exercised its discretion wrongly and wished to appeal. The rules provided that any dispute should 'be submitted to ... the Court of Arbitration for Sport'.

Korda argued that the ITF could not appeal because the first rule took precedence. To accept this argument would mean that the doping rules and decisions made under them were not appealable. In the High Court, Lightman J accepted Korda's argument. The words 'full, final and ... binding' should be given full effect. This meant that there was no further appeal. To take the case to the CAS would mean a 'second full scale appeal'. This was not the intention of the procedure. Lightman J added two further reasons. First, to allow the ITF to appeal would mean 'that a player acquitted ... should be subject to double jeopardy and would be required to face a retrial on appeal before the CAS'. Secondly, the CAS is clearly a legal body and, therefore, is not best equipped to hear a case anew. The judge said: '... looking at the respective composition of the two bodies [the Appeals Committee and the CAS] alone, the inference must surely be that there is not to be a full appeal with a re-hearing ... on the merits ... but rather a limited review of legal questions.' This asserts that the criminal and medical discourses are separate and need to be dealt with by separate institutions. This seems a sensible and accurate solution to the problem of appeals from doping decisions. The CAS is a substitute for a court. It can only hear those questions that the formula of 'final and binding' does not preclude an athlete from taking to a court. Lightman J gave as examples an unfair hearing, public policy grounds such as restraint of trade and 'the construction of the decision made'. It is a 'court of appeal' only.

The Court of Appeal undermined this distinction by reversing Lightman J's decision. They viewed the two contractual provisions as not necessarily inconsistent. The Appeals Committee's decision was a question of the legal interpretation of the rules and, therefore, appealable to the CAS. The parties were disputing whether a legal error had been made. This was a 'dispute arising out' of the Appeals Committee's decision and, as agreed, should go to the CAS. This interpretation allows the CAS a wider function than being solely an appeal body. It allows it to hear the case *de novo*.[57] Although *Korda* is essentially a narrow decision that ultimately turns on the correct construction of a contract, it indirectly raises a key question. Is the CAS the final appeal in a domestic tribunal's proceedings and, therefore, subject to the High Court's jurisdiction, or is it an independent arbitration panel whose awards cannot normally be questioned because there is a binding agreement to arbitrate?

---

56 Given the use of this phrase in the Olympic Code, it is interesting to note that the IAAF, in *Edwards v BAF* [1997] Eu LR 721, argued that their r 60.8 (the equivalent rule) was only applicable when a longer ban was unlawful under the domestic law of the athlete's federation.

57 This is also the CAS's own view of its functions. See *De Bruin v FINA* CAS 98/211.

One further aspect of the *Korda* case is that it appears wrongly to allow a sporting federation to appeal against a reduced sentence. If the criminal law discourse is dominant, then there is no good reason for a sporting federation to appeal against an acquittal. Lightman J's point against double jeopardy is well taken. The prosecution does not have an automatic right of appeal against either a conviction or even against the sentence in criminal discourses. This point was ignored by the Court of Appeal, which, in arguing that this was an appealable question of contract interpretation, sidestepped the point and did allow the ITF to appeal. Clarke LJ did say that, 'so far as I am aware, no one suggests that ... the machinery can be operated only by one party and not by the other'. This is to conceptualise the issue as one of contract where reciprocity is the norm. But if this is a criminal law discourse, there are good reasons why the prosecution does not always have reciprocal rights to the accused. The case therefore sets an unfortunate precedent that a sporting federation can reopen a doping case, at least on the question of sentence, if not on the question of acquittal, when its own committee has made a 'full, final and binding ruling'.

THE SPORTING EMPIRE STRIKES BACK

Sporting bodies have fought back against the incursion into their territory of State and legal intervention. They have done so in two major ways. They have addressed the justice discourse by trying to ensure procedural justice. This is represented institutionally by the CAS. They have addressed the sovereignty issue by helping to create an independent agency to police the internationalisation and harmonisation of the doping problem. That agency is WADA.

The CAS has developed a jurisprudence that makes sure that rules are followed and properly interpreted.[58] This uses the contractual discourse to ensure that doping regulations are properly construed. It also ensures procedural justice by insisting on a fair hearing. The governing bodies insist on their sovereignty to impose exclusive jurisdiction on athletes so that they can only go to the CAS.

WADA began to function in 2000. It has agreed a draft constitution. It has a draft mission statement, which declares that 'the mission of the Agency shall be to promote and co-ordinate at international level the fight against doping in sport in all its forms'.[59] Its initial funding has been provided by the IOC. It is still 'offshore', operating, like the IOC itself, out of Switzerland, although it

---

58 *Op cit*, Beloff *et al*, fn 13, pp 217–20.
59 Available at www.nodoping.org.

has begun a process of selection for its permanent headquarters. The Foundation Board has a mixture of representatives of the Olympic movement and government representatives, although the former are in the majority. It co-ordinated the testing programme at the Sydney Olympics and used an independent body to undertake the tests.

Both institutions have tried to become independent of the IOC. These extra institutions of self-regulation will need to acquire the legitimacy and power of independence to have the greatest impact upon the many discourses of doping.

CONCLUSION

This chapter has argued that the way in which doping in sport is constituted as being a problem is the key to answering the question: how is doping best regulated? The usual initial answer to this question has been to ask whether sporting federations are best left to regulate themselves. This poses the question as one of the autonomy of the sporting federation. Should they be left alone by national governments and should they be immune from legal intervention? Yet, there are more complex processes at work than simply intervention or not. Each of the regulators can operate at different levels from the national to the international. So there is a multitude of possible layers of regulation, all of which can potentially conflict with each other. This fragmented regulatory pattern creates its own problems of autonomy.

There are many different discourses at work in this field. The non-legal discourses are those over which the sporting federations have claimed sovereignty, for example, the ethical question as to what is right and wrong in sport. But, each of the non-legal discourses has been influenced by the courts. The ethical discourse of right and wrong is overlain by the criminal discourse of strict liability rules which, in turn, is modified by the justice discourse to allow a defence of innocent ingress or by the penal discourse that permits lesser penalties for non-intentional doping. The medical and scientific discourses have claimed autonomy, but even here courts have been prepared, as in the *Modahl* litigation, to allow the procedures of scientific testing to be challenged. The penal discourse has regularly been modified by courts using the workers' rights discourse to declare illegal certain types of sporting penalties that are restraints of trade. The discourses constantly interact and modify each other as the regulatory institutions are active in particular discourses. When the regulatory institutions act is itself a result of sovereignty and constitutional discourses about who should regulate doping in sport.

The English courts have had a limited impact on modifying these discourses. This is because they have given too much respect to the constitutional and contractual discourses. They have permitted the constitutional discourse, which allows private organisations to be autonomous and unaccountable, to prevail by refusing to recognise sporting federations as public bodies. This has been reinforced by empty statements that sport needs autonomy. The classic statement is that of Browne-Wilkinson VC, who once said that 'sport would be better served if there was no running litigation at repeated intervals by people seeking to challenge decisions of the regulating bodies'.[60] The courts have also emphasised the contractual discourse. In the *Wilander* litigation, the question of appeals was treated as merely a matter of the courts assisting in the interpretation of the club's rules. There has been, consequently, little use of the criminal discourse, for example, to limit the harsh interpretation of doping rules by relying on the maxim that criminal codes should be restrictively interpreted. There has been little use of the workers' rights discourses. English courts have been slow to acknowledge that professional athletes are workers. *Modahl* effectively denied workers any compensation for procedural defects by those who control their livelihood. The conceptual limitation has been to see the issues as clustered around the private/public divide. This leads to an implied policy choice of intervention or non-intervention. The choices are much more varied because there are many more discourses at work.

The English courts have also been slow to recognise that there are other regulatory institutions operating in this field. It is not simply a choice between self-regulation by sporting federations and legal interference by the courts. It is outdated to treat sporting federations as sovereign and private clubs. Their sovereignty is now shared with national governments. The new global institutions, such as WADA, are partnerships with shared sovereignty over the field of doping. This allows new inputs into the discourses and alters the power that different regulatory institutions have over the discourses. The courts could respond to the changing international politics of doping by recognising that intergovernmental treaties are setting international standards.[61] But most important of all will be their attitude to the developing jurisprudence of the CAS. If the English courts concentrate on the contractual discourse, they will allow this 'independent' court to claim exclusive jurisdiction over the criminal and justice discourses. Whether the CAS is worthy of this trust is an open question. It is surely better for the courts to keep a residual power of supervision that allows them to have the final word on how the legal discourse is constituted. To intervene is not necessarily to deny autonomy and sovereignty to sporting federations. To intervene is to contribute to the development to the discourses. To intervene is to regulate,

---

60 *Cowley v Heatley* (1986) *The Times*, 24 July.

61 The Court of Appeal in *Wilander v Tobin (No 2)* [1997] 2 Lloyd's Rep 293 did this by discussing whether the Council of Europe Anti-Doping Convention's basic right to a fair hearing had been infringed.

but to regulate for a better sporting 'rule of law' and to overrule the rule of 'sporting law' as an uncontrolled, independent legal order. Private justice must always be publicly accountable.

CHAPTER 13

DRUG TESTING IN AMATEUR SPORTS IN THE US

Paul M Anderson

When Major League Baseball home run hero Mark McGuire admitted that he used the drug androstenedione, the US media was on alert. Reports ran of rampant drug use by players in sports in the US, particularly that of professional athletes. The media claimed that players would do anything to avoid being caught, while owners and administrators would take any measures to restrict a player's personal freedom. But this was not the real issue.

In reality, the debate over drug use in sports in the US focuses on the legality of testing players for such use. Because players can be barred from participation as a result of positive testing, they often claim that their personal rights have been violated by any such testing programme. It is these claims that have become the focus of the drug testing issue in the US. Some groups claim that an individual's right to be free from such testing is very strong, while others claim that the risks of drug use are so great that testing is warranted.

This chapter will not endorse or debate drug use as an act of human behaviour. The purpose of the chapter is to dilute the issue down to its most legally relevant consideration – whether a sporting organisation can legally test sports participants for drug use. The issue's focus, then, is not on actual drug use itself; it is on individual rights of privacy and health concerns. In addition, when making these considerations, it is important to note the clear distinction between drug use by professional athletes and those at the amateur level.

At the level of professional team sports, any drug testing policy is governed by that particular sport's collective bargaining system.[1] Under this system, in the majority of the professional team sports in the US, players' unions and management negotiate over the terms of employment. This negotiation then becomes part of the agreement (called a collective bargaining agreement) which regulates all terms of employment. A drug testing policy can then become a negotiated term within the collective bargaining agreement that governs the relationship between the players and the owners. Consequently, such policies are generally not open to judicial scrutiny.

---

1   This would include Major League Baseball, the National Basketball Association, the National Hockey League, the National Football League and Major League Soccer.

In addition, certain specific drugs, such as steroids, are directly noted as banned drugs within the collective bargaining agreement. If an individual wants to play for the professional league, he or she must agree not to take the banned drugs. This also will not be open to judicial review. All such players are employees at will and are adults who have voluntarily agreed to be bound by the collective bargaining agreement by signing a player contract. There is no rights issue here because, as a negotiated condition of employment, American professional athletes must agree to these terms. Therefore, McGuire's use of androstenedione is not controversial because Major League Baseball specifically allows for such use. The National Basketball Association and National Football League would not.

Before moving to the amateur level of sports in the US, a note on amateurism is necessary. Many commentators have debated what qualifies as an amateur sport in itself. Some say that college athletes are amateurs because they do not play under professional employment contracts and are not given typical salaries. Some would say that only interscholastic athletes who merely play for the love of the game are amateurs. Whatever the definition, there is no such thing as a strictly 'amateur' athlete. Amateurism is defined by whatever regulatory body or organisation is in charge. The International Olympic Committee defines amateurs in one way; the National Collegiate Athletic Association defines amateurs very differently. Nevertheless, this chapter follows the typical American scholarship in this area, and amateur athletes are defined as any athletes in interscholastic and intercollegiate sports.

At the amateur level, then, the drug testing issue becomes more complex. Initially, this complexity focuses on the position of the student athlete involved. At the high school level, the athletes are generally below the age of 18 and do not possess the general rights of privacy that an American adult would have. At the college level, the athletes still have limited rights, due to the controlled environment of college sports participation.

In essence, the issue at the amateur level focuses on the justifications behind any sort of drug testing scheme. The rights of the individual are a consideration, but they are not paramount. As with most issues dealing with rights in the US, an understanding of the legality and possibility for drug testing in sports at this amateur level is defined by the courts. Courts have set the standard in terms of what types of drug testing policies will be allowed for amateur athletes, and what amount of judicial scrutiny such policies will be subject to. Bear in mind that it is not as if the athletes involved have sued, asserting some individual right to be free to use drugs in any way. The focus of their claims is a perception that they must have some privacy right, which right has been violated.

This chapter will discuss the legal requirements and the strictures put on drug testing policies in amateur sports in the US. It will begin with a discussion of a general legal framework for analysing a drug testing policy in amateur sports. The chapter will then move to a comparison of the different judicial models for review of drug testing policies in interscholastic (high school and lower grades) and intercollegiate (college) sports in the US. The aim of this chapter is to provide an overall US judicial model to use in assessing the validity of drug testing programs in amateur sport.

DRUG TESTING OF AMATEUR ATHLETES IN GENERAL

The issue of whether schools can test their student athletes for drug use is governed by many judicial decisions within the last 15 years. However, an early appellate court case at the high school level illustrates the issues involved in all testing procedures for amateur athletes.

In 1986, the Tippecanoe County School Corporation (TSC) implemented a drug testing policy for its student athletes.[2] Under the policy, all students desiring to participate in interscholastic athletics, and their parent or guardian, were required to sign a consent form agreeing to submit to urinalysis if chosen on a random basis.

The actual testing procedure was as follows: the randomly selected student would enter a bathroom, accompanied by a school official of the same sex, where the student would be given a specimen bottle. The student would enter a lavatory stall and close the door so as not to be under visual observation while producing a sample. The official would merely stand outside of the stall to listen to the normal sounds of urination and then check the sample produced for temperature and tampering.

If a sample tested positive for controlled substances or performance enhancing drugs, the student athlete was given an opportunity to provide an innocent explanation for the result and to have the sample tested by a laboratory of their choice. Barring any satisfactory explanation, a first positive test result would result in a suspension from 30% of the athletic contests, a second positive would result in suspension from 50% and a third positive would result in suspension for a full calendar year. A fourth positive result would mean the student being barred from athletic participation for the remainder of their high school career.

In 1987, two student athletes sued TSC, claiming that the policy violated their rights under the Fourth Amendment to the US Constitution.[3] The Fourth Amendment provides that:

---

2   The policy discussed here is similar to all of the policies discussed in the cases to follow in this chapter.

3   *Schaill v Tippecanoe County School Corp* 864 F 2d 1309 (7th Cir 1988).

> The right of the people to be secure in their persons, houses, papers, and effects, against unreasonable searches and seizures, shall not be violated, and no Warrants shall issue, but upon probable cause, supported by Oath or affirmation, and particularly describing the place to be searched, and the persons or things to be seized.[4]

In general, as a result of this language, any searches conducted by governmental officials (including officials at a public high school) must be based upon probable cause and a warrant, or at least some form of individualised suspicion of the individual being searched. The question in the cases at the amateur athletic level is under what circumstances these requirements can be avoided.

As the *Schaill* court discussed, the US Supreme Court has held that 'A "search" occurs when an expectation of privacy that society is prepared to consider reasonable is infringed'.[5] This mandate from the US Constitution and the Supreme Court serves as the framework under which all drug testing policies will be evaluated in the US. Such policies are assessed as searches, and must be analysed to determine whether they are still reasonable searches which may be allowed.

In this initial case, the Court of Appeals for the Seventh Circuit agreed that TSC's drug testing policy was a search because, as it said, 'There can be little doubt that a person engaging in the act of urination possesses a reasonable expectation of privacy as to that act, and as to the urine which is excreted'.[6] Yet this only began the court's inquiry.

In assessing the drug testing policy, the court turned to a test that would balance the individual student athlete's rights under the Fourth Amendment against the governmental interests allegedly used to justify the intrusion caused by the drug test itself. This balancing is then part of an assessment of the actual reasonableness of the testing policy itself.

In balancing the interests involved here, the court pointed out initially that such searches are generally more permissible where an individual already has a diminished expectation of privacy.[7] As the court explained, student athletes have a particularly diminished expectation of privacy, as reflected in the element of 'communal undress' inherent in athletic participation. This is clearly demonstrated by the mandatory medical examinations which students must undertake to participate in athletics, and the incredible regulation that they are under from their schools and governing athletic association while participating in athletics.[8]

---

4   US Constitution, Amendment IV.
5   *Schaill v Tippecanoe County School Corp* 864 F 2d 1309 (7th Cir 1988), pp 1311–12 (citing *USA v Jacobsen* 466 US 109 (1984), p 113).
6   *Ibid*, p 1312.
7   *Ibid*, p 1317.
8   *Ibid*, p 1318.

The next part of the balancing is the court's assessment of the governmental interest furthered by the particular search – here, the drug testing policy. As part of this analysis, the court also looked to whether any less intrusive means could be used that would still sufficiently serve the government's interests.[9] The court agreed with TSC that the use of drugs is a particular health and safety hazard to student athletes; as it stated, '[d]ue to alterations of mood, reductions of motor co-ordination and changes in the perception of pain attributable to drug use, the health and safety of athletes was particularly threatened'.[10] Moreover, the court found it important that the student athlete is viewed as a role model by other students and in the community and, therefore, a student athlete's drug use could lead other students to such risky behaviour.[11]

The plaintiffs attacking the policy also argued that a programme that would only test individuals based on individualised suspicion would have been a much less intrusive alternative. However, the court would not challenge the association's judgment that the random testing method was more effective and a better deterrent.[12]

In order to withstand constitutional scrutiny, the drug testing policy also had to incorporate certain safeguards to 'assure that reasonable expectations of privacy are not "subject to the discretion"' of the individual monitoring the testing itself.[13] In this regard, the court again found that the test was a reasonable search, because the official monitoring the test was not viewing the student athlete while giving the sample and had no involvement in selecting individuals who would be tested, and because student athletes were informed in advance of the procedures used and chances of being tested by signing a consent form.[14] On this last point, it is important to note that courts have been uniform in determining that participation in athletics at the high school level in itself is a privilege and not a right. And, therefore, even though athletes would not be allowed to participate in athletics without signing the form (clearly a sort of coercion in itself), as the court stated in this case, 'It is not unreasonable to couple these benefits [of participating in sports] with an obligation to undergo drug testing'.[15]

In the end, the Seventh Circuit found that the TSC drug testing policy, although clearly a search, was reasonable and did not violate the Fourth Amendment.

---

9   *Schaill v Tippecanoe County School Corp* 864 F 2d 1309 (7th Cir 1988), p 1318.
10 *Ibid*, p 1320.
11 *Ibid*.
12 *Ibid*, p 1321.
13 *Ibid*, p 1321.
14 *Ibid*, pp 1321–22.
15 *Ibid*, p 1320.

The *Schaill* case provides the framework for analysing the legality of all drug testing programs at the amateur level. Such programs will be analysed to determine whether they are searches that would normally be held to be violations of the Fourth Amendment to the US Constitution. This analysis focuses on the reasonableness of the drug testing programme itself that is measured by a balancing test. The test balances the individual's privacy interests in the form of an expectation of privacy in the procedure and results of such testing, against the government's interests generally in promoting the health and safety of student athletes and in not using some less intrusive means of testing.

Clearly, the issue of individual rights is not paramount. The courts have consistently stated that it is perfectly legal and legitimate for a school to institute a drug testing policy in the interests of protecting the health and safety of the student athletes themselves. American courts, schools and associations have repeatedly acknowledged and asserted the serious health and safety risks associated with any kind of drug use. In their roles as protecting the student athletes involved in their programmes, schools have found these safety concerns to be paramount.

In line with these health concerns, soon after the *Schaill* case, the US Supreme Court helped clarify the balancing test in two related cases, both decided on the same day. In the first case, *Von Raab*, US Customs Service employees were forced to submit to a drug screening programme if they were involved in drug interdiction, were required to carry firearms or required to handle classified material. Certain employees sued the Customs Service, claiming that the drug testing policy was an illegal search under the Fourth Amendment.[16] In using the same type of balancing test that the Seventh Circuit used in *Schaill*, the Supreme Court balanced the individual worker's privacy interests against the government's interests in the drug screening programme. The *Von Raab* court then added to the test, by stating that the government has a 'compelling interest' in screening the workers involved here due to the high level of risk involved in their jobs and the nature of the work they perform in detecting and eliminating drugs that enter the country.[17]

The companion case, *Skinner*, dealt with Federal railroad administration regulations requiring railway employees to submit to drug testing after certain major accidents or after violating certain safety rules. In this case, the court again stated that the government's 'compelling interest' in testing in this way outweighed the individual employee's privacy interests.[18] The court also explained that this 'compelling interest' was based on 'special needs' that allowed the government to test in this way, avoiding the normal requirements of probable cause and issuing a warrant.

16 *National Treasury Employees Union et al v Von Raab* 489 US 656 (1989).

17 *Ibid*, pp 668–72.

18 *Skinner v Railway Labor Executives Association* 489 US 602 (1989).

With the addition of these two Supreme Court decisions, the analysis of a drug testing policy of student athletes would focus on whether the policy is a reasonable search under the Fourth Amendment. This reasonableness is then assessed by balancing (a) the student athlete's expectation of privacy (generally considered to be diminished), and (b) the government's interest in promoting the policy, which must be a *compelling interest* based on *special needs*. These special needs focus on health and safety concerns, ranging from certain health and safety factors associated with drug use to the perception that student athletes are role models within the school and community and so their drug use could lead to drug use by others, who then would be subject to certain health and safety risks. Finally, a court will look to the nature of the policy itself and the possibility that there might be less intrusive means available to serve the governmental interest involved. The US Supreme Court would soon use this model in assessing for itself a drug testing policy at the interscholastic level.

INTERSCHOLASTIC ATHLETICS

The *Schaill* case, discussed above, was an important step in determining what type of drug testing programme would be allowed at the high school and grade school level. Seven years later, the US Supreme Court completed the steps by setting out the explicit rules for drug testing programmes at this interscholastic level.

Drugs had not been a problem for schools in Vernonia, Oregon. However, by the end of the 1980s, drug use and disciplinary problems had increased at an exponential rate in Vernonia schools. Student athletes were not only among the drug users; they were also the leaders of the drug culture at the schools. Because of the dangers associated with drug use (including deleterious effects on motivation, memory, judgment, reaction, co-ordination and performance), many coaches noticed their athletes being stricken with severe injuries attributable to their drug use.

In response to this problem, School District 47J, the regulatory association for several Vernonia schools, offered special classes, speakers, and presentations designed to enlighten students to the problems associated with drug use. However, the problems persisted. Consequently, the district held a parent's input night to determine if parents would approve of a student athlete drug policy. The parents uniformly agreed to the district's implementation of the policy, the express purpose of which was to 'prevent student athletes from using drugs, to protect their health and safety, and to provide drug users with assistance programs'.[19]

---

19 *Vernonia School District 47J v Acton* 515 US 646 (1995).

The policy applied to all student athletes. Initially, every student athlete and his or her parents had to sign a consent form agreeing to the testing. Athletes were tested at the beginning of the season for each sport and, once a week during the season, a random drawing was taken, representing 10% of the athletes.

During the testing, the student athletes entered the locker room with an adult monitor of the same sex. Each boy would produce a sample while standing fully clothed at a urinal with his back to the monitor. Girls were allowed to produce samples in a bathroom stall with the monitor outside the door. The monitor would then check each sample for tampering and temperature. An independent laboratory then tested these samples.

If a sample tested positive, a second test would be taken immediately to confirm the result. If the result was still positive, the student athlete and his or her parents then had to meet with the school principal, at which time the student could either decide to participate in a drug assistance programme that included weekly urinalysis, or be suspended from participation for the remainder of the current season and the next season entirely. The student athlete would then be tested again before being eligible to play. A second positive test resulted in an automatic suspension for the current year and next year, while a third positive test resulted in suspension for an additional year.

In 1991, James Acton signed up to play football at a Vernonia grade school. He was not allowed to participate when he would not consent to the drug testing programme. His parents sued the district, claiming that the policy denied him his rights under the Fourth and 14th Amendments to the US Constitution.[20] After making its way through the lower courts, the case found its way to the Supreme Court to resolve the issue finally.

As in the framework discussed above, the Supreme Court began by noting that any drug testing policy is a search under the Fourth Amendment, and the court also noted that the 14th Amendment extends the protection of the Fourth Amendment to searches by State officials like the public officials in the district.[21] The court then began to assess the reasonableness of the search as represented by the drug testing policy.

In judging the reasonableness of the district's policy, the court adopted the language in the *Skinner* case and stated the balancing test as follows: '... whether a particular search meets the reasonableness standard "is judged by balancing its intrusion on the individual's Fourth Amendment interests against its promotion of legitimate governmental interests".'[22] This is the Supreme Court's test, and the test that will be used in judging the

---

20 *Vernonia School District 47J v Acton* 515 US 646 (1995), p 651.

21 *Ibid*, p 652.

22 *Ibid*, pp 652–53 (citing *Skinner v Railway Labor Executives Association* 489 US 602 (1989), p 619).

reasonableness of any such drug testing programmes at the interscholastic level.

The court began its balancing by discussing the nature of the student athlete's privacy interests at issue. The court found it particularly important that the individuals tested were children and that they were in public schools. The court determined that, while at school, these student athletes were 'committed to the temporary custody of the State', that is, in a position of *'in loco parentis* over the children entrusted to them'.[23] Therefore, these students already have a lesser expectation of privacy than a normal individual because the school is in control and supervision of them while in school.

The court also looked to the *Schaill* case and found that student athletes have an even lesser expectation of privacy due to the basic elements of 'communal undress' which were described above.[24] Student athletes are under the control of the coaches or administrators of their sports programmes in regard to dress, training hours and other matters and should expect to have their privacy intruded upon while participating in sports.

The court looked to the nature of the drug testing policy as an intrusion on the clearly diminished privacy rights of student athletes. The court found it very important that the student athletes produced samples while under no direct aural viewing by the monitors: in the court's word, a 'negligible' invasion of privacy.[25] The court also found that the methods of testing the sample and confidentiality measures surrounding the testing were reasonable.[26]

In its final analysis, the court looked to the nature of the governmental concern prompting the drug policy itself. In looking at the type of governmental interest necessary to balance the test in favour of reasonableness, the court defined for the first time what a 'compelling interest' would be for purposes of evaluating the government's interest in this type of case. A compelling interest is one that 'appears *important enough* to justify the particular search at hand, in light of other factors that show the search to be relatively intrusive upon a genuine expectation of privacy'.[27]

In discussing this importance, the court recognised many factors that demonstrated that the Vernonia School District had a compelling interest in putting forth the drug policy. Studies showed that drug use by children was a serious health problem and affected the entire student body, as it disrupts the

---

23   *Vernonia School District 47J v Acton* 515 US 646 (1995), p 654.

24   *Ibid*, pp 656–57 (citing *Schaill v Tippecanoe County School Corp* 864 F 2d 1309 (7th Cir 1988)).

25   *Ibid*, p 658.

26   *Ibid*.

27   *Ibid*, p 661; emphasis in original.

educational process.[28] Student athletes who use drugs are at particular risk of immediate harm and of harming their competitors.[29] Moreover, the district's concerns were immediate and necessary to deal with 'an immediate crisis of greater proportions than existed in' the *Skinner* and *Von Raab* cases discussed above, 'caused by the sharp increase in drug use' among the student athletes and student body.[30] All of this led to a 'special need' which the court determined to exist in the public school context.[31]

As to the procedure used, the court determined that it was efficacious: as the court noted: 'It seems self-evident that a drug problem largely fuelled by the "role model" effect of athletes' drug use, and of particular danger to athletes, is effectively addressed by making sure that athletes do not use drugs.' As to the possible alternative of drug testing based on individualised suspicion, the court found that this alternative was at least impracticable, due to the risks associated with falsely accusing students who appear to exhibit drug induced behaviour, and due to the stigma attached to being singled out for such testing.[32]

In the end, in finding that the drug testing policy was constitutional, the court found that the most significant factor was that 'the policy was undertaken in furtherance of the government's responsibilities, under a public school system, as guardian and tutor of children entrusted to its care'.[33]

The *Vernonia* court defined more clearly the type of compelling governmental interest that would be needed to substantiate a drug testing programme, while also demonstrating that a student athlete in a public school has a significantly diminished interest in their own personal privacy, at least while at school. Moreover, the court agreed that the drug problem in public schools in the US had reached epic proportions and was a special need in support of the Government's interest in a drug testing programme. The background for this epidemic is the health and safety risks that student athletes can face as a result of such drug use.

While *Vernonia* may have clarified the judicial review of drug testing policies at the interscholastic level, several later cases refined this process even more. Two years after the *Vernonia* decision, the Supreme Court added to the judicial model in a case that did not involve student athletes. The case of *Chandler v Miller* dealt with a random urinalysis drug testing policy for candidates to public office in Georgia.[34] While the facts of the case are

---

28 *Vernonia School District 47J v Acton* 515 US 646 (1995), p 662.

29 *Ibid.*

30 *Ibid*, p 663.

31 *Ibid*, p 653.

32 *Ibid*, p 663.

33 *Ibid*, p 665.

34 *Chandler v Miller* 520 US 305 (1997).

unimportant for purposes of analysing student athlete drug testing, the court did go further in defining the 'special needs' prong of the model. According to the court: 'When such "special needs" concerns other than crime detection – are alleged in justification of a Fourth Amendment intrusion – courts must undertake a context-specific inquiry, examining closely the competing private and public interests advanced by the parties.'[35] It is this context specific inquiry that must then be followed in analysing a drug testing policy in interscholastic athletics that does not in any way have as its purpose the determination of criminal activity.

This special need must be 'substantial', that is, 'important enough to override the individual's acknowledged privacy interest, sufficiently vital to suppress the Fourth Amendment's normal requirement of individualized suspicion'.[36] Moreover, a 'demonstrated problem of drug abuse ... would shore up an assertion of special need', while '[p]roof of unlawful drug use may help to clarify – and to substantiate – the precise hazards posed by such use'.[37] If the special need is based on a potential risk to public safety, random suspicionless testing policies may become reasonable and be allowed, although they are searches under the Fourth Amendment.[38]

Soon after this case, the Supreme Court of Colorado explained that the Supreme Court's analysis in *Vernonia* was really reducible to a three part test. This test would consider:

(a) 'the nature of the privacy interest upon which the search ... intrudes';

(b) 'the character of the intrusion that is complained of'; and

(c) 'the nature and immediacy of the governmental concern at issue ... and the efficacy of the means for meeting it'.[39]

This test, in conjunction with the considerations discussed above, creates an overall model for judicial review of a drug testing policy. A drug testing policy will be analysed under the Fourth Amendment to determine whether the policy is a reasonable search that will be allowed as constitutional. A judicial model for this process is as follows:

---

35 *Chandler v Miller* 520 US 305 (1997), p 314.

36 *Ibid,* p 318.

37 *Ibid,* p 319.

38 *Ibid,* p 323.

39 *Trinidad School District No 1 v Lopez* 963 P 2d 1095 (Colo 1998), p 1106. This case dealt with a testing policy that extended to all students involved in any extracurricular activities, from athletics to marching band. The Colorado Supreme Court found that the special needs that may exist in the athletic setting do not exist in other extracurricular settings, and so the policy was found to be illegal.

Step 1   Balancing test

(1)   Balance – the nature of the student athlete's privacy interest.

(2)   Against – the nature and immediacy of the governmental interest:

    (a)   the governmental interest must be *compelling*;

    (b)   the governmental interest must be based on a *special need* focused on a health and safety concern.

Step 2   Character of the intrusion

(1)   Look to the efficacy of the procedure in meeting the governmental interest.

(2)   Determine whether there are other less intrusive means.

This model reduces the various language discussed in the courts to two basic steps that encompass all of the pieces discussed so far. As will be shown, this judicial model has been extended beyond the athletic context and possibly further than the Supreme Court envisioned.

After *Schaill* and *Vernonia*, and the Supreme Court's clarifications of special need in *Chandler*, it seemed that the extent of drug testing allowed in interscholastic athletics was clear. Public schools could legally test their student athletes due to the compelling government interest in such programmes, as based upon the special need caused by the incredible health and safety risks brought on by student athlete drug use. However, the courts did not stop here.

In 1998, the Seventh Circuit Court of Appeals, in *Todd*, used the same judicial model to uphold drug testing policies aimed at students involved in any extracurricular activities, and not just sports. The court found that 'the reasoning compelling drug testing of athletes also applies to testing of students involved in extracurricular activities'.[40] Therefore, students involved in extracurricular activities such as student council, foreign language clubs and the Fellowship of Christian Athletes also could be subjected to a random drug testing policy.

In a similar case, the Eighth Circuit Court of Appeals, in *Miller*, focused on the Supreme Court's recognition in *Vernonia* that students in public schools necessarily have diminished expectations of privacy, as it found that 'students who elect to be involved in school [that is, extracurricular] activities have a legitimate expectation of privacy that is diminished to a level below that of the already lowered expectation of non-participating students'.[41] Interestingly, the Eighth Circuit recognised that there was no immediate crisis, as there was in

---

40   *Todd v Rush County Schools* 133 F 3d 984 (1998), p 986.
41   *Miller v Wilkes* 172 F 3d 574 (8th Cir 1999).

Vernonia, yet the court saw no reason why 'a school district should be compelled to wait until there is a demonstrable problem with substance abuse among its students before the district is constitutionally permitted to take measures that will help protect its schools'.[42]

In May 2000, the Seventh Circuit Court of Appeals, in *Joy*, again reviewed a drug testing policy that was mandatory for students in all extracurricular activities. The court followed the judicial model above in looking to the nature of the privacy interest involved, the character of the intrusion, the nature and immediacy of the governmental concerns and the efficacy of the procedure itself in assessing the drug testing programme. However, in disagreeing with its decision in *Todd*, in this case, the court found that:

(a) students participating in extracurricular activities are not subject to the same rules and regulations as those in athletics, and so, although their expectations of privacy may be lessened, they are still greater than that of a student athlete;

(b) there was no special need demonstrating a crisis situation in drug use by students in non-sports extracurricular activities;

(c) there was no compelling governmental concern or interest with respect to these students; and

(d) there was no showing that this policy was the most efficacious in addressing any perceived problem of drug use by students merely involved in non-sports extracurricular activities.[43]

However, mindful of these shortcomings, in following principles of *stare decisis* and precedent, the court still had to follow its decision in *Todd* and uphold the drug testing policy.[44]

Although the Supreme Court of Colorado did not allow a drug testing policy to extend to students in any extracurricular activity, and the *Joy* court had some of the same misgivings, the decisions in *Todd* and *Lopez* demonstrate that some courts will allow such policies to remain in place by explicitly following the Supreme Court's *Vernonia* decision. Unfortunately, it is left to the Supreme Court to address this particular issue before the legality of testing of students in all extracurricular activities is resolved.

---

42 *Miller v Wilkes* 172 F 3d 574 (8th Cir 1999), p 581.

43 *Joy et al v Penn-Harris-Madison School Corp* 212 F 3d 1052 (7th Cir 2000), pp 1063–65.

44 *Ibid*, pp 1065–66.

INTERCOLLEGIATE ATHLETICS

American intercollegiate athletics are different from interscholastic sports in more respects than the age of the students involved. The student athletes who participate in college sports will be above the age of 18 and it would seem that they have a stronger set of personal privacy rights than would a minor athlete at the interscholastic level. However, this is not necessarily the case.

The analysis must begin with an explanation of college sports. Similar to the interscholastic level, college sports are governed by an overriding association. However, at the college level, this governance is by a national association, the National Collegiate Athletic Association (NCAA).

The NCAA comprises virtually all college athletic programmes in the US. These members then are classified in terms of their size and whether they provide athletics-based financial aid to their student athletes. In a general sense, schools range from the largest schools that provide significant amounts of financial aid to their student athletes (the Division 1 level) to smaller schools that do not offer athletics-based financial aid to student athletes (the Division 3 level).

This chapter will focus on the Division 1 level because it has proved to be the area that has seen the most litigation and so has had exposure to the judicial model for drug testing that was discussed at the interscholastic level.

For each division, the NCAA member schools must follow the rules and regulations put forth in an NCAA *Manual*. Therefore, in discussing the NCAA's drug testing policy, the place to begin is with the NCAA's *Division 1 Manual 2000–01*.

The NCAA's drug testing programme is very similar to the programmes discussed so far. The programme begins with the requirement that each student athlete must sign a drug testing consent form each year, to be eligible to participate in intercollegiate athletics.[45] Student athletes who do not sign this form are ineligible to practise or compete in their sport.

The specifics of the drug testing procedure vary in each sport; however, students selected for testing furnish a urine sample under the visual supervision of an NCAA monitor.[46] The NCAA provides an extensive list of banned drugs that it tests for recreational to performance enhancing drugs.[47]

If a student tests positive for one of the banned drugs, he or she will be ineligible to participate in all NCAA sponsored college athletics for one year.[48]

---

45 NCAA, *Division 1 Manual 2000–01*, Art 3.2.4.6: Drug-Testing Consent Form; Art 14.1.4: Drug-Testing Consent Form.

46 NCAA, *Drug-Testing Program Protocol 2000–01*, Art 6.0: Specimen Collection Procedures.

47 *Ibid*, NCAA, fn 45, Art 31.2.3.1: Banned Drugs.

48 *Ibid*, Art 18.4.1.5.1: Duration of Ineligibility.

A second positive result after having been restored to eligibility will lead to the student athlete's loss of eligibility to participate in any remaining regular season and post-season contests in any NCAA sports.[49] Further details of the NCAA's drug testing policy are unnecessary in order to assess the legality of drug testing at the college level. The courts have provided this assessment.

As the majority of colleges in the US are members of the NCAA, they must follow the NCAA's rules and regulations in order to sustain their membership and give their student athletes the chance to become eligible to participate in NCAA sponsored athletics. Therefore, many schools have adopted drug testing policies of their own, which follow the NCAA model.

One such school is the University of Colorado (CU). In the 1980s, CU implemented a random suspicionless drug testing policy for all student athletes. Under the policy, potential student athletes were required to sign a consent form to the policy in order to become eligible to participate in CU athletics. In 1993, several student athletes sued CU, claiming that the drug testing policy was a violation of their constitutional rights under the Fourth Amendment, in the case of *University of Colorado v Derdyn*.[50]

The case made its way to the Supreme Court of Colorado, which began its review of the validity of the policy by performing the same balancing of individual privacy interests against the governmental interests involved as in the judicial model discussed above. It is important to note, as well, that, although the court recognised that, as a public university, CU was clearly bound by the strictures of the US Constitution, a private entity would not necessarily be.

The court also noted that it did not find the interscholastic cases discussed above (such as *Schaill*) to be of any particular relevance to its decision, because the college students in this case were not the minors in an *in loco parentis* position while in school.[51] The college students were adults, and so this factor of protecting the students, which was so important in the interscholastic cases, was of no importance here.

Regardless, CU argued that the student athletes' privacy interests were diminished for several reasons, including: (a) the fact that each student athlete must already submit to an annual physical, which includes the provision of a urine sample;[52] (b) student athletes must also submit to the NCAA's random testing policy in order to participate in NCAA athletics;[53] and (c) that the consequences of refusing to submit to the programme were not severe because a students would only lose the privilege of participating in intercollegiate

---

49 *Op cit*, NCAA, fn 45, Art 18.4.1.5.1: Duration of Ineligibility.
50 *University of Colorado v Derdyn* 863 P 2d 929 (Colo 1993).
51 *Ibid*, p 938.
52 *Ibid*, p 939.
53 *Ibid*, p 941.

sports at CU – they would not lose their jobs or be kicked out of school.[54] The court disagreed with CU at every step and found that the fact that student athletes must submit to a medical examination does not result in a diminishment of their expectation of privacy, the NCAA's policy also had no direct relation to a diminishment of their rights herein, and the loss of the privilege of participating in sports was very significant.[55]

The court then moved to an analysis of the governmental interest that CU proposed in support of its drug testing policy. CU argued that its interests were in preparing its athletes for the NCAA's drug testing programme, preventing other students from following role model athletes who used drugs, ensuring fair competition, and protecting the health and safety of the student athletes.[56]

In assessing these interests, the Colorado Supreme Court would not specifically follow the 'compelling interest' language of the judicial model. Instead, 'rather than trying to characterize CU's interests as "compelling" "strong", "substantial", or of some lesser degree of importance', the court found it more helpful to 'compare them with other types of commonly asserted interests that have been held sufficient or insufficient to justify similar intrusions'.[57] Still, by doing this, the court then found that 'a concern for public safety animates the general acceptance of drug testing by courts'.[58]

In looking for this concern for public safety, the court found CU lacking. Therefore, since CU's justifications were not sufficient, and in fact had insufficient factual evidence in their support, the balancing of the private versus government interests fell in favour of the private interests of the student athletes. All this, even though the court acknowledged that CU's interests were valid and significant in a general sense.[59]

In the end, the court found that CU's drug testing policy was an unconstitutional violation of the Fourth Amendment.[60] Yet, what does this say about the judicial model proposed above? The court did follow the normal balancing test and, although it would not directly associate itself with the language of compelling interest or special needs, it seems clear that the result is the same. What changes the analysis and causes the programme to be declared unconstitutional is that the individuals involved are adults and so their privacy interests are much stronger than the children involved in the interscholastic cases.

---

54 *University of Colorado v Derdyn* 863 P 2d 929 (Colo 1993), pp 941–42.

55 *Ibid*, pp 939–42.

56 *Ibid*, p 943.

57 *Ibid*, p 944.

58 *Ibid* (citing *International Brotherhood of Electrical Workers Local 1245 v Skinner* 913 F 2d 1454 (9th Cir 1990), p 1462).

59 *Ibid*, pp 945–46.

60 *Ibid*.

The NCAA's drug testing policy has also come under direct attack. The most important case found its way to the Supreme Court of California. In this case, *Hill v NCAA*, student athletes sued the NCAA, claiming that its drug testing policy (as it was in 1994) violated their rights under the California Constitution.[61] Much of the case is a description of the history behind the NCAA and its drug testing policy and a discussion of the specifics of California law, both of which are unimportant for the discussion in this chapter. For the purposes of assessing the judicial model, however, the California Supreme Court was in line with the other cases discussed so far, even though the NCAA has long been determined to be a private entity and not a State actor. Therefore, as the court noted, the NCAA had no obligation to use the least intrusive means available in its drug testing model because it could not be held up to the same scrutiny as a State actor, like all of the public schools discussed above.[62]

In this case, the court also looked to a balancing of the individual privacy interests involved against the NCAA's interest in promoting its drug testing policy. The court agreed with the majority of other courts discussed – the student athlete's expectation of privacy is already diminished for several reasons. The court pointed out that student athletes have advance notice of the policy as a requirement to participate in NCAA athletics and must consent to the policy before participating.[63] As to this consent, the court found it unimportant that a lack of consent would result in ineligibility because participation in NCAA sports is merely a benefit and not a right in itself, and so a lack of this benefit could not be a serious violation of one's rights.[64]

The court did note that the NCAA's method of visual monitoring of sample production was more invasive than the other methods discussed herein.[65] However, the court found that the NCAA's justifications for this method – (a) safeguarding the integrity of competition, and (b) protecting the health and safety of student athletes – were very significant. Moreover, the drug testing programme was reasonably calculated to serve these goals of the NCAA, and so counterbalanced the privacy interests at stake.[66]

Three years after this decision, a case dealing with the drug testing programme initiated by the University of Southwestern Louisiana (USL) reached the First Circuit Court of Appeals – the *Brennan* case. Here, a student athlete who tested positive for drug use after two tests, and so was suspended by USL in accordance with the NCAA's policy, sued the school to enjoin its enforcement of the NCAA rules because the policy violated his privacy

---

61   *Hill v NCAA* 7 Cal 4th 1 (1994).

62   *Ibid*, p 50.

63   *Ibid*, p 42.

64   *Ibid*.

65   *Ibid*, p 43.

66   *Ibid*, p 43–44.

rights.[67] The court initially made clear that a State university's imposition of sanctions in accordance with NCAA rules is State action and so could be attacked as violations of his privacy rights.[68]

The court then turned to the *Hill* decision discussed above, and followed the California Supreme Court's analysis that, while 'the drug testing program impacts privacy interests ... there was no constitutional violation when the student athlete's lower expectations of privacy were balanced against the NCAA's countervailing interests'.[69] Although the student athlete in this case had sued the school, and not the NCAA, the First Circuit found that the student athlete also had a diminished expectation of privacy, while USL 'shares the NCAA's interests in ensuring fair competition in intercollegiate sports as well as in protecting the health and safety of student athletes' and that the 'significant interest by USL and the NCAA ... outweighs the relatively small compromise of privacy under the circumstances'.[70]

In following this case and the *Hill* case, it is clear that judicial review of drug testing policies at the intercollegiate level will also follow the judicial model introduced above, especially in the use of a balancing of the individual and governmental, or at least governing bodies' interests involved. The college cases do not literally discuss the other parts of the judicial model concerning an assessment of special need and a thorough assessment of the intrusiveness of the search itself for several reasons.

Initially, the *Vernonia* case and the cases after it predate all but the last college case provided in this chapter. In addition, as *Vernonia* followed the *Hill* case in great detail, the judicial model had just not been developed at this early stage for these decisions to follow. More importantly, the schools, NCAA and student athletes in these college cases are not involved in the same protective environment found at the interscholastic level. Therefore, the judicial model's grounding in the nature of the relationship between interscholastic student athletes and their schools or regulatory associations is absent. Still, the analysis is very similar at both levels, and it is anticipated that, at the college level, more discussion of special need and compelling interest should be anticipated.

---

67   *Brennan v Board of Trustees for University of Louisiana Systems* 691 So 2d 324 (1st Cir 1997).
68   *Ibid*, p 328.
69   *Ibid*, p 329.
70   *Ibid*, pp 329–30.

CONCLUSION

Drug testing of student athletes at the interscholastic and intercollegiate levels of sports participation has been, and will continue to be, allowed as long as the drug testing programme meets the Fourth Amendment to the US Constitution's requirements of reasonableness. This reasonableness is assessed by judicial review following some form of the general judicial model proposed in this chapter.

In US amateur sports, drug testing is not an issue of assessing the legitimacy of drug use, or even arguments concerning the differences between the effects of recreational and performance enhancing drugs. Drug testing programmes can be implemented to require student athletes to submit to testing as long as the governmental entity or association ultimately in charge of the testing programme can demonstrate a compelling interest in the programme. This compelling interest must be based on some special need in protecting student athletes and others from the dangers of drug use, which counterbalances any alleged impact on an individual's right to privacy.

The crux of the issue is special need. All of the courts dealing with student athletes at this amateur level have agreed that the health and safety risks of drug abuse supersede any potential individual rights that student athletes may have. The courts have also agreed that student athletes at the high school and college level are even more restricted because of the regulation that they voluntarily subject themselves to.

This consideration is similar to the courts' willingness to allow drug testing at the professional level due to the nature of the collective bargaining agreements in professional sports and the fact that players voluntarily agree to be bound by these agreements. Similarly, players in high school and college voluntarily agree to participate and, consequently, to submit themselves to many forms of regulation, including drug testing.

At this point, it may seem that the personal rights of the athletes involved have been superseded, if not eliminated, but this is not the case. One of the basic tenets of sports participation at the amateur level is that students do not have any right to participate in sports in any way. At the amateur level, individuals only have a privilege to participate, there is no property or other right associated with this privilege. Restrictions on this privilege are perfectly acceptable as long as they do not infringe any other protected rights, such as privacy rights. In addition, as the cases demonstrated, an amateur athlete's privacy rights are already diminished.

This may seem paternalistic and controlling. In some sense it is. The US legal system has often been set up to protect the health and safety of individuals at the expense of their personal privacy rights. The drug testing cases follow this paradigm.

The drug testing cases also do not really focus on the issue of drug testing itself. The focus is on the privacy rights of the individuals involved versus the government's right to serve the health and safety interests of its individuals. Drug testing is then the forum; it is not the issue.

The judicial model studied in this chapter may not be applicable to any European system, because it is grounded in rights jurisprudence and not interpretations of sport itself. As they continue to expand, European sports may strive to emulate the business of sports in the US; however, European courts would have to begin following the jurisprudence of US courts as discussed herein, in order for this judicial model to become applicable beyond the US.

Drug testing programmes in high schools and colleges are here to stay, because US courts have been persuaded by the arguments demonstrating the different negative health and safety affects associated with drug use. Unfortunately for student athletes at any amateur level, who have nothing more than a privilege to participate in athletics, the choice is simple – submit to a drug testing programme or do not participate in interscholastic or intercollegiate athletics.

CHAPTER 14

CRIMINAL LAW REGULATION OF PERFORMANCE ENHANCING DRUGS: WELCOME FORMALISATION OR KNEE JERK RESPONSE?

Jason Lowther

INTRODUCTION

This chapter considers certain impacts that might be consequent upon the criminalisation of aspects of the use of certain performance enhancing drugs. The use of such a powerful regulatory and socialising machinery against a statistically minute group of people is worthy of closer scrutiny. Central to the wider issues in relation to the use of such drugs is the submission that criminal controls, beyond those that one would expect for consumer protection, help neither the image of sport nor the health of the non-competitive user.

The public perception of the Corinthian ideal might be slightly tarnished. Leaving the vast amounts of money available to leading sports stars aside; ignoring the petulance that at times would seem more in character with the music industry's 'brat pack', the perceived desire to win at all costs would seem to be that which is harming the public image of sport. Drugs issues are at the forefront of this aspect of sporting controversy, with various high profile cases pending or punished by the appropriate sports governing bodies in the last few years. The massive personal gain available to those who are able to succeed at the highest level is obviously a temptation to some to cheat. A wider effect can be seen in the construction of sport as a powerful social cement. Images of sporting excellence and prowess are presented as socially desirable, to be aspired to, emulated and, ultimately, packaged for sale.

In the current climate, the drugs issue, unfortunately for sport, transcends mere cheating through performance enhancement. It goes far beyond even the correct and legitimate concerns for the health of the drug using competitor, or even the image of the controlling bodies. The drug user as criminal and the drug user as cheat are comfortable and complementary representations. There is an identifiable attempt to form a link between the drug user in society as a whole and the drug user in competitive sport,[1] witnessed through statements such as: 'Athletes are often looked to as heroes and role models by our youth and so must be held to a *higher standard* regarding drug use in sport.'[2] It

---

1   See, eg, US Drug Enforcement Agency Conference on Anabolic Steroids Control Act, Annapolis, Maryland, 1995.

2   *Ibid*, finding 7. Emphasis added.

should be pointed out, however, that very few of the athletes so idolised have ever faced a criminal charge consequent on their drug taking. It is perhaps important to realise that the people most likely to be affected by a proscriptive use of the criminal law would be those who are not actively competing in any sport but keen to improve their image, or in some cases self-perception. The use of performance enhancing drugs is firmly ingrained within certain sectors of the non-sporting community, perhaps keen to appear to have attained a socially desirable physique, power or image of healthy athleticism.[3]

The use of anabolic steroids (AS) for cosmetic purposes, or in those sports where there is no proscriptive control over the use of commonly prohibited substances, is well documented.[4] The perception and the reality are that the drugs do work, although the side effects might be potentially harmful for the user who is unable or unwilling to take steps to mitigate them. That there are adverse effects consequent upon irresponsible use is not in doubt, and the most comprehensive study in the UK reported that most users were able to identify at least one unwelcome side effect.[5] Certain of these side effects can be mitigated to a greater or lesser degree through a more informed approach to their use, however: for example, the use of anti-oestrogen drugs, such as Tamoxifen™, to combat certain of the aromatising effects of the more androgenic compounds. More education might be a sensible reaction to perceived problems. The lack of effective advice and counselling has been identified by commentators[6] and, in the current climate, any message is less likely than ever to reach its target audience effectively.

MAINTAINING THE SOCIAL STATUS OF SPORT

In an Olympic year, the anti-drugs hyperbole obviously increased in fervour and frequency. In preparation for this showcase world event, the International Olympic Committee (IOC) prepared a new policy[7] to combat doping and set up a new testing agency to facilitate its implementation. The agency has already received criticism, perhaps unfairly, doubting its ability to police the

---

3   See, eg, Bahrke, MS *et al*, 'Psychological and behavioural effects of endogenous testosterone and anabolic-androgenic steroids' (1996) 22(6) J Sports Medicine 367.

4   See, eg, Korkia PK and Stimson GV, *Anabolic Steroid Use in Great Britain: An Exploratory Investigation*, 1993, Report for the Department of Health, The Welsh Office and the Chief Scientists Office, Scottish Home and Health Department, Centre for Research on Drugs and Health Behaviour, London: HMSO; Clarkson, PM and Thompson, HS, 'Drugs in sport research findings and limitations' (1997) 24(6) J Sports Medicine; Yesalis, C and Bahrke, MS, 'Anabolic-androgenic steroids current issues (1995) 19(5) J Sports Medicine.

5   *Ibid*, Korkia and Stimson.

6   *Ibid*.

7   See below, fn 10.

drug problem effectively, from Barry McCaffrey, the American 'Drug Tsar'.[8] If evidence were needed about the cross-cultural issues involved in contemporary drugs in sport issues, the musings of a zero tolerance, prohibition absolutist such as McCaffrey should provide some indication of it. It may be that the failures of legislators and policy makers effectively to deal with drugs issues in wider society has resulted in sport being seen as a soft target where success can more easily be demonstrated.

It would appear that there is a trend towards the blurring of the lines of demarcation between the criminal law controls placed upon certain drugs of abuse and the anti-doping codes of sports governing bodies in terms of the drugs scheduled as attracting penalties for recalcitrant competitors. To illustrate the point, the supplementary notes to the Olympic Movement Anti-Doping Code, accepted by the Lausanne Declaration of the World Conference on Doping in Sport,[9] state that:

> ... [the] Olympic Movement alone cannot regulate all of the aspects of the fight against doping in sport ...

The IOC stress the need for a partnership approach involving 'public authorities'.[10] The actual Declaration itself goes further still when it states that:

> ... the collaboration in the fight against doping between sports organisations and public authorities shall be reinforced according to the responsibilities of each party. Together, they will also take action in the areas of education ... *and co-ordination of legislation relative to doping.*[11]

It is not explicitly clear, however, which responsibilities the IOC is attributing to whom. The meanings are vague at best. Thus, certain drugs with a very limited, if any, performance enhancing nature, for example, LSD, are controlled under the auspices of the fair competition rules of the IOC. It might be that, in this circumstance, the health and safety of the athlete would provide the justification for this sort of inclusion, or it may, perhaps, be more of a reflection of concern over the sports bodies' image. Recreational use of illegal drugs, such as LSD or ecstasy, by sports people would undermine the perceived wholesomeness of sport, challenging its position as a social good if it were to remain unpunished. By subjecting the drugs used by athletes to assist their performance to similar criminal control as drugs more commonly used for recreational purposes, the inter-relatedness of the drugs issue is brought into sharp focus. Conversely, the fact that a body builder takes growth hormone or anabolic steroids for merely aesthetic purposes does not

---

8   Institute for the Study of Drug Dependence, *Druglink,* January/February 2000, London: ISDD, p 4.
9   Lausanne, 4 February 1999.
10 IOC, *Explanatory Memorandum Concerning the Application of the Olympic Movement Anti-Doping Guide,* 1999, Lausanne: IOC.
11 Lausanne Declaration on Doping in Sport, 1999, para 6; emphasis added.

denigrate the image of sport, but can only be attacked on the grounds of some notional harm that is inextricably linked to manufactured societal attitudes to all drugs. It does seem faintly ridiculous to present a wholesome, and thus acceptable, version of fitness and health only to then castigate those who take drugs to fulfil that vision. If the same logic were applied to other potentially dangerous means of cosmetic enhancement, may there be an argument for the criminalisation of cosmetic surgery?

The next section will examine how the law is structured to regulate the availability and use of performance enhancing drugs and how this fits into the overall framework of drug laws.

CURRENT LAW IN THE UK

Two main legislative controls exist in relation to drug use in the UK: the Medicines Act 1968 and the Misuse of Drugs Act (MDA) 1971. The former is more concerned to regulate how drugs are marketed and sold, whereas the latter is effectively just applied to countering the criminal supply and possession of various compounds scheduled within it. The Medicines Act provides controls over the marketing and distribution of medicinal products through a scheme of licensing. To produce or market such products without the requisite authority is in breach of the provisions of the Act and attracts criminal sanction. The MDA is, in comparison, solely concerned to limit to defined groups, for legitimate purposes, the availability of a range of drugs which have been determined as posing a significant threat to society. It should be pointed out that AS were not originally subject to control under the MDA 1971.

A wide selection of performance enhancing drugs were scheduled to be regulated under the MDA in 1996. Up until this time, the only controls that existed were those in place under the Medicines Act 1968, in common with most other drugs. At the time of the law change, it was difficult to understand the purpose to which the law was being directed. Home Office press releases at the time were kept very much with the *'war on drugs'* mantra in mind,[12] declaring a *'battle* to stamp out abuse of steroids ...'. At the time, however, there was, and there remains, little evidence of the drugs so controlled moving beyond the relatively small and specialist pockets of use they inhabit. Departmental opinion, based on research further explored below, did not offer any conclusive reasons why the drugs should be subject to criminal control. Some clue may be found in the rhetoric of the then Health Minister, Dr Brian Mawhinney, which was firmly linked to the support of the normative proposition that the use of these drugs was inconsistent with notions of fair

---

12   News Release 082/96, 1996, London: Home Office; emphasis added.

play.[13] If anything, as will be suggested below, the introduction of the law has led to uncertainty: an uneasy position for the user, and a less than clear mandate for intervention for the enforcement authorities. In seeking to register disapproval at the *perceived* social harm consequent upon drug taking, the effect of the law change could be that *actual* harm is inflicted upon a relatively small group of users.

A substance becomes subject to classification, and consequent criminal regulation, under the MDA 1971 upon the recommendation of the Advisory Council on the Misuse of Drugs (ACMD). The ACMD describes itself as a statutory and non-executive non-departmental public body established as a result of the MDA,[14] and comprises medical and veterinary professionals, as well as 'people who have a wide and recent experience of social problems connected with the misuse of drugs'.[15] The Council has a statutory remit as provided for in the MDA 1971, which places it under a duty to:

> ... keep under review the situation in the [UK] with respect to drugs which are being or appear to them to be likely to be misused and of which the misuse is having or appears to be having harmful effects sufficient to constitute a social problem ...[16]

The Council is then required to provide advice to ministers on measures necessary to combat both the abuse and the social harm that might be consequent on that abuse. In particular, the ACMD is required to consider such means as: restricting the availability of the drug(s); ensuring the provision of 'proper' treatment or rehabilitation facilities; co-ordinating professional services with impact in the area; providing for education; and promoting research into matters necessary for the prevention of the misuse of the drug in question or on any of the social harms that it may create. A current example involved the question as to whether GHB[17] should be brought under the control of the MDA 1971: the powers and sanctions available under the MDA being considerably more robust than those presented by the Medicines Act 1968, which currently regulates the compound. Sold to clubbers as 'liquid ecstasy' and as a training aid to body builders, it is not yet considered pressing enough a problem to require rescheduling.

It is against a backdrop of these requirements that the ACMD considered AS. The drugs were first considered for their harm potential in the late 1980s, but the Council concluded at that time that the necessary social harm test was

---

13 Press Release H/93/766, 1993, London: Department of Health.

14 Advisory Council on the Misuse of Drugs, *Annual Report Financial Year 1998/99*, 1999, London: Home Office, available at www.homeoffice.gov.uk/cpd/anrep99.htm.

15 *Ibid*, p 2. It is worth noting, however, that there is no representative from the sports world in the current membership of the ACMD, which is perhaps surprising.

16 MDA 1971, s 1.

17 Gammahydroxybutyrate, considered by the ACMD in 1999, but not recommended for rescheduling.

not fulfilled and, thus, the drugs remained outside of the control of the MDA 1971. The issue was revisited in 1993 on the basis of the publication of a Department of Health sponsored piece of research, investigating patterns of use and potential public health concerns.[18] The report resulted in a further consideration of the steroid issue by the ACMD, which, on this occasion, felt compelled to recommend that AS be brought under the control of the MDA 1971. It was believed at this time that the necessary social harm caveat to rescheduling was satisfied on the basis of the harms identified through the report, although the report itself explicitly stated that it did not consider the social implications of use and remained confined to medical concerns.[19] In particular, the public health implications of the injection of AS were examined, and the conclusion was that there was a risk of the spread of blood borne disease such as HIV and hepatitis through the adoption by users of unsafe injecting practices. Harm reduction methods such as greater education and other health promotion activities were recommended. The Council advised that mere possession of AS should not be an offence under the Act and the Secretary of State for the Home Office, Michael Howard, set forth the legislative machinery accordingly.

Once the necessary statutory instruments[20] were drafted and the decision about what to include within the schedules of the MDA 1971 was taken, the law itself should have been relatively unproblematic. There is little controversy attaching to the actual operation and purpose of the majority of the MDA, the basic offences being clearly set out. The MDA attempts to control those substances scheduled within it through creating offences in relation to, *inter alia*, their possession,[21] supply,[22] and their possession with intent to supply.[23] The Act also criminalises the import and export[24] of the drugs scheduled subject to certain statutory defences.[25] The Act proceeds by placing all the scheduled drugs within a classification system. The initial classification relates to the perceived danger of the drug in terms of its abuse potential and the possibility for harm, in a wide sense, to be done to the user or society. Thus, Class A drugs are considered to be the most harmful drugs of abuse and they are, therefore, subject to the most vigorous criminal penalties. Simple possession, for example, as well as the supply and manufacture

---

18 See, above, fn 3.

19 Although it might be argued that *serious* medical concerns may, of themselves, become a social concern.

20 Misuse of Drugs Act 1971 (Modification) Order 1996 (SI 1996/1300); Misuse of Drugs (Amendment) Regulations 1996 (SI 1996/1597).

21 MDA 1971, s 5(2).

22 *Ibid*, s 4.

23 *Ibid*, s 5(3).

24 *Ibid*, s 3.

25 See, eg, those provided in s 28.

without an applicable defence, attracts potentially lengthy imprisonment.[26] Of lesser seriousness are the subsequent Classes B and C, with their perceived dangers reflected in the lesser penalties they attract. The controls placed on AS have classified them as Class C drugs, subject also to the requirements of Scheds 3 and 4 to the Act, regulating trafficking offences and possession in the form of a medicinal product.

Class A drugs include drugs such as heroin and LSD. Obvious stimulants such as cocaine excepted, drugs of this class would not seem to be the usual sorts of compound that would be traditionally associated with an enhanced sporting performance, although UK Sport offers a view that the use of illegal drugs, whether or not performance enhancing, might damage the 'image' of sport.[27] However, there have been studies linking cocaine[28] use with AS use and, perhaps more worrying from a harm reduction perspective, anecdotal reports of the use of a synthetic opiate, Nubain™,[29] reportedly marketed by dealers as an aid to recovery after intensive training. In assessing the potential social problems that may be consequent on the use of AS, the criminalisation of the market for them could perhaps lead to greater harm than the previous regime of control under the Medicines Act 1968. Certain of the possibly detrimental effects that have been predicted as a result of this changed status will be examined below. At a general level, concerns would attach to the *de facto* lack of positive influence that the authorities are able to exert over an illicit market, which, by definition, operates outside the normal conventions of command and control. Furthermore, concerns exist in relation to the inconsistency of application of the law, despite guidance on the issue.[30]

Thus, the current application of the law would seem problematic. The scheduling under the MDA 1971 has raised complex issues of interpretation for the enforcement authorities. The main problem would appear to relate to the fact that the definition of a medicinal product does not appear in the MDA itself. Given that this term is crucial to the operation of the schedule, this would appear to be a major oversight. In the past, the issue has not presented such a conundrum. Conversation with Drug Squad officers in the Derbyshire force revealed a distinct lack of faith in the schedule and, in relation to steroids particularly, a lack of direction from the Home Office. The main criticism seemed to be founded on the lack of any real guidance on what might be

---

26 MDA 1971, Sched 2.

27 UK Sports Council, 'Drugs and sport, classes of substances subject to certain restrictions', in *Competitors' and Officials' Guide to Drugs and Sport*, 1998, London: UKSC.

28 See, eg, Middleman, A and DuRant, R, 'Anabolic steroid use and associated health risk behaviours' (1996) 21(4) J Sports Medicine.

29 Manufactured and licensed by DuPont.

30 Home Office Circular No 29/1996, 3 July 1996, London: Home Office.

considered sufficient amounts to frame a charge of possession with intent to supply.

One drug squad officer contacted explained the ease with which a possession with intent charge might be framed for a drug like heroin. He stated that it would be quite conceivable to secure a conviction in relation to possession with intent to supply for only a very small amount of heroin, as officers are familiar with the patterns of use and distribution. The same would not apply to steroids. Much as Korkia and Stimson discovered that there was little accurate information available to illicit steroid users about the optimum and safest ways to take the drugs, there is as much ignorance within the average drug squad as to how to police them. One drug squad[31] contacted had obtained some underground steroid magazines/guides and used these as a basis for understanding current trends. Guidance is needed for the enforcement authorities if they are to implement the law in an even handed and consistent manner. The drafting of the law has left a lot to be desired as there is, apparently, little consistency of approach.[32] The majority of the AS actually seized by the authorities were recovered by HM Customs and Excise, the drugs representing 20% of the seizures of all Class C drugs.[33]

STATISTICAL CONSIDERATIONS

The Home Office Research and Statistics Directorate produces annual figures to ascertain the levels of drug use in the UK by reference to the number of seizures, the amounts of drugs seized and statistics relating to the disposal of offenders. Over time, these statistics enable the authorities to gain insight into current drug trends and the effectiveness of enforcement measures. The fact that there has been an exponential rise in the number of drug offences and offenders over the last 10 years[34] might be indicative of the increased prevalence of drugs in society, or it could reflect the prohibitionist stance, and the resulting change in enforcement priority. AS have been included in the statistics since 1996 and, anomalies apart, they also present with a year on year increase in the level of seizures, the amount of the drugs seized[35] and the number of people brought into the criminal justice system. As would be

---

31 Conversation with Derbyshire Drug Squad officer, February 2000.

32 Only five of the 51 police authorities in the UK (including Scotland and Northern Ireland) had made any seizure as at the most recent Home Office statistics: Corkery, J, *Drug Seizure and Offender Statistics 1998 (Area Tables)*, 2000, London: HMSO.

33 *Ibid.*

34 Running at about an average of 13% pa 1988–1998; see *ibid.*

35 Eg, the relatively large seizure figures for 1997; see *ibid.*

expected, the levels of both seizure and conviction are low when compared to other drugs commonly misused, reflecting the relatively small using community. It is estimated that only around 1% or less of the population are involved in using AS.[36]

The most recent data[37] show that, in 1998, 171 seizures of the drugs were made. This represents an 11% increase from the 154 seizures made in 1997, and a proportionate increase in the 34 seizures made in 1996, the first year of criminal control. The 1996 figure, however, only represents the last quarter of the year, as legal restrictions only came into force on 1 September that year. It is only to be expected, in common with most other drugs, that the levels of seizure will continue their year on year rise as the effect of the criminalisation of the substances continues to have an impact and enforcement agencies become more familiar with the patterns of use.

The amounts seized have also risen fairly significantly. Home Office statistics show a rise from 3.8 kg in the last quarter of 1996 to a level of 17.6 kg in 1998. There was a relatively large seizure of 455.5 kg in 1997, effectively a blip in the general trend upwards, although it is conceded that it is difficult to ascertain any concrete trends with such a limited amount of data to draw on. It could be that the increased levels of detection and seizure also have something to do with the fact that the enforcement authorities are actively looking for the drugs in a way that they were not previously. It is submitted that the fact that the drugs seized are measured in kilograms demonstrates a lack of understanding of the methods of use and distribution on the part of the enforcement authorities. Ecstasy tablets and LSD, for example, are reported by virtue of the amount of doses seized, perhaps a more appropriate way to record the seizures of steroids, especially since they are counted differently when in ampoule form.[38]

The level of convictions for those people convicted in breach of the provisions of the MDA 1971 that relate to AS are not, in themselves, significant, if one considers the Home Office statistics. However, what is more interesting is that there has been a steady increase in the number of people being convicted on a charge of possession of the drugs. The regulations are absolutely clear that the drugs as scheduled are excepted from the prohibition on possession 'when in the form of a medicinal product'.[39] In addition, the regulations also provide that they are 'excluded from the application of offences arising from the prohibition on importation and exportation when

---

36 *Op cit,* Home Office, fn 32.

37 *Op cit,* Home Office, fn 32. Corkery J, *Drug Seizure and Offender Statistics 1998,* 2000, London: HMSO.

38 *Ibid,* Corkery. 94,583 ampoules were seized by HM Customs and Excise in 1998.

39 Misuse of Drugs (Amendment) Regulations 1996 (SI 1996/1597), para 2(2), amending the Misuse of Drugs Regulations 1985 (SI 1985/2066).

imported or exported in the form of a medicinal product by any person for administration to himself'. This particular aspect would thus seem to permit the possession of the drugs for self-administration, even if the person involved is crossing a border into or out of the UK. Thus, increases in convictions for the offence of possession of AS under the MDA 1971 can only suggest two things. First, that there is an increase in the illegal manufacture or counterfeiting of these drugs and thus, the drugs are unable to be classed as *medicinal products*; or, secondly, that there is a level of confusion as to the precise meaning of the terminology.

MEDICINAL PRODUCT?

The term medicinal product is, as highlighted above, crucial to the operation of the scheme of control of both the Medicines Act 1968 and the Misuse of Drugs Act 1971. In the case of the former, it has import in terms of the regulation on the production, sale and marketing of particular compounds. It also classifies drugs as being able to be openly sold or limited to prescription only. From the perspective of the MDA, it is able to offer a limited ground for the possession of a drug. The UK legislation in force implements the requirements in Directive 65/65/EEC,[40] which seeks to approximate Member States' laws regarding the treatment of proprietary medicinal products.

The Directive provides the definition of a proprietary medicinal product as '[a]ny ready prepared medicinal product placed on the market under a special name and in a special pack'.[41] This definition is given further specificity by virtue of a separate definition of *medicinal products*. The basic definition in Art 1(2) implies that a medicinal product consists of any substance (itself widely defined in Art 1(3)), alone or in combination, which is presented for the treatment or prevention of disease in humans or animals. It is interesting to note that the definition includes reference to 'restoring, correcting or modifying physiological functions', which one would assume must include the vast majority of AS that are legally available. Indeed, the European Court of Justice has gone as far as to hold that a product could be a medicinal product if it were able to satisfy either of the definitions offered.[42] The issue at hand required a determination of the question as to whether hair-restorer was capable of being a medicinal product. It was held that it could be. Given that a large proportion of the AS currently abused and/or those available on the unregulated market are imported, or diverted, legitimate medical supplies, it must surely follow that the classification as a medicinal product should apply.

---

40 Council Directive 65/65/EEC, OJ 022 9.2.65, pp 0369–73, as subsequently amended.
41 *Ibid*, Art 1(1).
42 Case C-112/89 *The Upjohn Co v Farzoo Inc* (1991) *The Times*, 3 June.

It is submitted that to argue otherwise would be to import a degree of uncertainty in the law that is unnecessary and able to be inconsistently applied.

In the UK, the responsibility for the regulation of medicinal products placed on the market and intended for human use falls on the Medicines Control Agency (MCA). The Agency is so empowered through both primary[43] and secondary legislation.[44] The MCA provides guidance notes to explain further certain of the definitions that are important. It is clear from the Medicines Act,[45] as well as from the guidance provided by the MCA,[46] that there are various factors used in the determination of what is or is not held to be a medicinal product for licensing purposes. Drawing on the criteria set out in regulations from time to time, and the jurisprudence of the European Court of Justice, the MCA is obliged, as the competent authority, to take all characteristics of the product into account, as well as 'what impression of the product "an averagely well informed consumer" would be likely to gain'.[47] One might assume that the committed AS user is well aware of what they are taking (a well informed consumer) and the reason why they are taking it. Thus, it would seem to be stretching the boundaries of logic to suggest that what would, in normal use, be a *proprietary medicinal product* by virtue of the Directive definition set out in Art 1, would not satisfy the test for being exempt from the prohibition on possession of AS under the MDA 1971.

So far, there would appear to be two reasons why any person caught in simple possession of a substance controlled under Sched 4 to the MDA 1971 should not be held to commit an offence. In terms of both the appearance, that is, the form of the product, and, further, the therapeutic effect, it would appear to be abundantly clear that the majority of these compounds *are* medicinal products. This point is also reinforced when considering that amyl nitrates are considered medical products by the MCA.[48] The compound, a vaso-dilator with a medicinal use in the treatment of, amongst other things, angina, has long been used recreationally as a sex aid, as well as being firmly established as a part of the night clubber's experience. By ensuring that the drug is classed as a medicinal product, more effective controls are able to be imposed to restrict its sale.

Although the MCA is at pains to stress the non-definitive nature of the guidance, a further conundrum is provided later in the guidance note[49] when

---

43 Medicines Act 1968.

44 Medicines for Human Use (Marketing Authorisations, etc) Regulations 1994 (SI 1994/3144).

45 Medicines Act 1968, s 130.

46 MCA, *Guidance Note: A Guide to What is a Medicinal Product*, 1995, London: MCA.

47 *Ibid*, para 8.

48 Institute for the Study of Drug Dependence, *Druglink*, September/October 1999, London: ISDD.

49 See *ibid*, MCA, specifically paras 13–16.

attempting to establish the second part of the Directive definition, in relation to the restorative, corrective or modifying nature of the substance in question, as outlined above. The guidance states: 'If [the product] contains any ingredients with a significant pharmacological effect, this will indicate that the product may be medicinal by function.' The guidance then considers various herbs that have well documented pharmacological effects, such as the sedative effects of valerian, and states that, if they are present in sufficient quantity in a product, this will be 'considered as evidence that the product is intended for a medicinal purpose'.

Finally, in this connection, it is offered that[50] certain products which may be claimed as being primarily cosmetic or nutritional may still be classed as medicinal products if they possess 'significant' pharmacological effect. It would be on this basis, for example, that any reclassification of substances such as St John's wort (so called natural Prozac™), or perhaps even creatine, may occur in the future. There is obvious utility in the law by ensuring some basic standard of protection for consumers. Marketing a substance that has a profound pharmacological effect by any other claims as to its effects, as a means to avoid the rigours of the necessary licensing demanded by prudence and the law, is potentially dangerous and rightly prohibited.

On the basis of this definition and the reasoning offered above in relation to other aspects of the Directive and its interpretation, it is difficult to sustain the argument that AS are not in the form of *medicinal products*, at least in the majority of cases, and to suggest otherwise is a seemingly perverse application of the law. It is surely inconsistent with the policy of the Directive and the Medicines Act to be able to choose a favourable and, frankly, unsustainable interpretation of the term medicinal product merely to secure convictions under the MDA. It would appear that prosecution claims that AS, at least when used outside medical supervision, are not capable of definition as medicinal products, are incorrect and the law is being misapplied unjustifiably. To offer a particularly simple example, a prescription only or pharmacist supervised sale painkiller, such as an analgesic containing both paracetamol and codeine, does not cease to be a medicinal product even though the person in possession of it takes an overdose. It is difficult to offer even a purposive interpretation of the fact that certain people caught in simple possession of AS are convicted, if one considers that the Home Secretary of the day had no intention to criminalise their mere possession, stating that:

> ... we propose to change the law and make it an offence, without authority to produce, supply or possess or import or export with intent to supply, anabolic steroids and other similar drugs. In accordance with the recommendation of the ACMD *it would not, however be an offence simply to possess these drugs* in the United Kingdom.[51]

---

50 *Op cit*, MCA, fn 46, para 15.
51 *Hansard*, written answer No 92, 2 November 1994; emphasis added.

The then Home Office Minister, Tom Sackville MP, was more blunt when he stated that 'these measures are aimed primarily at those who profit by selling these drugs to body builders and sportsmen'.

It could also be observed that the real policy of the Directive, that of consumer protection, is undermined if such arbitrary interpretations are to be adopted and continued. This would remain so, in the case of scheduled AS, even if the product in question were inert, or a counterfeit preparation marketed illegally under the guise of a proprietary product. The issue, therefore, remains clouded and it would be sensible to argue for some clarity and consistency of approach in the application of the law.

In order to ascertain the likely implications of the rescheduling in the UK, it is perhaps useful to draw a comparison with the position in another legal system, which has an established legal regime in place criminalising all aspects of the illicit use of AS. The US, for example, is often regarded as providing the definitive stance in relation to a prohibitionist drugs policy. The American model is based on zero-tolerance of drugs it classifies as illegal and is characterised through the rigorous prosecution of offenders and the imposition of severe penalties. The following section will outline the US experience in relation to the prohibition of AS and consider the rationale, substance and perceived effectiveness of the measures that have been adopted.

THE US EXPERIENCE: ANY PARALLEL?

As with the current position in the UK, US law has changed over time to reflect a more rigorous and less tolerant legislative attitude. It is interesting to note that initially, as with the UK experience with the ACMD, there was little interest in placing AS under criminal control. The prime movers were politicians rather than doctors.[52]

With federal legislation based primarily on public health grounds, AS were the subject of increasing control through the period 1970–1990. Similar in certain respects to the regime employed under the Medicines Act 1968 in the UK, AS were governed in an analogous way to a prescription only drug, but without attracting the status of a controlled substance, and thus were outside the control of the draconian Controlled Substances Act, which represents Title II of the comprehensive Drug Abuse Prevention and Control Act 1970. Concern over the proliferation of the use of AS in the US led to their being subject to a more repressive legal regime. The basic rationale offered by those in favour of stricter controls, later echoed by the Home Office at the launch of

---

52 See, eg, Collins, R, *Does the Anabolic Steroid Control Act Work?*, available at www.decriminalisesteroids.com

the UK legislation, was threefold. First, illicit trafficking could be more easily targeted, enforced and thus deterred. Secondly, a decreased supply of the drugs, coupled with the deterrent effect of criminal sanctions imposed on possession, would mitigate the perceived threat to the health of users. Finally, emphasis on drug free sports competition was, and is, seen as an objective good to be promoted.

The US has had specific criminal legal controls targeting AS in place for a decade. The Anabolic Steroid Control Act (ASCA) 1990 places criminal legal controls over a variety of compounds. The ASCA provides for the inclusion of AS in Sched 3 to the Controlled Substances Act.[53] The US approach is clear, if somewhat more extreme. It does not suffer the torturous complications of interpretation that the equivalent UK law appears to. The drugs are subject to an absolute ban on use outside legitimate medical prescription and supervision. Legislation controls the manufacture, import/export, supply and possession of AS. Further, the US laws adopt a line which is unusual in UK drug laws, that of proscribing the *use* of a banned substance.[54] Although the penalties applicable to Sched 3 substances are not the most severe, the hard line attitude taken to drug crime enforcement in the US provides that simple possession could involve a penalty ranging from a minimum $1,000 fine to a lengthy jail sentence.[55] Possession with intent to supply (to adopt the UK's terminology) and/or supply is treated more seriously, as a felony, and would subject the offender to a maximum of five years' imprisonment and/or a fine of $250,000. Individual States have adopted a raft of legislative provisions, in some cases with higher penalties than those imposed by the federal law. Policy makers have declared criminalisation a qualified success. Criticisms have been levelled in more libertarian quarters that the unduly harsh penalties and subsequent ancillary impacts, such as losing the right to a driving licence, consequent on any drug conviction in the US are counter-productive.[56] Unsurprisingly, as will be considered below, this view is not shared by the enforcement authorities.

IMPACTS: THE ENFORCEMENT PERSPECTIVE

The extent to which the criminal regime can be evaluated as successful or otherwise was the subject of a Drug Enforcement Agency (DEA) sponsored conference in 1994. The Conference Report[57] evaluated the law as a qualified success in its Executive Summary:

---

53 Along with amphetamines and certain classes of opiates.

54 Note: the UK MDA 1971 bans the *use* of opium only.

55 Up to three years for a persistent offender.

56 See, eg, www.steroidlaw.com, an excellent site maintained by New York Attorney Rick Collins.

57 Haislip, GR, *Conference on the Impact of Natural Steroid Control Legislation in the United States*, DEA, June 1995, available at www.usdoj.gov/dea/programs/ diversion/divpub/confer/steroids.htm.

Although experts presented evidence of considerable achievement, the data continues to show that abuse of anabolic steroids constitutes a significant threat to the general public health and safety, especially with respect to adolescents and young adults. It was determined that, while there have been notable accomplishments under this legislation, there are several serious obstacles to its effectiveness.

Evidence presented to the conference identified a variety of shortcomings concerned with both the impact and the operation of the law. In terms of operational concerns, the conference was critical of the alleged inadequacies of federal sentencing guidelines, which it was claimed do little in terms of providing an effective deterrent to the use or supply of the drugs. Further, it drew attention to the fact that these inadequacies made steroid cases difficult to prosecute and that, as a result, some federal prosecutors come to the 'conclusion that the investigation and prosecution of steroid traffickers is not a justifiable expenditure of resources'.[58] Finally, the conference was critical of the fact that 'steroids are not controlled in many key countries, nor are they controlled by international treaty',[59] thus making the task of effective policing of the phenomenon additionally problematic. Indeed, the DEA appears fatalistic about its prospects in reducing the supply from imported drugs, despite its claimed success at stemming the flow of steroids diverted from legitimate domestic medical supplies.

Operational difficulties apart, the conference also identified a growing problem in relation to the smuggling of steroids into the US. The conference concluded that international trafficking had increased, which one would assume would be an obvious effect of more rigorous controls on the domestically produced product; and that the traffickers themselves had become 'more sophisticated and organized'.[60] There is, perhaps, a certain inevitability in both of these circumstances: in the latter case, the draconian penalties attaching to the supply of drugs under the Controlled Substances Act 1970 would necessarily imply that a calculated risk for considerable reward was being undertaken by the importer. It is interesting to note that the DEA observes a particular problem in relation to the postal service. With increased internet access and a proliferation of sites offering various nutritional supplements and training aids, including AS, for sale from offshore locations, this is a problem that will only potentially increase.

---

58 *Op cit,* Haislip, fn 57, p 1.

59 *Op cit,* Haislip, fn 57, p 1. For international controls in this area see, eg, Single Convention on Narcotic Drugs 1961; UN Psychotropic Substances Convention 1971; Convention Against the Illicit Traffic in Narcotic Drugs and Psychotropic Substances 1988.

60 *Op cit,* Haislip, fn 57, p 2.

A further corollary of increased criminality involved in the supply chain relates to the counterfeiting of various compounds. Just as there is a market in counterfeited sportswear, perfumes and computer software, there is also a market in fake drugs. The DEA has noted this as a problem and, somewhat bizarrely, links this to the success of the programme of criminalisation in halting the flow of diverted medical supplies.[61] The DEA's Office of Diversion Control sets out a case study of an investigation into a counterfeiting operation. The agency reported that steroidal cattle implant pellets were being used to manufacture illicit drugs and, further, identifies cases where non-sterile injectable products were being produced. The extent of the operation can be visualised when the DEA reported that it had 'obtained fraudulent packaging, labels, bottles, vials and package inserts ... two million counterfeit or bogus dosage units'.[62] This is obviously a phenomenal amount of a potentially dangerous product, and can be linked without too much difficulty to the increased risks inherent in the market for AS consequent on criminalisation. At the current time, data are not available to determine the extent to which this is occurring in the UK, however, anecdotal evidence suggests that there is a problem. One can only assume that this will increase.

A further impact to add to the decline in quality and availability of certain compounds has been a reported rise in prices. In the UK, this is a conclusion that can, again, only be drawn anecdotally, although there are data available from the US. The illicit market in AS in the US is estimated at $400 million,[63] showing a $100 million rise since the passing of the Anabolic Steroids Control Act in 1990. At the time of the Act, Congress was advised that the estimated value of the trade was $300 million.[64] It has been suggested by some commentators that the increased value of the illicit market is fostered and maintained by the imposition of the criminal law.[65] The DEA conference also noted that prices had risen and preferred compounds were not consistently available, thus prompting people to move toward the use of even more unpredictable drugs with potentially worse side effects. It is interesting to note that this phenomenon is offered as evidence of the success of the criminalisation policy. It might be argued that, as the criminal law was imposed under the auspices of protecting the health of, *inter alia*, American youth, this impact should be viewed from a somewhat more negative

---

61 See, eg, DEA, *The Diversion of Drugs and Chemicals: A Descriptive Report of the Programs and Activities of the DEA's Office Of Diversion Control*, May 1996, available at www.usdoj.gov/dea/programs.

62 *Ibid*, p 7.

63 Yesalis, C and Cowert, V, *The Steroids Game*, 1998, Champaign, Ill: Human Kinetics, p 108, cited at www.steroidlaw.com

64 Hearings on HR 4658, Sub-Committee on Crime of the House Committee on the Judiciary, 101st Cong, 2d Sess 90 (17 May 1990).

65 *Op cit*, Haislip, fn 57, Executive Summary.

perspective. The reality of diminished quality, sporadic availability and increased prices, combined with the lack of opportunity for objective health advice or education, surely cannot further the aims of the law.

Thus, it would appear that the UK's declared rationale to deter trafficking and supply offences in relation to AS are comparable to those adopted in the US. It could also be concluded that the failures inherent in the system, as identified by the enforcing authorities, prove more of a threat to public health, or at least that of the consumer of these drugs, than a means to combat the perceived problem of AS use. Of course, as the criminal law regime in the UK is less rigorous in its application than that in the US, then certain of the negative effects experienced would be expected to be concomitantly reduced. However, the main thrust would still be expected to apply. Criminalisation undoubtedly increases the criminality involved in the supply chain and, whilst tautologous at first glance, it can be observed through commentators on the American experience that it is indeed the case. The criminality involved alters, it becomes more intense, more professional and with more at stake. Year on year increases in the numbers of those convicted of steroid offences and, perhaps of more concern, the effects of the uncertainties in the UK law, especially in relation to the definition of a medicinal product, can only lead to more people being involved in the criminal justice system where otherwise they would not.

The increased formalism of the doping process, combined with the fact that there is unlikely to be any major success in the 'war on drugs' at a wider societal level, perhaps suggests an outmoded and invalid response to the doping issue. As with the erythropoietin developments,[66] the inability to test for certain compounds such as IGF-1, HGH, etc, and other problems suggest that there are wide flaws in the regulatory system as currently presented which cannot be solved in any more effective way by the criminal law. It can be concluded that the criminalisation of AS will have an effect far beyond the sporting arena and the flaws in the US approach will be replicated in the UK. The image of sport is worthy of some protection, but there remains the potential for greater societal and individual harm consequent upon AS use being driven even further underground.

---

66 IOC Declaration on EPO testing, 30 August 2000.

CHAPTER 15

DRUGS, HEALTH AND SPORTING VALUES

Edward Grayson and Gregory Ioannidis

Much of the objection to the use of drugs in sport is founded on issues of unfair competition and health. These two issues have been used consistently by sports governing bodies as major justifications for the ban on doping in sports. The central objective of this chapter is to provide a further justification for the ban on drugs by focusing on the health dangers to athletes by their use of doping techniques. It will concentrate on contemporary and topical examples illustrating that the health risk to athletes is still *the* fundamental issue in doping. Athletes do not, or are not prepared to, realise that the 'win at all costs' attitude is catastrophic for them as individuals as well as their sport. It will then consider means by which governing bodies and the law can ensure healthy sporting competition.

HEALTHY SPORTING ACTIVITY?

The Symposium mounted in 1985 by the Sports Council at London University's King's College, backing the Sports Council's campaign for drug testing among sporting governing bodies, presented a formidable body of oral, documentary and visual evidence. The evidence explained graphically the adverse health consequences of doping violations both internationally and domestically. It identified the fundamental interrelationship between the health and ethical sporting problems.[1]

Since then, however, governing bodies have done little to produce a solution to this fundamental and difficult issue. The absence of Corinthian sporting ideals based on ethical and moral consensus has created a controversial and complicated cheating 'culture'.

Shortly after Ben Johnson's positive test for the steroid stanozolol at the 1988 Seoul Olympics, the Government of Canada appointed the Honourable Charles L Dubin to lead the Commission of Inquiry into the Use of Drugs and Banned Practices Intended to Enhance Athletic Performance. This was the most detailed and innovative legal report that has been published on this subject. Dubin J said of the problem in sport: '... the evidence shows that banned performance enhancing substances and in particular anabolic steroids

---

1   Grayson, E, *Sport and the Law*, 3rd edn, 1999, London: Butterworths.

are being used by athletes in almost every sport, most extensively in weightlifting and track and field.'2

Robert Armstrong QC, a member of the Canadian Bar Association and Commission Counsel to the Dubin Inquiry, stated at an International Symposium on Sport and the Law, held in Monaco in 1991, that Canada had lost its innocence as a sporting nation in Seoul. The Dubin Inquiry showed that the use of drugs within sport had no national boundaries. Sport had lost the fundamental Corinthian values that had for so long underpinned healthy sporting competition.

Dr Robert Kerr testified before the Dubin Inquiry that he had prescribed anabolic steroids to approximately 20 medallists in the 1984 Olympics. Pat Connolly, a coach of the women's track team, at the US Senate Judiciary on Steroid Abuse in the US estimated that five out of 10 gold medallists in the US men's Olympic track team used anabolic steroids at Seoul.

Many commentators have argued that interference with the individual's liberty is unacceptable and, therefore, the ban on drugs cannot be justified. However, this argument cannot rebut the fact that doping is both extremely dangerous and destructive. In particular, the 'individual liberty' argument fails to take into account the coercive nature of doping that is at its most insidious at the State level.

Manfred Ewald, the former head of the East German Sports Federation, and his former medical director, Dr Manfred Hoppner, were charged with complicity in causing bodily harm for administering performance enhancing drugs to young athletes. They were both found guilty of doping and received suspended sentences in a trial that came to an end in July 2000.

Ewald, now 74, was found guilty of making 142 East German sportswomen, mostly swimmers and athletes, take performance enhancing drugs. He was given a suspended prison sentence of 22 months. His co-accused, Hoppner, 66, was given an 18 month suspended sentence.

During the two month trial, the prosecution had submitted that the two men ran a secret programme of doping during the 1960s and 1970s, providing athletes with performance enhancing substances. Part of the prosecution's case was that most of the athletes were unaware of the drugs they were receiving and, therefore, unaware of the health risks. Former athletes testified in order to substantiate and justify these arguments. According to the indictment, the female athletes who were given performance enhancing substances (mainly anabolic steroids) suffered side effects including hormonal disturbances, developing male characteristics such as excessive body hair, muscles and deep voices, and liver and kidney problems. Some of these athletes still suffer from menstrual and gynaecological problems.

---

2   Grayson, E, *Ethics, Injuries and the Law in Sports Medicine*, 1999, London: Butterworth-Heinemann Medical.

Details concerning East Germany's drugs programme began to emerge three years ago in Berlin, when a special team of the Central Investigative Agency for Government and Institution poured over thousands of files seized from the Stasi, the German Democratic Republic's (GDR's) notorious State Security Service, and questioned dozens of former athletes. In all, 90 investigations are underway and 680 coaches, doctors and former officials are under suspicion. Nine of them have been prosecuted and two, in the present case, have been found guilty.

The Stasi evidence suggests that, in the years since 1969, when the GDR made sports a priority to try to humiliate West Germany at its 1972 Munich Olympics, as many as 10,000 athletes received drugs. Many did not know what they were taking. When they found out, they were forced to sign pledges of silence. 'There was this psychosis to prove that socialism was better than capitalism,' says Giselher Spitzer,[3] a sports historian at Potsdam University. 'The party was pathologically ambitious about beating West Germany and gave sports free rein and gobs of money. The only goal was brilliant results.'

The price was heavy, however. The cost of brilliance was physical damage, sometimes of grotesque proportions. In a 1977 report to the Stasi, Hoppner listed known side effects of performance enhancing drugs given to women, including growth of body hair, deepening voice and aggression resulting from unfulfilled sexual desire. But Hoppner concluded that sporting success could be achieved only with continued drug taking. Years later, Rita Reinisch, a GDR swimmer who won three gold medals at the 1980 Moscow Olympics, recalled: 'Taking pills was normal, though I had no idea what I was taking. My coach told me, that's good for you, it will help your body recover quicker after training, and I trusted him blindly.'[4] He did not tell her that it would also cause inflamed ovaries and the growth of cysts, forcing her to take premature retirement.

Reinisch, now a TV sports broadcaster in Munich, was relatively lucky – she overcame the damage and had two children. Others ended up infertile and young gymnasts sometimes found themselves in wheelchairs when their bodies rebelled against unnatural regimes. Some men have grown breasts: under artificial stimulation, their own systems lost their capacity to produce sufficient male hormones. In one of the most important and unfortunate cases of all, a top East German shot putter, Heidi Krieger, European gold medallist in 1986, changed her sex after 10 years of drug taking in GDR. Unusually high doses of anabolic steroids – as much as 2,590 mg per year – could be the reason why she not only started looking like a man, but also developed transsexual feelings. Krieger, now 34, underwent sex change surgery in 1997.

3   Bonfante, J, 'Sports officials confront the legacy of Communism's State approved abuse of steroids', Reuters, February 1998.

4   *Ibid.*

It is likely that State controlled doping programmes continue in some countries today. Whilst individuals in most States practise doping as a matter of choice, doping can never be tolerated so long as it give scope for wide-scale institutionalised abuse that removes from individual sportsmen and women the very freedom of choice that the pro-doping lobbies seek to protect.

'ARE THEY ALL AT IT?'

Equally damaging to sport are the rumours that undermine outstanding athletic performance. Rumours often stem from alterations in health and physical conditions.

The sudden death of Florence Griffith-Joyner from suspected heart seizure in California in September 1998 has developed into one such rumour. It was claimed that 'Flo-Jo' was using performance enhancing drugs during her career, despite the fact that she had never tested positive.

The case of Flo-Jo – like many doping stories – is based on hearsay and rumour. So far, there have been no medical reports to suggest that her death is the direct result of drug abuse.

According to a coroner's report on 23 October of that year, the American sprinter, who won three gold medals and one silver at the 1988 Seoul Olympic Games, suffered an epileptic seizure that caused her to suffocate. According to post mortem examination, the seizure was brought on by a congenital defect called a cavernous angioma. The doctors found that she died as a result of positional asphyxia, secondary to an epileptic seizure. Despite the criticisms as to the cause of her death, friends and family have refused to comment and have condemned those who have spread rumours about drugs.

There has been considerable reported speculation as to the cause of her death. Cardiologist Dr Jonathan Halperin argued that the theory that anabolic steroids can damage the heart of an athlete is disputable and not accepted by many cardiologists. The endocrinologist Dr Stanley Feld believes that the amazing development of her muscles might have been due to a special diet and hard training.

Rumours of doping are compounded by rumours of cover-ups. As Robert Voy MD, a former Chief Medical Officer for the US Olympic Committee, alleges:[5]

> Allowing national governing bodies (NGBs), international federations (IFs), and National Olympic Committees (NOCs) such as the United States Olympic Committee to govern the testing process to ensure fair play in sport is terribly ineffective. In a sense, it is like having the fox guard the henhouse. There is

---

5   Voy, R, 'Drugs, sport and politics', in *Testing Gone Afoul, Cover-ups, Lies and Manipulation – All for the Sake of Gold*, Champaign, Ill: Human Kinetics, p 101.

simply too much money involved in international sports today. One needs to understand that the officials in charge of operating sport at the amateur level need world-class performances to keep their businesses rolling forward. The sad truth is that people don't pay to watch losers, and corporations don't sponsor teams that can't bring home the gold. The athletes and officials realise this, so they're willing to do whatever it takes to win. And sometimes that means turning their backs on the drug problem.

Another sport that has been blighted by rumour is football, as a recent case from Italy illustrates.[6] In July 1998, the former Roma coach Zdenek Zeman claimed that the former Chelsea manager, Gianluca Vialli, and the Juventus forward, Alessandro Del Piero, were two players whose muscular development had 'surprised' him, implying that both were using performance enhancing drugs.

Subsequent interviews led to an investigation into doping practices in Italian football being carried out by magistrate Raffaele Guarinielo. The inquiry discovered systematic malpractice and cover-ups at Coni's (the Italian Olympic Committee) dope testing laboratory at Acqua Acetosa in Rome. According to the Milan newspaper *Corriere Della Sera*, an unnamed Udinese player had tested positive after Udinese played Roma on 19 January 1997, but, it was alleged, the laboratory physicians were told to keep the discovery quiet. As a result of these revelations, the president of Coni resigned and the director of the laboratory was sacked. The story, however, has another chapter. The latest revelation showed that tests taken from 24 Parma players in July of that year revealed an abnormally high level of red blood cells. It is well known that increased numbers of oxygen carrying red blood cells can enhance performance. Although Parma officials claimed that this was a defamatory campaign to harm the club, the tests showed that goalkeeper Alessandro Nesta had a hematocrit level of 63%, 11% higher than the normal.

It is impossible to assess the truth of these rumours. However, it is far easier to assess their impact. Rumour is the parasite that feeds off illness and positive tests.

IS THERE AN IN-HOUSE SOLUTION?

If Flo-Jo's performances were drug enhanced, then responsibility should lie with the governing bodies as a lack of appropriate education for the athletes, as much as with the athletes themselves. The buck must stop at the door of the governing bodies. If they are unable, ultimately, to prevent the tide of doping abuse, they should at least be seen in the vanguard of the movement. All

---

6   Ioannidis, G, 'Drugs in football' (1998) 1(5) Sports Law Bulletin 14.

necessary steps need to be taken in order to ensure that participants in sport compete in a healthy environment. Doctors and physicians have an important role to play. Any medical or paramedical practitioner practising without an awareness of the daily conflicts between regulatory bodies in sport and society generally is acting inappropriately.[7]

The President of the IOC, Juan Antonio Samaranch, on the eve of the 50th anniversary of the opening of the first post-Second World War Olympic Games in London, stated that: 'Substances that do not damage a sportsman's health should not be banned.'[8] This was a bold and encouraging statement. The IOC is in a powerful position to dictate to the sporting world the focus and intention of doping regulation that has, over the years, become subverted by mixed messages. Samaranch's statement appears to suggest that issues of health are at the centre of doping policy.[9] As yet, however, words have not been translated into deeds.

At the very heart of the fight must be a concerted effort between doctors and administrators. At a UK Sports Council Seminar on 30 October 1996, under the banner of 'Tackling ethical issues in drugs and sport', Dr Malcolm Brown, Medical Adviser to the near bankrupt British Athletic Federation (BAF) (at the date of writing in receivership), explained:

> ... under the IAAF [International Amateur Athletics Federation] regulations as opposed to the IOC regulations, and this is where problems sometime begin, there's no restriction on the use of inhaled cortico-steroids and rightly so. Oral cortico-steroids are not allowed and the mechanisms by which you might have been able to persuade the IOC to give exceptional permission are not well publicised.

Clearly, there is a need for general practitioners to be better informed of current and updated guidelines. Doctors in sport must be aware of the regulations that affect the administration of drugs in different sporting jurisdictions. Parents and schools, all acting *in loco parentis*, have duties to protect their infant charges. Club coaches and governing bodies owe a duty to their respective sports and those who participate in them to create practical regulations which are effective against the misuse of drugs but which do not preclude *bona fide* medical treatment when appropriate for general health circumstances.

Thus, doctors who treat patients competing athletically must familiarise themselves with the requirements of the particular sport in question, both at

---

7 *Op cit*, Grayson, fn 2, pp 42–49.

8 (1998) *The Daily Telegraph*, 26 July.

9 The message was not received with universal acclaim, however. One of Britain's leading and most respected international sports writers, Ian Wooldridge, wrote in London's *Daily Mail* on that anniversary, 29 July 1998: 'He betrayed the youth of the world.'

domestic and international levels – and must pass on this information to their patients. Lawyers who advise administrators must see that any regulations to prevent cheating do not either transgress natural justice rules and the opportunity to be heard, or contravene the spirit of the British parliamentary defence that ignorance of the facts can be a defence in a drug case. Administrators should try, with doctors, pharmacists, lawyers and drug manufacturers, to attain a balance between the sport's rules and the individual's medicinal requirements, in the interests of fair play, health and the avoidance of cheating. Competitors must familiarise themselves with their own medical requirements within the rules laid down by their particular sport. If the various parties with sports cannot or will not address these issues, then it may become necessary for the law to mediate.

THE INVOLVEMENT OF THE LAW

The Sports Council in London governs dope testing in Britain with an accredited IOC laboratory and has implemented one of the most stringent programmes in the world. In 1992, over 4,000 samples were taken from athletes in 53 different sports, with a higher number than ever before coming from out-of-competition testing. It is difficult to assess how effective dope testing is as a deterrent. Taking as a touchstone Ben Johnson, who was tested positive for the second time in March 1993 after suffering so much humiliation following the Seoul Olympics, it is apparent that, for some athletes, it is not an effective deterrent.

There is a limit, however, on the extent to which the law is prepared to assist in the quest for healthy sporting activity. Apart from a few countries such as Greece[10] and Belgium,[11] which criminalise the use of performance enhancing drugs by sportsmen and sportswomen, the law should be viewed more as a means of bolstering the doping regulations of governing bodies rather than providing an alternative front on which to fight the battle for healthy sporting activity. In Britain, Pt 1 of Sched 4 to the Misuse of Drugs Act 1971 deals with the problem of the supply of steroids. It is a provision mirrored in many jurisdictions, but it has had little positive impact on doping in British sports. As a result, judicial activity revolves around the lawfulness of the provisions of governing bodies.

The British sprinter Jason Livingstone was sent home from the Barcelona Olympics as he was tested positive for the drug methandianone in a random out-of-competition test before the Olympics. He appealed to the BAF Appeals

---

10 Law 1646/1986, Arts 7–11.
11 Law of 2 April 1965 of the French Community of Belgium; Decree of 27 March 1991 of the Flemish Community of Belgium, Art 43.

Panel, which dismissed his appeal by a 2:1 majority in April/May 1993. In the appeal, there was some doubt cast over the positive test as, in fact, a metabolite of methandianone had been found, not the actual substance. Livingstone argued that, just because a metabolite of the substance had been found, this was not conclusive proof that he had actually used methandianone. This view was supported by the evidence of Professor Arnold Beckett, previously a member of the IOC's medical commission. However, the majority of the panel felt that the evidence which was before them put beyond reasonable doubt that Livingstone had taken the drug and had indeed cheated. Livingstone did not pursue his action through the courts. However, it illustrates just how careful governing bodies must be in the drafting of their anti-doping provisions.

At an international level, harmonisation of doping regulations is essential. Andrew Saxton and Andrew Davies, two British weightlifters, were sent home from the Barcelona Olympics in 1992 for being tested positive for clenbuterol. Davies and Saxton have argued that their use of the substance did not justify disqualification, as the drug was not on the IOC's list of banned substances at the time of competition.

Following a rugby international between France and Wales in Paris during 1992, Anthony Clement and Jean-Baptiste Lafond were allegedly tested positive for the use of prohibited drugs. In due course, it emerged that Malcolm Downes, the Welsh Rugby Union honourary surgeon, had prescribed Clement drugs for sickness and dysentery. Lafond had been administered with pholeodine for a cough by a French doctor.

In due course, each player was exonerated, but what emerged is that the Welsh Rugby Union uses the same list of banned substances as the IOC, which differs from the list adopted by the French Rugby Union. Correspondingly, after an international conference of rugby doctors in Bermuda had recommended criteria for drug testing, the International Rugby Board, which was not renowned for its consistency over discrepancies in financial compensation for loss of time from normal employment, required reminding of the necessity for creating sanctions for findings of positive tests. The role of the law is clear. Rather than lawyers being the means of undermining the doping regulations, they should be the means by which anti-doping policies become immune to challenge. The role of the lawyer is to work with governing bodies to ensure healthy competition – not against them.

Perhaps the fact that legal action in this area is relatively rare illustrates the positive involvement of the lawyer. What little there is illustrates that the law is not oblivious to the rights of athletes and courts will not necessarily adopt a non-interventionist stance. Indeed, Katrin Krabbe, from Germany, successfully overturned one IAAF ban for drug abuse when a German court held that the regulations of the IAAF were incompatible with those of German national law.

Sandra Gasser, a Swiss athlete who had attained international standard in the 800 m and the 1,500 m, appealed to the Chancery Division of the High Court after she was suspended for two years from eligibility to enter athletics competitions held under IAAF rules, following a positive test of the metabolite of methyl testosterone at the 1987 World Championships in Rome. An Arbitration Panel of the IAAF affirmed the decision. Scott J refused declaratory relief by writ (not by the usually misconceived judicial review procedure) that the suspension was unreasonably in restraint of trade (although he accepted that the restraint of trade principles applied to the facts of the case).

More significantly, however, in his unreported judgment he made two observations which suggest that a different approach by the plaintiff's lawyers (as so often happens) might have had different consequences. First, he found, in relation to one of the two tested samples of urine: 'The Panel might have found that the other explanation was too conjectural to be accepted. But no evidence to incline them to the view had been put before them by the plaintiff or the SVL.'

Secondly, he explained that the Panel:

> ... accepted the other explanation. They may have been wrong in doing so. They may have been wrong in regarding the identified procedural failure as not material. But unless they exceeded their jurisdiction, exceeded, that is to say, their terms of reference, the Plaintiff is stuck with their conclusions. Any remedy of appeal to the High Court under the Arbitration Acts is long since time-barred.

Furthermore, Robert Armstrong QC, at an international symposium, said: '... basically, Dubin recommended that, in order to have a fair right of appeal, athletics should be in a position to be able to test the scientific validity of the test results.' The question, therefore, remains, could *different evidence* in the *Gasser* case of the kind contemplated specifically by Scott J have produced a different result? For that reason, the decision and reliance upon it as a binding precedent must always be challenged as based upon a debatable foundation because of apparent inadequate or insufficient preparation *in the eyes and mind* of the trial judge for reliance upon it by those who wish to challenge tribunal practices in this area.

More recently, in July 2000, Doug Walker won his fight to get back on the track[12] after he was granted an interim relief order by a High Court judge. Hallett J, after considering the evidence, argued that, if interim relief was not granted to Walker following the adjournment of the case, the consequences for him would be incalculable.

---

12 Ioannidis, G, *'Doug Walker v UK Athletics and IAAF* [2000] HC, 25 July, unreported' (2000) 3(5) Sports Law Bulletin 3.

The athlete was originally suspended by UK Athletics after he was tested positive in an out-of-competition test in December 1998. Six months later, in July 1999, a disciplinary committee set up by UK Athletics reinstated Walker after deciding that the athlete was not guilty of any doping offence. However, the IAAF decided to refer the matter to an arbitration panel, prohibiting Walker at the same time from participating in any competition.

The main argument for Walker was the incorrect construction of strict liability rules. Walker's counsel, Andrew Hunter, argued that Walker was originally exonerated by UK Athletics, and the IAAF's intervention was highly unjust because there was no suggestion that Walker was guilty of deliberate misuse of drugs.

After his opening statement, counsel submitted that, although UK Athletics (UKA) had unanimously exonerated Walker of any doping offence, he remained suspended from all athletic competitions, simply because IAAF referred the matter to arbitration. Mr Hunter argued:

> The IAAF commenced an arbitration against UKA but in which the only relief sought was a declaration that Mr Walker is ineligible to compete in athletics competitions. That intervention was highly unjust to Mr Walker. It was not a case where there was any suggestion that Mr Walker was guilty of deliberate dope-taking. The UKA disciplinary committee unanimously concluded there was no question of this. The IAAF does not challenge this decision ... The reason for the IAAF's intervention is that it disagrees with the committee's construction of the IAAF's prohibited substance list. Mr Walker has therefore been caught up in a dispute between UKA and the IAAF about the correct construction of strict liability rules.

Mr Hunter submitted that the IAAF changed its own rules to provide for interim suspension of athletes in arbitration cases. They applied this new rule to Walker. He argued: 'He [Walker] fully accepts and supports that the IAAF plays an important rule to ensure there is a uniform high standard applied throughout the world against dope taking, but what he says is that the IAAF can't do that at the expense of riding roughshod over the rights of individual athletes ...' Hallett J, after a careful consideration of the arguments, granted the athlete a temporary court order pending the outcome of arbitration proceedings in his case.

Unfortunately for Walker (and the other two athletes involved in the nandrolone controversy, Cadogan and Christie), the Arbitration Panel of the IAAF, meeting in Monte Carlo in August 2000, decided that UK Athletics misdirected itself and reached an erroneous conclusion when clearing the three British athletes. As a result, the Panel confirmed that all three committed doping offences and received two years' suspension.

At this juncture, the Human Rights Act 1998 must be mentioned briefly. Its impact on sport generally is, as yet, unknown; however, there may be some impact in the area of doping, as Art 8 of the European Convention on Human

Rights aims to protect rights of privacy. In the doping context, this could involve a re-examination of the legitimacy of urine and blood testing and fair hearings by sports governing bodies. Whilst emphasising the importance of the Act in strengthening individual liberty, the provision could prove counterproductive if such liberties impacted on the ability of anti-doping measures to protect the health of sports participants. The application of the Human Rights Act to sporting situations is awaited with some anxiety.

CONCLUSION

Whilst there are those in sports management who advocate the controlled use of performance enhancing drugs, the vast majority of sports medical practitioners are firmly against such a development. Healthy competition demands attention and action at every level where medicine, sport and the law merge. Doctors, patients, parents, schools, club coaches, and governing bodies must all address the issues raised and the implications for modern sport.

The detrimental side effects of the use of steroids must be constantly stressed in order that sports participants who are tempted to use them will understand that a better performance is not the only effect of this practice.

When yet another sportsman or woman is tested positive, the public become resigned to the view that certain sports are not 'clean' and, subsequently, suspect that innocent participants may be cheating. Undoubtedly, the real victims are the competitors who choose to compete using their own natural resources and refuse to compromise their own integrity in order to be better, stronger or go faster.

There is no doubt that good health in sport can be achieved with continuous education and legal assistance. The cases discussed above confirm that, without a uniform application of the doping rules based on a strong legal foundation, inconsistency and confusion will undermine the fight for healthy sporting competition.

In the interests of health and fair play, which in the end is what sport, in and out of court, is all about, sporting ideals can and should play the most important role in the fight against doping. As Dubin J comments:

> Cheating in sport, I fear, is partially a reflection of today's society. Drugs and the unprincipled pursuit of wealth and fame at any cost now threaten our very social fabric. It is little wonder the immorality has reached into sport as well. Of course, cheating as such is not a new phenomenon in Olympic competition, but the methods used to cheat have become more and more innovative and more pervasive. Moreover the use of drugs as the method of cheating has reached epidemic proportions.[13]

---

13 Dubin, C, *Commission of Inquiry into the Use of Drugs and Banned Practices Intended to Increase Athletic Performance*, 1990, Ottawa: Canadian Government Publishing Centre.

What is needed, ultimately, is a change in attitude. As Hubert Doggart[14] comments:

> Three groups whose efforts could be harnessed to stop the rot and ensure the survival, relatively intact, of the Corinthian ideal. First, the doctors, whose Hippocratic oath can be construed as an upholding of the Corinthian ideal in medicine. Secondly, the lawyers, who once played without a thought that their services *qua* lawyers would be needed, but cannot now be sure. And, thirdly, school teachers, whose *raison d'être* could be called 'the upholding of the Corinthian ideal in body, mind and soul' ...

---

14 Doggart, H, 'The Corinthian ideal' (an ideal which is almost unattainable in the ever increasing realistic commercialisation of sport), in *op cit*, Grayson, fn 1.

CHAPTER 16

DOPING SOLUTIONS AND THE PROBLEM WITH 'PROBLEMS'

John O'Leary

INTRODUCTION

The essays contained within this book provide insight into the diversity of issues related to doping in sport. It may appear that the essays are so diverse that a synthesis of their ideas would be impossible. However, this is not necessarily the case. The dynamic nature of the relationships both inside and outside sport requires such disparate views if it is to be understood in its totality. What the essays have in common is that they all acknowledge certain shortcomings of the present system – these are the 'problems'. Most of the essays seek to offer means of redressing those problems – the 'solutions'. The complexity arises because, as the contributors approach the same subject from different perspectives, there is no consensus as to the nature of the problem, so it might appear there cannot be a consensus as to the solution. The object of this final chapter is to analyse the nature of the problem and to suggest a solution. The solution is the relaxation of doping regulation. This is not a solution that will meet with the approval of all of the parties within sport, but it is the only solution that addresses the diverse identified problems.

THE 'PROBLEM'

Representatives of the European Union (EU) have stated, rather candidly, that it's now or never for anti-doping measures. Jaime Andreu[1] of the European Commission stated recently that harmonisation represents the very last chance for the sports world to resolve the problem of doping. If this effort fails, he envisages two possibilities: governments will try to rectify the situation via strict legislation; or doping will become more or less tolerated.[2] Those who campaign against the evils of doping should not become over alarmed by the latter alternative. The evocation of this particular bogeyman should be seen as no more than a threat to recalcitrant governing bodies. Europe and the

---

1 Head of Unit, European Commission; Education and Culture DG; Directorate C – Culture, Audiovisual Policy and Sport; 5 *Sport.*
2 Round Table Sports Conference, 2 December 1999, TMC Asser Institute, The Hague, The Netherlands.

Olympic movement seem to be basing their last stand on measures to harmonise doping regulations and the World Anti-Doping Agency (WADA) is seen as the standard bearer of this final assault.

It is not, however, possible to find a solution to the doping problem until one exactly defines the problem. What this book illustrates is that there is no consensus of opinion. It is axiomatic that any issue such as doping which impacts upon such a diverse range of interests is likely to elicit a number of different possible solutions and these will depend upon whether, for example, that solution emanates from the governing bodies, the athletes or the politicians. What one would expect, though, is that the suggested solutions would have a common outcome. Unfortunately, this is not the case.

Critiques of the current system of doping control tend to fall into two distinct categories. These could be labelled 'insiders' and 'outsiders'. Insiders' solution's to the problem are those which seek to reinforce the current system or its ideological subtext. The insider philosophy is that doping is wrong and a system is needed to ensure that those competitors who use doping are punished. If there are problems, they arise out of an imperfect system.

From the perspective of the governing bodies it appears that the danger is legal challenge. Diane Modahl continues her long running battle for compensation against athletics' national governing body. The former body, the British Athletics Federation, is currently in receivership. This is due, in part, to the cost of defending Modahl's action. To this extent, there is a direct link between the problems associated with the nandrolone athletes and Modahl. Athletics UK, the new national governing body of athletics, has trodden carefully in its dealings with Dougie Walker and Linford Christie. Whatever the logic of the national body's decisions to exonerate these athletes, there must have been a concern that further legal challenge by athletes could result in the demise of the latest incarnation of British athletics' national governing body.

Further tensions are caused through the different stance taken by the International Amateur Athletics Federation (IAAF), the international body. In imposing a penalty on Walker and Christie, the IAAF has taken an approach that is consistent with earlier decisions – if you test positive and there are no valid excuses as to why that should be, then you will be punished. This position causes UK Athletics further problems, for it is placed in the position of having to enforce the policy of the IAAF while reconciling that policy with its own precarious financial condition. If it is the national body that hears the doping conduct cases and it is the national body that bans, then it will be the national body against which any legal action will be taken. If the national body exonerates a sportsman or woman then it will have to answer to the IAAF. So, the problem from the perspective of national governing bodies is to develop a system of doping control which effectively immunises against legal challenge.

Applying the same logic at a higher level, the IOC also wishes to protect itself. Its response is to create the Court of Arbitration for Sport (CAS). The idea of the CAS is to create an additional layer of disciplinary hearing in an attempt to install a legal buffer between the governing bodies and the courts. This is merely a more sophisticated attempt to achieve what governing bodies at a lower level are attempting to achieve by a watertight construction of their doping regulations, ensuring self-autonomy, free from interference by courts of law.

Sportsmen and women, despite the irony of the fact that they are the partial cause of the governing bodies' problem, are also 'insiders'. Their perspective on the problem of doping is the lack of confidence in their governing body's abilities to get it right. Getting it right involves punishing the dopers, but providing an effective mechanism to ensure that 'innocent' sportsmen and women can compete, and earn their living, without the fear of being labelled drug cheats. In every material way, sportsmen and women condone the present system. Their concerns address the effectiveness of the system rather than the system itself. Competitors are concerned that their drink bottles cannot be tampered with, that laboratories correctly process their samples, and that they receive the correct advice regarding 'safe' and 'unsafe' supplements.

However, what if the real problem is more profound – that doping control does not work? Those with the temerity to take this view are usually 'outsiders'. There are a number of grounds upon which the logic or principles of the current doping regulatory framework can be criticised, such as the impossibility of imposing a uniform system of doping control across a range of countries and cultures or the inevitable tensions inherent in any effective system of doping control which purports to provide the competitor with a system of rights equivalent to or better than those enjoyed under national jurisdictions. Their common theme is that the 'insider' view is predicated on a presumption that the present system is fundamentally 'right', and this presumption precludes the possibility of a more holistic solution.

The most damning criticism of the present system levelled by 'outsiders' is that it fails to prevent competitors doping. If this is so, then it undermines the basis on which the present system is constructed and makes the views of 'insiders' appear little more than tinkering at the edges.

If rumours may be believed, a significant number of sportsmen and women use some form of doping to assist them in their bid for sporting glory. Rumours are unsatisfactory as a form of evidence, but this is one area where there is unlikely to be anything more substantial. Governing bodies would argue that the low level of positive tests is an accurate reflection of the proportion of sportsmen and women who use doping. They would ascribe the low levels to continually improving testing techniques, a fear of detection, and better education of athletes. The 'outsider', however, may consider that to ascribe a reduction in positive tests to an improvement of the testing system would be to ignore other variables that should rightfully be considered. For example, are the International Olympic Committee (IOC) and the governing bodies of sports punishing the positives? More than one Olympic Games has had its image tarnished by allegations that positive tests had been 'overlooked'.

The vast majority of doping tests are negative, but the system does give scope for abuse. Positive tests are not necessarily an accurate reflection of the number of competitors who are doping. Blood testing was introduced in Sydney as a means of identifying those competitors using erythropoietin (EPO). EPO aids pain control and muscle growth – very useful in long term training. However, blood tests are only useful in detecting the presence of EPO that has been used in the weeks immediately prior to testing. Most competitors who wished to enhance their performance with EPO could have avoided detection by the simple expedient of discontinuing use a few months prior to competition. Also, there are doping techniques in use that cannot at present be detected, such as the use of human growth hormone.

Equally, it is possible to change an innocent competitor into a doping cheat simply by adjusting the levels of a substance that need to be present in an competitor's sample to denote a positive test. The limits of nandrolone in a sample imposed by the IAAF and the IOC are two nanograms of nandrolone per millilitre of urine. At a recent meeting of high level sports officials, lawyers and administrators in Cologne, the IOC was advised that two nanograms of nandrolone per millilitre of urine was not scientifically based and could, therefore, be subject to successful legal challenge. If this is so, the legitimacy of many other substances on banned lists may be questioned. Many upper limits are highly questionable in terms of scientific authority and substances ranging from caffeine to recreational drugs such as cannabis could be challenged on the basis that there is a lack of logic of appropriateness in their inclusion.

THE SOLUTIONS

When Mr Andreu speaks of problems, it is necessary to appreciate that there is no single problem, merely alternative problems and their alternative solutions. The EU believes that harmonisation is the solution. If the problem is, as according to governing bodies, one of developing a challenge-proof system, then harmonisation may well be the solution. The idea of harmonisation is to regularise the doping regulations across a range of sports in different countries. This, inevitably, will result in a watering down of some regulations in order that it satisfies national laws. It may be of benefit in establishing equality of treatment. However, harmonisation is a term that defies common interpretation. There cannot be one system of doping regulation that applies equally to all sports because the nature of sporting activity varies. A two year ban on competitors in some sports may effectively be a life ban, while in other sports where competition is less frequent, a two year ban could represent the loss of a few competitions. So there are question marks over whether or not harmonisation can even be successful as a solution to one of the problems.

Harmonisation is not a solution to the problems of all 'insiders', let alone to all the problems. Competitors will find little satisfaction in a harmonised system of doping control if that system does not address the problem of strict liability or an improved system of sample testing or hearings procedure. Harmonisation promises neither of these. Harmonisation is the solution to the problems of governing bodies.

Therefore, when Mr Andreu offers the solution as being harmonisation, one is able to identify the problem according to the EU, that inconsistency in the doping regulations of governing bodies affects the ability of those governing bodies to regulate themselves without the intervention of the law.

Mr Andreu's alternatives are the imposition of strict national laws or a relaxing of the system. These two alternatives appear to be from opposite ends of the solutions spectrum. Strict national laws may satisfy governing bodies, but they would not resolve the problems identified by competitors or 'outsiders'. A relaxing of the regulations may satisfy some 'outsiders', but would not satisfy any of the 'insiders'.

There are many administrators within sport who would welcome national parliaments creating specific criminal offences related to competitors' use of doping techniques. The IOC, on its site detailing its anti-doping conference in Lausanne this year, promoted in positive terms a list of countries and their doping sanctions. In Britain, drug use in society generally is controlled by the Misuse of Drugs Act 1971. The Act is consistent with legislation in many countries and outlaws the use of various substances, some of which appear on the doping lists of sports governing bodies. An increasing number of countries, including Britain, outlaw the supply of steroids – this is also an offence according to sports governing bodies. Very few countries go any further than this. Belgium and Greece are exceptions, in that they criminalise the competitor for doping activities as well as their suppliers.[3] Inevitably, some of these substances, which would be present on the list of governing bodies, would not otherwise be subject to criminalisation in any other social context.

To what degree are further criminal sanctions an effective solution to the problem of doping, however? Many governing bodies' anti-doping regulations are constructed around the principle of strict liability. It is not a defence under these regulations to claim that there was no intention to take

---

3   Greek Law 1646/1986, Arts 7–11; Law of 2 April 1965 of the French Community of Belgium; Decree of 27 March 1991 of the Flemish Community of Belgium, Art 43.

the drugs. This appears to eliminate as an argument that the athlete's food or drink had been tampered with or that they were given drugs on the understanding that they were not banned under the doping regulations.

While not all governing bodies operate a system of strict liability for doping offences, an increasing number do. A rule that a positive test leads to an automatic ban is attractive in its clarity and simplicity; however, it denies what many would view as the fundamental right of an opportunity to prove a lack of fault, knowledge or intent. In practice, this would mean that even if a competitor could prove that the consumption of the drug was accidental or as a result of malice on the part of another, the competitor would still be found 'guilty'.

This may appear to be a draconian provision. However, the reason for it is a fear that rules requiring proof of intent would be impossible to implement and it is likely that athletes would find little difficulty in producing a coach or doctor prepared to take responsibility and vouch for the athlete's innocence. As Scott J explained, in *Gasser v Stinson*:

> Mr Blackburne submitted with great force that a rule which did not permit an athlete even to try to establish his or her innocence, either in resisting conviction or in mitigation of sentence, was unreasonable and unjustifiable. But the consequences if the absolute nature of the offence was removed or if the length of the sentence became discretionary and not mandatory must be considered.

> Suppose an athlete gives evidence that he or she did not take the drug knowingly and that it must therefore be inferred that the drug was digested unknowingly. How is the IAAF to deal with such an explanation? How can credibility be tested? Suppose a third party, perhaps a member of the athlete's team of coaches, perhaps a medical adviser, perhaps a malicious prankster, gives evidence that he or she administered the drug to the athlete and that the athlete had no knowledge that this was being done. How is the credibility of the third party's evidence to be tested? The pressure for success in international athletics, as well as domestic athletics, and the national pride and prestige which has become part of international athletics has to be borne in mind. Will the credibility of the athlete or the third party vary depending on the nation to which he or she belongs? If a competitor or third party from nation A is believed, what will be the position when similar evidence is given by a competitor or third party from nation B? The lengths to which some people will go in order to achieve the appearance of success for their nation's athletes in athletics competitions is in point. The long jump in last year's World Championship illustrates the point. Cynicism, sadly, abounds. Mr Holt in his evidence, said that in his view, if a defence of moral innocence were open, the floodgates would be opened and the IAAF's attempts to prevent drug-taking by athletes would be rendered futile. He had, in my opinion, reason for that fear.

> Mr Blackburne submits that it is not justifiable that the morally innocent may have to suffer in order to ensure that the guilty do not escape. But that is not a submission that is invariably acceptable. The criminal law in this country (and

in, I would think, all others) has various absolute offences and various mandatory sentences.

For my part I am not persuaded that the IAAF's absolute offence and mandatory sentence applicable to an athlete who is found to have dope in his or her urine is unreasonable.[4]

Any provision purporting to criminalise doping by the competitor themselves would not be subject to such a strict liability offence. Most criminal sanctions in Britain depend on the establishment of *mens rea*, a 'guilty mind'. Section 28 of the Misuse of Drugs Act 1971 is no exception. Section 28(3)(b)(i) makes it clear that a person shall be acquitted if he proves that he neither believed, nor suspected, nor had reason to suspect that the substance or product in question was a controlled drug. This means that any criminal sanction mirroring the regulations of sports governing bodies would be less effective than those regulations because the competitor may be able to show a lack of the requisite 'guilty mind' for such an offence.

There are other fundamental problems relating to criminalisation. The relationship between a sportsman or woman and the governing body is a contractual one. In essence, a doping offence on the part of a competitor is a breach of contract, leaving the competitor subject to the doping penalties prescribed in the contract. To criminalise these doping offences would, in effect, be to impose a criminal sanction for a breach of a contract.

It would also leave the sportsman or woman at a disadvantage compared to the rest of society. If the list of banned substances were to remain the same, then a competitor may be imprisoned for consuming too many cups of coffee after dinner, while his or her dinner companions would be guilty of no offence. If the criminal sanction omitted some substances such as caffeine, then, due to strict liability, the competitor who tests positive for caffeine has a more difficult task in disproving the allegation than would a fellow competitor who is prosecuted under a country's criminal law for testing positive for, say, steroids.

The ambit of the sanction would need to be carefully drawn. Would the sanction apply only to international-standard competitors and apply to an even smaller minority of society, or would the law apply to situations such as a group of friends kicking a ball around the park, which would necessarily involve a degree of discretion by the authorities in its application?

Equally, it is unclear exactly who would carry out the doping tests. It is unlikely that Parliament would be content to leave the testing to a body such as the Ethics and Anti-Doping Unit that is affiliated to the governing bodies, or WADA, with its IOC connections.

It is difficult to imagine many countries wishing to criminalise behaviour which is fundamentally an employee disciplinary issue, or the cheating of a

---

4   *Gasser v Stinson* (1988) unreported, 15 June.

competitor while playing a game which, incidentally, provides that individual with an income. In one country, Greece, where competitors can be prosecuted for doping, there is no record of any prosecutions. This is no surprise, as effective criminalisation of the competitor is impossible.

From the perspective of the governing body, this is not a solution to their problem anyway. If the State takes the place of the governing body in actions against competitors, then it does reduce the risk of legal action against governing bodies; however, the creation of the CAS is indicative of a *desire to keep doping control within sport*. The intervention of the criminal law would remove doping from its control.

The final alternative is a relaxation of doping. It is hard to believe that this alternative is meant in any other way than a hollow threat, bearing in mind that it represents an 'outsider's' solution. The governing bodies would maintain that this solution is in conflict with the philosophy that underpins its fight against doping. This philosophy is usually presented as having two strands. First, the regulations are there to protect the health of competitors. Secondly, sport is based on the notion of fair and equal competition and drugs create an uneven playing field. These arguments are familiar and well rehearsed – if a little confusing. If health and fair competition are the objectives of doping regulation, then why should governing bodies become so embroiled with issues such as harmonisation, which cannot possibly assist in the protection of health and fair play?

To most sporting participants, the side effects of these drugs outweigh the advantages of taking them. However, at the highest level, the competitive instincts of many participants may blind them to the dangers. This, the governing bodies argue, justifies what amounts to a paternalistic approach to doping control within sport. In *Death in the Locker Room 2*, Dr Bob Goldman and Dr Ronald Klatz undertook a survey to test the lengths to which competitors would go in order to be a success at their chosen sport. Asked whether or not they would take a drug that would make them unbeatable in any sporting competition, but would cause their death in five years, 52% said yes. They concluded:

> The desire to win is so great that people sometimes lose the concept of right and wrong due to being single-minded driven individuals. Sometimes it is very difficult to view life as a whole, as sports goals for the obsessed individual are the only true tangible goal. It can totally dominate your life, and effectively shut out any vision of the world beyond. Mental perceptions of right and wrong may become misty and clouded, and your attempts at experiencing the ethics and fun of sport are so nebulous, that it is hardly worth mentioning, let alone planning for in your mind. In some athletes' minds, the present is a set of stair steps of relatively minor competitions leading up to the moment when they have the opportunity to be the best in their designated sport.[5]

---

5   Goldman, R and Klatz, R, *Death in the Locker Room 2*, 1992, Chicago: Elite Sports Medicine, p 23.

There is no doubt that doping can damage your health. Anabolic agents such as stanozolol and testosterone increase strength and endurance but can lead to aggressive behaviour, impotence, kidney damage and breast development in men, and the development of male features, facial and body hair in women. Beta blockers reduce heart rate and blood pressure, but can lead to dangerously low blood pressure. Blood doping where blood is taken from the athlete's body re-oxygenated and then pumped back into the athlete[6] can lead to allergic conditions, blood clotting and kidney damage. Diuretics such as frusemide and triameterine encourage weight loss, but cause nausea, cramps and dehydration. Stimulants such as amphetamine increase mental and physical stimulation, but raise blood pressure and make the heartbeat irregular. The much publicised EPO aids pain control and muscle growth, but can cause abnormal growth of internal organs and increase the risk of blood clots and strokes. Human growth hormone, in adults, increases the number of red blood cells, boosts heart function and makes more energy available by stimulating the breakdown of fat. However, inflated levels of human growth hormone can cause acromegaly, a disease characterised by excessive growth of the head, feet and hands. The lips, nose, tongue, jaw and forehead increase in size and the fingers and toes widen and become spade-like. The organs and digestive system may also increase in size, which may eventually cause heart failure.

If the governing bodies genuinely wished to protect the health of sportsmen and women, however, they would introduce a provision which forbade a competitor competing whilst injured. Women's gymnastics would also need to be reviewed, bearing in mind the incidence of arthritis and other diseases of the joints suffered by competitors in later life. There are also a number of contact sports which, by the nature of that activity, are likely to cause injury. No doubt the governing bodies of sport would argue that the risks of injury in certain sports are well known and that competitors are in some way consenting to the possibility of harm. The difficulty with this argument is that it could apply equally to doping. As JS Mill argued:

> ... the sole end for which mankind are warranted, individually or collectively, in interfering in the liberty of action of any of their number, is self protection. That the only purpose for which power can be rightfully exercised over any member of a civilised community, against his will, is to prevent harm to others. His own good, either physical or moral, is not a sufficient warrant. He cannot rightfully be compelled to do or forbear because it will be better for him to do so, because it will make him happier, because, in the opinions of others, to do so would be wise, or even right. These are good reasons for remonstrating with him, or reasoning with him, or persuading him, or entreating him, but not for compelling him, or visiting him with any evil in case he do otherwise. To justify that, the conduct from which it is desired to deter him must be

6   See Perry, C, 'Blood doping and athletic competition' (1983) 1(3) Int J Applied
     Philosophy 39.

calculated to produce evil to someone else. The only part of the conduct of any one, for which he is amenable to society, is that which concerns others. In the part which merely concerns himself, his independence is, of right, absolute. Over himself, over his own body and mind, the individual is sovereign.[7]

This argument applied to doping is clearly simplistic, but it contains, in essence, the distinction that is drawn in other sporting situations. If doping regulation is justified on the grounds that competitors feel coerced into doping as the only way of competing with the cheats, then that excuse is no more or less persuasive than any form of negative peer pressure; for example, the pressure to over-train.

It is necessary, of course, to distinguish situations such as the State controlled doping scheme in the former East Germany or where children are involved. However, examples such as these can be controlled effectively by national law, which threaten greater sanctions than could be imposed by doping regulation.

The second, but equally unconvincing argument is that taking drugs will give the taker an advantage over a competitor who has not taken drugs and is therefore cheating.[8] Governing bodies argue that this is both unfair on the honest competitor and that there is a risk that the image of their sport would be undermined by a belief that it was being conducted on an uneven playing field. This knowledge would undermine the validity of the sport and lead to a loss in popularity.

Following the drugs revelations surrounding Ben Johnson, the Canadian sprinter, a governmental inquiry chaired by Charles Dubin J concluded:

> The use of banned performance enhancing drugs is cheating, which is the antithesis of sport. The widespread use of such drugs has threatened the essential integrity of sport and is destructive of its very objectives. It also erodes the ethical and moral values of athletes who use them, endangering their mental and physical welfare while demoralising the entire sport community.[9]

---

7   Mill, JS, *On Liberty* (1859), 1999, Ware, Herts: Wordsworth. See, also, Dworkin, G, 'Paternalism' [1972] The Monist 56, pp 64–84; Dworkin, G, 'Paternalism: some second thoughts', in Sartorius, R (ed), *Paternalism*, 1983, Minneapolis: Minnesota UP; Feinberg, J, 'Legal paternalism' [1971] 1 Canadian J Philosophy 106.

8   Simon, RL, *Fair Play: Sports, Values, and Society*, 1991, Boulder: Westview, Chapter 4; Gardner, R, 'On performance-enhancing substances and the unfair advantage argument' (1989) XVI J Philosophy of Sport 59; Brown, WM, 'Drugs, ethics, and sport' (1980) VII J Philosophy of Sport 15; Fraleigh, W, 'Performance-enhancing drugs in sport' (1985) XI J Philosophy of Sport 23; Brown, WM, 'Comments on Simon and Fraleigh' (1984) XI J Philosophy of Sport 14.

9   de Pencier, J, 'Law and athlete drug testing in Canada' (1992) 4(2) Marquette Sports LJ 259.

However, eradicating all the unfair advantages that one participant may have over another may not only be impossible to achieve, but also undesirable. Competitive sport is all about one athlete being better than another and, therefore, it is desirable to have physiological and psychological differences between the participants.

There are many advantages inherent in, for example, the nationality of an athlete. The skier raised in Austria or Switzerland has an advantage over one raised in Belgium; the runner living at altitude over the runner at sea level; the height advantage of the average American basketball player over the average oriental player; or the technological, training and dietary advantages of the rich nation over the impoverished third world country. All these are advantages, and may be considered unfair in terms of sporting equality:

> In the first case we do not object to differences in the endurance capabilities of athletes resulting from increased haemoglobin count, provided that increase is the result of high altitude training. In the second case, we do not object to discrepancies in the size of skeletal muscles, providing that size results from genetic endowment or training (for example, weight lifting). In each case, we are not objecting to the advantage but to the way in which the advantage is gained. So what is it about blood doping or human growth hormone that somehow distinguishes these methods of securing an advantage and seems to render their effects unacceptable? The obvious difference is the advantages gained by blood boosting and HGH are achieved through the use of a (supplemented) substance. However, if the basis of our objection is to be that using a substance is an unacceptable means to gaining an advantage, then the inconsistencies are more than apparent ...

> There are many legal substances used by athletes in their attempt to gain an advantage over competitors – for example, amino acids, protein powders, vitamin and mineral supplements (sometimes injected), caffeine (legally limited to 12 micrograms per millilitre of urine, about seven cups of coffee), glucose polymer drinks, and injections of ATP (a naturally produced chemical involved in muscle contraction). The list could go on and on. Clearly we do not object to gaining an advantage through the use of a substance; it is only particular substances to which we are opposed. This being the case, it seems that some form of definitive criteria would have to be established in order to differentiate between permissible and prohibited substances. Yet, such criteria do not seem to exist.[10]

An alternative argument is that, rather than cheating fellow competitors, the drug taker is cheating the sport itself. Clearly, the essence of a sport would be compromised by certain breaches of the rules. It would be totally unacceptable for Linford Christie to be beaten in an Olympic 100 m final by a competitor on a motor cycle or for Tiger Woods to lose the Masters to a player with a radio controlled golf ball.

---

10 *Op cit*, Gardner, fn 8, pp 59, 66.

However, not all tactical or technical deviations from the norm are prohibited. Carbon fibre racquets have dramatically altered the game of tennis, Chris Boardman's radically different bicycle has revolutionised pursuit cycling, and Cathy Freeman's bodysuit may well become standard apparel for 400 m runners of the 21st century, yet these developments were accepted by the respective sports. Secondly, the question presumes that performance enhancing drugs are an extrinsic aid unrelated to the skills and physical condition of the athlete. However, it is clear from the benefits of doping detailed above that, generally, doping directly enhances training rather than performance. In other words, it is no substitute for the Corinthian value of hard work.

Therefore, rather than being an idle threat, the notion of relaxing doping control should be taken seriously as a solution if the problem is that doping is out of control. In order to achieve some level of acceptance, however, the relaxation of doping must resolve the problems of 'insiders'.

CONCLUSION

Inherent in the finding of a solution to any problem is the accurate identification of the problem itself. Doping is no exception. Those with vested interests in the administration or performance of sport, or 'insiders', have an interest in maintaining the status quo. Although different 'insiders' identify different problems, they can be grouped together on the basis that their solutions are predicated on a continuation of the present system. 'Outsiders' have the luxury of taking a broader, more holistic view in that they are not shackled by any loyalty or sense of adherence to the present system of doping control. Rarely do 'insiders' express the views of 'outsiders'. When Wilf Paish, coach to Tessa Sanderson (amongst others), dared to speculate last year that the problems in doping may best be solved by allowing competitors controlled use of doping techniques and products, he was almost universally condemned – not least by sportsmen and women themselves. Perhaps, however, the impact of Paish's message was amplified by the fact that it came from an 'insider'.

Philosophically, there is nothing preventing sport from constructing its regulations in any way that it chooses. However, justifying the doping regulations on the basis that they protect competitors from harm, or that they uphold a form of equality of opportunity, is difficult. If these justifications represent the only reasons for a continuation of doping regulation, then allowing competitors to use doping products and techniques represents a logical 'outsider's' solution. Ironically, it may also resolve the problems identified by 'insiders'. There would be no danger of legal challenge and competitors would not have the concerns of false positive tests. If the levels of doping are as high as rumour suggests, then we would expect to see no changes in the nature of sporting competition. Once competitors could openly use doping, then the terrible side effects of some drugs could be prevented by their effective administration by medical staff.

The IOC would claim that governing bodies could never condone such heresy, but then it could be said that, whether doping regulations are ultimately relaxed or not, it would have little impact on the IOC. The adage that there is no such thing as bad publicity can readily be applied to doping scandals. The IOC declared publicly that it wanted the Sydney Games to be free of doping revelations. Did it have in mind that competitors testing positive before the Games should be prevented from competing, or that those testing positive at the Games should escape the glare of the world's media? Either way, the IOC remains the focus of media attention. As for the public perception, once the regulations had been relaxed, the media would be denied their 'doping scandal' and, in a short period of time, the problem of doping would be a thing of the past.

BIBLIOGRAPHY

Adoninno Report, *A People's Europe*, 1985, Brussels: Commission of the European Communities

Advisory Council on the Misuse of Drugs, *Annual Report Financial Year 1998/99*, 1999, London: Home Office, available at www.homeoffice.gov.uk/cpd/anrep99.htm

Australian Government, *Drugs in Sport: Interim Report of the Senate Standing Committee on the Environment, Recreation and the Arts*, 1989, Canberra: Australian Government Publishing Service

Bahrke, MS *et al*, 'Psychological and behavioural effects of endogenous testosterone and anabolic-androgenic steroids' (1996) 22(6) J Sports Medicine 367

Beale, H, *Chitty on Contracts*, 28th edn, 1999, London: Sweet & Maxwell

Beloff, M, Kerr, T and Demetriou, M, *Sports Law*, 1999, Oxford: Hart

Bellotti, P *et al* (eds), *IAAF World Symposium on Drug Use in Sport*, 1988, London: IAAF

Birkinshaw, P, *Government by Moonlight: The Hybrid Parts of the State*, 1990, London: Unwin Hyman

Birley, D, *Sport and the Making of Britain*, 1993, Manchester: Manchester UP

Black, T and Pape, A, 'The ban on drugs in sports: the solution or the problem?' (1997) 21(1) J Sport and Social Issues 83

Bonfante, J, 'Sports officials confront the legacy of Communism's State approved abuse of steroids', Reuters, February 1998

Bourdieu, P, 'Sport and social class' (1978) 17 Social Science Information 819

Brown, WM, 'Comments on Simon and Fraleigh' (1984) XI J Philosophy of Sport 14

Brown, WM, 'Drugs, ethics, and sport' (1980) VII J Philosophy of Sport 15

Cashmore, E, *Making Sense of Sport*, 2nd edn, 1996, London: Routledge

Clarkson, PM and Thompson, HS, 'Drugs in sport research findings and limitations' (1997) 24(6) J Sports Medicine

Cohen, S, *Folk Devils and Moral Panics*, 1980, London: Robertson

Collins, R, *Does the Anabolic Steroid Control Act Work?*, available at www.decriminalisesteroids.com

Corkery J, *Drug Seizure and Offender Statistics 1998*, 2000, London: HMSO

Corkery, J, *Drug Seizure and Offender Statistics 1998 (Area Tables)*, 2000, London: HMSO

Council of Europe, *Explanatory Report on the Anti-Doping Convention*, 1990, Strasbourg: COE

Council of Europe Monitoring Group, *Meeting Report: Working Party on Legal Issues*, T-DO (94) 22, 1994, Strasbourg: COE

De La Chappelle, A, 'The use and misuse of sex chromatin screening' (1986) 256 J American Medical Association 1920

de Pencier, J, 'Law and athlete drug testing in Canada' (1994) 4(2) Marquette Sports LJ 259

Devetak, R and Higgott, R, *Justice Unbound? Globalisation, States and the Transformation of the Social Bond*, Working Paper No 29/99, Centre for the Study of Globalisation and Regionalisation, available at www.csgr.org

Donohue, T and Johnson, N, *Foul Play: Drug Abuse in Sports*, 1986, London: Blackwell

Drug Enforcement Agency, *The Diversion of Drugs and Chemicals: A Descriptive Report of the Programs and Activities of the DEA's Office Of Diversion Control*, May 1996, available at www.usdoj.gov/dea/programs

Dubin, C, *Commission of Inquiry into the Use of Drugs and Banned Practices Intended to Increase Athletic Performance*, 1990, Ottawa: Canadian Government Publishing Centre

Dunning, EG, Maguire, JA and Pearton, RE (eds), *The Sports Process: A Comparative and Developmental Approach*, 1993, Champaign, Ill: Human Kinetics

Dworkin, G, 'Paternalism' [1972] The Monist 56

Eassom, S, 'Drugs and ethics' (2000) 3(2) Sports Law Bulletin 2

Entine, J, *Taboo: Why Black Athletes Dominate Sports and Why We are Afraid to Talk About It*, 2000, New York: Public Affairs

Feinberg, J, 'Legal paternalism' [1971] 1 Canadian J Philosophy 106

Fraleigh, W, 'Performance-enhancing drugs in sport' (1985) XI J Philosophy of Sport 23

Franke, WW and Berendonk, B, 'Hormonal doping and androgenization of athletes: a secret program of the German Democratic Republic' (1997) 43(7) Clinical Chemistry 1262

Fuller, R and LaFountain, J, 'Performance-enhancing drug use in college athletics: a different form of drug abuse' [1987] Adolescence 115

Galluzzi, D, 'The doping crisis in international athletic competition: lessons from the Chinese doping scandal in women's swimming' (2000) 10 Seton Hall J Sport Law 65

Gardiner S, Felix, A, James, M, Welch, R and O'Leary, J, *Sports Law*, 1998, London: Cavendish Publishing

Gardner, R, 'On performance-enhancing substances and the unfair advantage argument' (1989) XVI J Philosophy of Sport 59

Goldman, R and Klatz, R, *Death in the Locker Room 2*, 1992, Chicago: Elite Sports Medicine

Grayson, E, *Ethics, Injuries and the Law in Sports Medicine*, 1999, London: Butterworth-Heinemann Medical

Grayson, E, *Sport and the Law*, 3rd edn, 1999, London: Butterworths

Guttmann, A, 'The diffusion of sports and the problem of cultural imperialism', in Dunning, EG, Maguire, JA and Pearton, RE (eds), *The Sports Process: A Comparative and Developmental Approach*, 1993, Champaign, Ill: Human Kinetics

Haislip, GR, *Conference on the Impact of Natural Steroid Control Legislation in the United States*, DEA, June 1995, available at www.usdoj.gov/dea/programs/diversion/divpub/confer/steroids.htm

Halsbury's Laws of England, 4th edn, 1991, London: Butterworths, Vol 44

Harris, DJ, OnBoyle, M and Warbrick, C, *Law of the European Convention on Human Rights*, 1995, London: Butterworths

Hart, HLA, *The Concept of Law*, 2nd edn, 1997, Oxford: Clarendon

Hay, E, 'Sex determination in putative female athletes' (1972) 221 J American Medical Association 998

Hill, CR, *Olympic Politics*, 2nd edn, 1996, Manchester: Manchester UP

Hirst, P and Thompson, G, *Globalization in Question: The International Economy and the Possibilities of Governance*, 1996, Oxford: Blackwell

Hood-Williams, J, 'Sexing the athletes' (1995) 12 J Sociology of Sport 290

Houlihan, B, 'Anti-doping policy in sport: the politics of international policy co-ordination' (1999) 77 Public Administration 311

Houlihan, B, *Dying to Win: Doping in Sport and the Development of Anti-Doping Policy*, 1999, Strasbourg: Council of Europe

Howard, M, *Phipson on Evidence*, 15th edn, 1999, London: Thomson Professional

International Amateur Athletics Federation, *Handbook 1992–1993*, 1992, London: IAAF

International Amateur Athletics Federation, *Handbook 2000–2001*, 2000, London: IAAF

International Olympic Committee, *Explanatory Memorandum Concerning the Application of the Olympic Movement Anti-Doping Guide*, 1999, Lausanne: IOC

International Olympic Committee, *Financial Considerations: Summary of Conclusions from the Meeting of the Working Group*, 1998, Lausanne: IOC

International Olympic Committee, *Medical Code and Explanatory Document*, 1995, Lausanne: IOC

International Olympic Committee, *Policy Commitment of the IOC*, paper submitted to the International Summit on Drugs in Sport, Sydney, Australia, 14–17 November 1999, available at www.nodoping.org/pos_drugsinsports_e.html

International Olympic Committee, *Preventing and Fighting Against Doping in Sport*, 1994, Lausanne: IOC

International Olympic Committee, *The International Olympic Charter Against Doping in Sport*, 1990, Lausanne: IOC

Ioannidis, G, '*Doug Walker v UK Athletics and IAAF* [2000] HC, 25 July, unreported' (2000) 3(5) Sports Law Bulletin 3

Ioannidis, G, 'Drugs in football' (1998) 1(5) Sports Law Bulletin 14

Jennings, A, *The New Lords of the Rings*, 1996, London: Simon & Schuster

Josling, JF and Alexander, P, *The Law of Clubs*, 5th edn, 1984, London: Oyez

Kaufman, SA, 'Issues in international sports arbitration' (1995) 13 Boston U International LJ 527

Korkia, PK and Stimson, GV, *Anabolic Steroid Use in Great Britain: An Exploratory Investigation*, 1993, Report for the Department of Health, The Welsh Office and the Chief Scientists Office, Scottish Home and Health Department, Centre for Research on Drugs and Health Behaviour, London: HMSO

Landry, F, Landry, N and Yerles, M (eds), *Sports ... The Third Millennium*, 1990, Sainte-Foy: Université Laval

Lob, J, 'Dopage, responsabilité objective ("strict liability") et de quelques autres questions' (1999) 12(95) Schweizerische Juristen Zeitung 272

McGrew, A and Lewis, P (eds), *Global Politics*, 1992, Cambridge: Polity

Medicines Control Agency, *Guidance Note: A Guide to What is a Medicinal Product*, 1995, London: MCA

Middleman, A and DuRant, R, 'Anabolic steroid use and associated health risk behaviours' (1996) 21(4) J Sports Medicine

Mill, JS, *On Liberty* (1859), 1999, Ware, Herts: Wordsworth

Nafziger, JAR, *International Sports Law*, 1988, New York: Transnational

O' Leary, J, 'Drugs update: nandrolone' (2000) 3(2) Sports Law Bulletin 11

O'Gorman, T, 'Ed Giddins v TCCB' (1997) 5(1) Sport and the Law J 23

Oswald, D, *Doping Sanctions: Guilty or Innocent*, FISA No 6, 1995

Ougaard, M, *Approaching the Global Polity*, Working Paper No 42/99, Centre for the Study of Globalisation and Regionalisation, available at www.csgr.org

Panagiotopoulos, D, 'Court of arbitration for sports' (1999) 6 Villanova Sports and Entertainment LJ 49

Paulsson, J, 'Arbitration of international sports disputes' (1994) 11 Entertainment and Sports Lawyer 12

Perry, C, 'Blood doping and athletic competition' (1983) 1(3) International J Applied Philosophy 39

Polvino, AT, 'Arbitration as preventive medicine for Olympic ailments: the International Olympic Committee's Court of Arbitration for Sport and the future for the settlement of international sporting disputes' (1994) 8 Emory International L Rev 347

Raber, N, 'Dispute resolution in Olympic sport: the Court of Arbitration for Sport' (1998) 8 Seton Hall J Sport Law 75

Redhead, S, *Unpopular Cultures: The Birth of Law and Popular Culture*, 1995, Manchester: Manchester UP

Reeb, M (ed), *Digest of CAS Awards 1986–1998*, 1998, Berne: Staempfli Editions SA

Sakamoto, H et al, 'Femininity control at the XXth Universiad in Kobe, Japan' (1988) 9 International J Sports Medicine 193

Sanger, J, The Compleat Observer: A Field Research Guide to Observation, 1996, Sussex: Falmer

Sartorius, R (ed), Paternalism, 1983, Minneapolis: Minnesota UP

Siekmann, RRC, Soek, J and Bellani, A (eds), Doping Rules of International Sports Organizations, 1999, The Hague: TMC Asser/Kluwer

Simon, RL, Fair Play: Sports, Values, and Society, 1991, Boulder: Westview

Simpson, J et al, 'Medical examination for health of all athletes replacing the need for gender verification in international sports' (1992) 267 J American Medical Association 850

Simson, V and Jennings, A, The Lords of the Rings: Power, Money and Drugs in the Modern Olympics, 1992, London: Simon & Schuster

Soek, J and Vrijman, EN, 'De Olympic Movement Anti-Doping Code: de moed van de herder', (2000) 13 Sportzaken 76

Starmer, K, European Human Rights Law, 1999, London: Legal Action Group

Tarasti, L (ed), Legal Solutions in International Doping Cases Awards 1985–1999, 2000, Milan: IAAF

Tomlinson, A and Garry, W (eds), Five Ring Circus: Money Power and Politics at the Olympic Games, 1984, London and Sydney: Pluto

UK Sports Council, Competitors' and Officials' Guide to Drugs and Sport, 1998, London: UKSC

UK Sports Council, Doping Control, 1993, London: UKSC

UK Sports Council, Doping Control Unit, Directory of Anti-Doping Regulations of International Sports Federations, 2nd edn, 1993, London: UKSC

UK Sports Council, Ethics and Anti-Doping Directorate, Annual Report 1997–98, 1998, London: UKSC

van Dijk, P and van Hoof, GJF, Theory and Practice of the European Convention on Human Rights, 1998, The Hague: Kluwer

Voy, R, Testing Gone Afoul, Cover-ups, Lies and Manipulation – All for the Sake of Gold, Champaign, Ill: Human Kinetics

Voy, R, *Drugs, Sport and Politics: The Inside Story about Drug Use and its Political Cover-Up*, 1991, Champaign, Ill: Leisure

Vrijman, EN, 'Towards harmonization: a commentary on current issues and problems' (2000) 3(2) Sports Law Bulletin 13

Vrijman, EN, *Blood Sampling and Doping Control*, 1995, Rotterdam: NeCeDo

Vrijman, EN, *Harmonisation: Can it Ever be Really Achieved?*, 2nd edn, 1995, Rotterdam: NeCeDo

White House Office of National Drug Control Policy, *Recommendations Concerning Strengthening the Anti-Drug Programs Within the Olympics and International Sport*, 1999, available at www.whitehousedrugpolicy.gov/newscommentary/paper/intro.html

Wise, A and Meyer, BS, *International Sports Law and Business*, 1998, The Hague: Kluwer

Wise, A, 'Strict liability drug rules of sports governing bodies' (1996) 146 NLJ 1161

Yesalis, C (ed), *Anabolic Steroids in Sport and Exercise*, 1993, Champaign, Ill: Human Kinetics

Yesalis, C and Cowert, V, *The Steroids Game*, 1998, Champaign, Ill: Human Kinetics

Yesalis, C and Bahrke, MS, 'Anabolic-androgenic steroids current issues' (1995) 19(5) J Sports Medicine

Young, RR, 'Drug testing in sport, legal challenges and issues' (1999) 20 Queensland ULJz

Young, RR, 'Problems with the definition of doping: does lack of fault or the absence of performance enhancing matter?' (1999) 20 Queensland ULJ

INDEX